THE
STATE AND
DEMOCRACY

Alternative Policies for America

THE
STATE AND DEMOCRACY

Revitalizing
America's Government

MARC V. LEVINE
CAROL MacLENNAN
JOHN J. KUSHMA
CHARLES NOBLE
with JEFF FAUX
and MARCUS G. RASKIN

Routledge
New York, London

The Institute for Policy Studies, 1601 Connecticut Street N.W., Washington, D.C., 20009, U.S.A., founded in 1963, is a transnational center for research, education, and social invention. IPS sponsors critical study of U.S. policy, and proposes alternative strategies and visions. Programs focus on national security, foreign policy, human rights, the international economic order, domestic affairs, and knowledge and politics.

First published in 1988 by

Routledge
an imprint of
Routledge, Chapman & Hall, Inc.
29 West 35 Street
New York, NY 10001

Published in Great Britain by

Routledge
11 New Fetter Lane
London EC4P 4EE

© 1988 by Routledge, Chapman & Hall, Inc.

Printed in the United States of America

Library of Congress Cataloging in Publication Data

The State and democracy: revitalizing America's government / Marc
    V. Levine . . . [et al.].
       p. cm.—(Alternative policies for America)
       Bibliography: p.
       Includes index.
       1. Political participation—United States. 2. United States—
Politics and government—1981– 3. United States—Economic
policy—1981—Citizen participation. I. Levine, Marc V., 1951–
II. Series.
JK1764.S83 1988
323'.042'0973—dc19   88-18323
ISBN 0-415-90045-X
ISBN 0-415-90076-X (pbk)

British Library Cataloging in Publication Data

The State and democracy: revitalizing
America's government.
1. United States. Government
I. Levine, Marc V., 1951–
353
ISBN 0-415-90045-X
ISBN 0-415-90076-X (pbk.)

Contents

Series editor's preface

The "Alternative Policies for America" series offers a concrete set of programs for dealing with some of the country's most pressing domestic problems. It answers, in very specific terms, what radical analysts of the failure of the U.S. economic and social system can offer in the way of alternatives. We seek to make clear that there are ways of ensuring that all Americans can have a decent standard of material well-being and public services, a healthy and safe environment, and real participation in the political processes of governance and how goods and services are provided. The problem, this series attempts to show, is not the inability to create workable alternatives, but our system's unwillingness to effect the basic economic, social and political changes in the structure of American society that will permit such alternatives to take root.

The Institute for Policy Studies sees this intellectual work as a first and necessary step in building a movement for political change. (A more comprehensive international as well as domestic program, framed in terms of platform proposals, has also been prepared by the Institute.*) The analyses and ideas put forward in these books must take concrete form as demands for change at the federal, state and community levels. In many cases, model legislation embodying the proposals put forth here are being developed for introduction into the policy debate, and as a means of public education and constituency-building. The many individuals and groups who have been involved in the discussions and review which led to these books provide the nucleus for a continually expanding circle of activists who, we hope, some day will turn these ideas and proposals into a more just and humane America.

Chester Hartman
Institute for Policy Studies
Washington, D.C.

* Marcus Raskin and Chester Hartman, eds. *Winning America: Ideas and Leadership for the 90s* (Boston: South End Press and IPS, 1988).

Acknowledgments

This book has been a genuinely collective enterprise. It emerged from an Institute for Policy Studies working group on revitalizing democratic government. Coordinated by Carol MacLennan and comprising the four lead authors, this IPS group provided a congenial setting for frank, critical discussions of the basic themes of the book. While each chapter is the work and responsibility of the specified author, we have benefited from ongoing collective discussions, and each chapter has been rigorously reviewed by the other lead authors. The rewards of this collective endeavor have been great in improving the quality of the individual chapters as well as forging a thematic coherence in the book.

Many colleagues and friends have helped in reading drafts of the chapters and providing insightful comments. Above all, we wish to thank Chester Hartman. As editor of the series in which this book appears, he has been instrumental in pulling this project together. His incisive comments on early chapter drafts were crucial in sharpening our arguments and improving our writing. His gentle prodding nudged us toward deadlines and helped make this book a reality.

Other individuals read specific chapters or sections of the book and offered much appreciated advice and criticism. In particular, we wish to thank Arnie Anderson, Margo Conk, Wally Katz, Andie King, Todd Swanstrom, and John Zipp, whose insights and suggestions were especially valuable. Ellen Herman provided superb copyediting assistance.

1 Introduction: The State and Democracy in America—Historical Patterns and Current Possibilities

Marc V. Levine

"Government is not the solution to our problems . . . government is the problem." That statement, trumpeted in Ronald Reagan's first inaugural address, neatly captured the central intellectual theme of the post-Great Society conservative ascendancy that culminated in Reagan's 1980 victory (Reeves 1985, 15). Throughout the 1970s, lavishly funded by a mobilized business community, conservative politicians and intellectuals unremittingly attacked the concept of a strong, activist state. Government spending, taxation, and regulation, it was argued, *caused* economic decline; government social programs *created* rather than solved social problems; and state expansion had overloaded the political system with too many participants and demands, creating a "governability" crisis that threatened political "bankruptcy."

There was, as Kevin P. Phillips and others argue, a populist dimension to the 1970s attack on the state (Phillips 1982, 120–24). The proportion of Americans who felt that the government was run "by a few big interests looking out for themselves" grew from 29 percent in 1964 to 50 percent in 1970 and reached 69 percent in 1980 (Schneider 1987, 52). Moreover, in the wake of Vietnam, Watergate, and the seeming inability of the federal government to manage the economy widespread disillusionment surfaced over the efficacy of government. Polls showed that the percentage of Americans who believed that they could trust government in Washington "to do what is right" most or all of the time dropped from 76 percent in 1964 to 54 percent in 1970, 33 percent in 1976, and 25 percent in 1980 (52).

Nevertheless, the recent attack on the state is best understood in class terms, as Frances Fox Piven and Richard Cloward persuasively argue. The expansion of government activity between 1930 and 1970 enlarged the "market leverage of American workers" (1981, 31). Blurring the lines between politics and economics—a separation at the core of capitalist ideology—enabled economically disenfranchised groups to mobilize successfully in the political arena. Moreover, the 1930–1970 period witnessed the emergence of "new institutional arrangements that helped expose the state to democratic influence in a continuing way" (118). For corporate America, facing the profit crunch of the late 1960s and

1

1970s, a state "susceptible to popular influence" was increasingly viewed as a threat to power and privileges (119).

The corporate response was to launch a full-scale assault on the state—or, to be precise, those state functions that did not serve corporate class interests (Gordon 1986, 23). In the context of 1970s anxiety over deteriorating economic conditions, business elites and their intellectual supporters plausibly argued that "runaway" government was America's foremost domestic problem. Their solution was to cut back the "liberal" state to three main functions: 1) providing the legal framework for private sector market transactions; 2) collecting *minimal* revenues to support *minimal* "safety net" services and the other "proper" functions of government; and 3) supporting a national security apparatus capable of maintaining U.S. power, mainly the interests of U.S.-based multinational corporations in the world. Despite the populist appeal of 1970s anti-statism, it was this corporate offensive that, more than any single factor, undermined support for progressive, activist government in the United States and helped pave the way for the triumph of what Reg Whitaker calls "the free enterprise ravings of the Reaganites" (1987, 6–7).

The central argument of this book is that the time has come to revitalize the notion of a progressive, democratic state in the United States. The legacy of the Reagan administration—*genuine* economic and political bankruptcy in the form of the Iran-*contra* affair, trade and budgetary deficits, the moral miasma of Wall Street, and the erosion of the living standards of millions of low- and middle-income people—makes clear the necessity of reasserting "public" values over "market" values.

This is *not* a book about statism; we are not advocates of stifling, centralized, and essentially *undemocratic* bureaucracies. But it is a book that recognizes—unlike the neo-liberal wing of the Democratic Party—that without an *effective* public sector, corporate-dominated private markets will skew the U.S. political economy in fundamentally undemocratic and socially destructive ways. If we are to grapple successfully with the serious social and economic problems facing this country in the years ahead, then political institutions that are democratic and encourage participation must be reinvigorated.

The laissez-faire rhetoric of conservatives has, in part, been a hoax. In the name of reducing the overall role of government, conservatives have actually eliminated progressive state activities while strengthening pro-business and pro-national security areas of public policy. Our argument here is that we will either dispense with this conservative brand of statism—epitomized by the cowboy politics of Oliver North and associates and the pro-wealthy redistributionist economics of David Stockman and his successors—or continue to suffer the wrenching consequences. History has caught up with America.

Understanding the Attack on the State

The positive social welfare state is a recent phenomenon in the United States. It emerged out of the Depression and the New Deal, solidified in the post-World War II consensus on Keynesian macroeconomic management, and expanded in the 1960s under the social reform impulses of the Great Society.

It is important to recognize, however, that positive progressive government has nineteenth century roots, primarily at the state and local levels. In his path-breaking study of pre-Civil War Pennsylvania, Louis Hartz demolishes the myth that laissez-faire economic policies dominated before 1860. While the federal government intervened little in economic affairs during this period, state governments "assumed the job of shaping decisively the contours of economic life" (289). In Pennsylvania, for example, the economic landscape included extensive public regulation, mixed and public enterprises, and elaborate theories of public spending as "the responsibility of a democratic state to its people" in pursuit of the public interest (301). According to Hartz, Pennsylvania's leading economic theorists developed the notion of "public profit," which conceptualized

> . . . a positive profit-making state—a state in which taxes were abolished, poorhouses obsolete, governmental institutions supported by public works revenues, and public schools universal. The dream of great wealth which motivated land speculators and mining investors captured the imagination of the state itself. The concept of profit led to the concept of public service, and the state became a gigantic entrepreneur whose gains were to be publicly shared. (299–300)

By the late 1850s, however, this expansive notion of state enterprise was under attack as growing corporate power challenged "the traditional intervention of the state," particularly in the area of public enterprise (319). In the absence of any mass movement suggesting otherwise, the notion of "popular community" was swept away as a rationale for state action.

The Progressive Era—roughly 1900–1920—is another historical period in which government action became an important antidote to the failures of capitalist markets. As several historians have noted, much of what is considered Progressive Era reform reflects attempts by corporate elites to use the state to smooth out deficiencies in capitalist markets while at the same time defusing potential challenges to the system (Kolko 1977). Nevertheless, important streams of Progressive reform did emphasize the fundamental inadequacies of a market economy and called for activist government to transcend those inadequacies. As Richard Fogelsong points out, the emerging urban planning movement in the early 1900s

> . . . complained that the process of city building was being determined by real estate speculation rather than by public policies based on the long-term interests of the community. They objected to this excessive reliance on the market system

on the grounds that it stymied the development of collective facilities of general benefit to the community, and it allowed private developers to run roughshod over the interests of the public . . . [T]here was general agreement that some form of government intervention was necessary to prevent these abuses . . . (1986, 3)

In the realm of social policy many of the first welfare state programs were put into place at the state level between 1900 and 1930. State governments in Wisconsin, Massachusetts, and New York, among others, passed legislation on workers' compensation, pensions for widowed mothers with children, and unemployment insurance (Skocpol and Ikenberry 1983; Orloff and Skocpol 1984; Leff 1973). These programs were bitterly contested by business interests, who believed that expanding the role of government to meet public needs left unsatisfied by private markets would infringe on the power and privileges of capital.

In short, despite persistent and powerful anti-state ideology, the concept of positive government does have some important historical roots. Nevertheless, it was the post-New Deal development of the welfare state and acceptance of Keynesian economic policy that represents the genuine emergence of positive government in the United States. The state was brought deeply into management of the economy and became "the direct focus of demands by social movements for a 'fair social share' through better access to good jobs, the reduction of wage discrimination, and provision of greater access to education and training" (Carnoy, Shearer, and Rumberger 1983, 43).

Between 1930 and 1970—but particularly in the tumultuous 1960s—government's role expanded dramatically in response to demands from social movements representing disenfranchised groups and individuals. As Bowles and Gintis point out, the development of positive government "gave notice that profit-making business activities would be monitored and that the capitalist corporation, while permitted a considerable expansion, would be subject to social scrutiny" (1986, 5).

To be sure, positive government in the United States was carefully circumscribed in what Joan Robinson calls "Bastard Keynesianism" (Kuttner 1984, 27). In the United States, the Keynes who emphasized macroeconomic demand management in a neo-classical framework took precedence over the Keynes who argued that a redistribution of economic power was central to full employment in capitalist societies. Thus, the Keynesian revolution in the United States denied the public arena control over the allocation of investment where democratic impulses might direct it in socially useful ways. In addition, the galloping depoliticization of mass politics—exemplified by dramatic declines in voter participation—enhanced the power of business elites over the policy process (Burnham 1983).

Nevertheless, the development of positive government did result in important gains for low-income people, workers, and racial minorities, and, as Piven and

Cloward point out, "the new programs of the 1930s and the 1960s produced pervasive new linkages between the state and democratic publics" (1981, 118). Moreover, as John Schwarz has demonstrated, positive government made important strides toward reducing poverty, improving access to health care, and cleaning up the environment, among other crucial problems (1983).

The expanding state and corporate America co-existed uneasily through the late 1960s. This "Keynesian accommodation" worked as long as economic growth underwrote increased corporate profits and a growing "social wage" (Wolfe 1981). However, the economic crisis of the 1970s—coupled with the political challenges to authority that bubbled over in the 1960s—persuaded corporate elites that Keynesian accommodation was no longer workable. As Bowles and Gintis put it, "By giving citizens the power to encroach upon the capacity of capital to invest profitably and to discipline its labor force, democratic institutions challenged the basic operations of the capitalist economy and sapped its dynamism" (1986, 60). Profits were being squeezed, and the state, along with "too much democracy," was the culprit.

It was in this economic context that business elites and their conservative intellectual allies launched a full-scale assault on the democratic state. Their argument against positive government contains four main components:

1. The U.S. economy had gone sour and government interference in private markets was to blame (Gilder 1981). "Indulgences" by government, in the words of David Stockman, "override the outcomes of the marketplace . . . introducing inefficiencies, arbitrary wealth transfers, and resource misallocations" (Blumenthal 1986, 219).

2. Government programs exacerbate rather than alleviate social problems. Irving Kristol hones this argument in his analysis of the law of "unintended consequences" (1983, 68) and Charles Murray provides empirical "proof" in his study of how anti-poverty programs actually cause poverty (1984).

3. Expanded government programs provided a nest for a "new class" of leftist, activist intellectuals, who used their positions to undermine the activities of private enterprise (Steinfels 1979, 56–58). Cutting programs such as the Legal Services Corporation and the Environmental Protection Agency was touted by conservatives as central to curtailing "the New Class assault on American institutions" (Blumenthal 1986, 231). "They're stashed all over the government," said David Stockman about the "New Class." "We'll find out where they are and throw them out" (231). One conservative member of Congress summed up the attack on the state this way: "We're going to defund the left" (Mollenkopf 1983, 282).

4. Expanded government had created an "overloaded political economy" (Rose and Peters 1978, 3–42), in which the system threatened to be "engulfed by a rising tide of entitlement" (Dickson and Noble 1981, 275). Theorists such as Samuel Huntington warned that the U.S. political system was becoming ungovernable because too many demands were being placed on the system; too

much democracy, in short, was dangerous (Huntington 1975, 50–118). The "intrusion of popular economic demands into political contexts" threatened corporate leaders (Piven and Cloward 1981, 123), and the ungovernability argument provided a convenient justification for cutting back government activities—particularly activities addressing the needs of low-income and working people.

Making these ideas the central themes in American politics took a concerted—and expensive—effort on the part of the business community. As Thomas Edsall has documented, much time and money was devoted to mobilizing business organizations, lobbying Congress, and supporting politicians sympathetic to the message that positive government was a bad thing. In an era in which political elites rely less on mobilized mass constituencies and party organization and more on capital-intensive, direct-mail and media campaigns, politicians were particularly susceptible to the pressures exerted by the politicized business community. Organizations such as the Business Roundtable and a revitalized Chamber of Commerce worked in various ways to get the anti-government message out (Edsall 1984, 107–140).

Corporations also spent millions financing the research and scholarship activities of intellectuals supportive of the anti-state argument. Think tanks and research institutions such as the Heritage Foundation, the American Enterprise Institute, the Hoover Institution, and the National Bureau of Economic Research received millions of dollars in the 1970s and 1980s from Fortune 500 companies and conservative foundations (Edsall 1984, 107–140; Blumenthal 1986, 32–68). The research emanating from these bodies invariably proved that positive government had a destructive impact on all areas of life, particularly management of the U.S. economy.

By the late 1970s, the mobilized corporate community was spending an estimated $1 billion a year on "corporate advocacy advertising," designed to undermine public support for positive government. As Thomas Edsall concludes, "The success of corporate advocacy advertising has been to cast public doubt on the solutions offered by the adversaries of business. The most consistent theme of corporate advocacy and public-interest advertising has been a sustained attack on the use of government money and regulation to solve social problems" (1984, 116).

Thus, it was not through serendipity or even a blinding flash of collective insight that the anti-state theme became "conventional wisdom" in 1980s politics. In the context of generalized fears over the trajectory of the U.S. economy and in the absence of any coherent or adequately organized alternative the well orchestrated attack on positive government by the business community and its intellectual allies *became* the conventional wisdom. The growth of a democratic state *was* a threat to business-class interests; positive government *could* provide an alternative to corporate-controlled markets. The debate over the role of the state was the crucial battle in what Piven and Cloward call "the new class war." As Sidney Blumenthal observes, "Unraveling the government becomes a form of control over it and a method to concentrate planning in private hands" (1986, 53).

Liberal defenders of the state proved no match for the corporate/conservative attackers for three reasons. First, it is inherently difficult to make the case for positive government in the absence of sustained traditions of support for "collective enterprise." As Karl Frieden persuasively argues,

> Unwieldiness of collective consumption erodes public confidence in government. Regardless of their relative merits, market goods or services that can be purchased on an individual basis, without conflict over goals, ability to pay, or democratic procedures, are likely to be appreciated more than collective output that can only be procured in a roundabout and politicized way. . . .
>
> . . .Since government is always spending money on programs that some people dislike, we all believe that the government budget is too large in relation to the benefits we receive from it. Even if we believe that a larger government is warranted, there are existing programs whose elimination we would applaud. This helps explain why citizens tend to be programmatically pro-government, but ideologically anti-government. (1986, 19,21)

Second, liberalism provides a weak ideological foundation on which to base public authority. Rather than basing state action on public purposes and communitarian values, liberalism defines the public good as the aggregation of private interests; thus, the role of government is to manipulate and channel self-interest into a social equilibrium. As Theodore Lowi points out in his brilliant analysis of "why liberal governments can't plan," this "interest-group liberalism" helped produce the 1970s crisis of public authority by failing to delineate the *public* purposes to which expanded governmental authority should be dedicated; instead, "interest group liberalism seeks to justify power . . . by parceling out to private parties the power to make public policy" (1979, 44). The idea of a New Deal "planning state"—advocated by progressives such as Rexford Tugwell—effectively gave way to a pluralist, "broker state" whose main function was as arbiter of competing private claims (Graham 1976, 88).

Finally, liberals failed to deflect the corporate assault on the state because they never challenged the central assumption of the corporate analysis: that the workings of private markets are a sound basis on which to organize the U.S. political economy. As a leading "liberal" text in policy analysis, aimed at people planning careers in government service, puts it, "The history of interventions to deal with market failure is a history of disappointments. In a variety of areas, programs have accomplished much less than we had hoped, at a cost far greater than we expected. . . . We should learn to be modest about our abilities to create and operate government programs that will achieve their intended purposes" (Stokey and Zeckhauser 1978, 309–310). Today, this position has degenerated to the technocratic, neo-liberal notion that the proper role of government is limited to facilitating economic growth (mainly by enhancing corporate competitiveness in the global economy) and providing compassionate assistance to the "losers" in the game of economic change. In a very real sense, neo-liberalism is market conservatism with a human face; there is no concept of democratic, *positive* government *transcending* the limits of market capitalism.

What We Believe

As the attack on the state is best understood in class terms, so too is our notion of revitalized government. A theme which runs through virtually all of our chapters is that a rejuvenated public sector is essential to meeting the needs of workers and communities ill-served by private markets. We reject the conservative attack on the state, and we also reject the neo-liberal emphasis on marketplace solutions instead of government solutions. Such an approach only reinforces existing inequalities in power and privilege. Moreover, as Chapters 3, 5, and 6 clearly indicate, marketplace solutions are notably deficient even in a technocratic sense: the most serious problems we face simply are not amenable to primarily market-based approaches.

We agree with George F. Will, of all people, who condemns those who would limit government to "policing the arena to limit anarchy" (1983, 35). Perhaps the most destructive consequence of the conservative ascendancy has been the glorification of the pursuit of private gain and the denigration of public action and communitarian pursuits. Public action, representing common goals determined through democratic debate, is off limits in this conservative era. It is supposedly more efficient—and democratic—to leave public problem-solving to the profit-motive or noblesse-oblige of business elites. It is, for example, more appropriate for the Donald Trumps of the world to determine urban land use patterns and housing policies than for democratically elected and accountable city governments to make such decisions. Ada Louise Huxtable, in her analysis of recent trends in New York City architecture, has nicely captured how such a privatistic philosophy impoverishes public life:

> What is new and notable in New York City's unprecedented building boom
> is that all previous legal, moral, and esthetic restraints have been thrown to the
> winds, or more accurately, to the developers, in grateful consideration of contributions to the tax base and the political purse. It is as if conflict of interest
> were a quaint, outmoded idea. . . . The city is wide open. Greed has never
> been so chic. The public interest has never been so passe. (1987, 1)

In the absence of positive government, community standards and public values are corroded by a public philosophy that says "the market is always right." Ivan

Boesky and the Wall Street criminals are in many ways the appropriate symbols of conservative policy; they are the logical products of marketplace solutions.

Robert Kuttner points out that there are two main arguments against public action and *for* a market-based political economy. First, in a free market, people supposedly get what they deserve: if the state tampers with the "principle of dessert," then efficient producers will have their incentives dampened—and all of society will suffer as growth is stifled (1984, 13). Second, as Kuttner summarizes the anti-statists, "If you love the Post Office, you'll love socialism" (23). In other words, government action, lacking the immediate profit or "hire/fire" incentives of the private sector, is inherently inefficient.

Kuttner's own analysis—as well as Jeff Faux's in Chapter 6—effectively refutes the first claim. An activist state, promoting equality, does not necessarily slow economic growth—and the evidence from advanced capitalist economies is compelling (Kuttner, 1984). As for the inherent-inefficiency-of-public-action argument, supporting evidence is generally anecdotal, impressionistic, and propagandistic. Critics tend to cite isolated cases of administrative bungling or bureaucratic insensitivity, or else, as the tendentious Grace Commission does, *define* social programs as "waste, fraud, and abuse." Curiously, the most significant examples of private sector bungling—disastrous investment decisions of U.S. auto and steel manufacturers in the 1960s and 1970s, for instance—are rarely mentioned by efficiency-minded critics of public action.

The fact is that public action is necessary because of inherent inadequacies of private markets in our corporate-dominated economy. Consider the following common examples of market failure:

1. the existence of "externalities," where the costs of private action—pollution, for example—are passed along to society at large;

2. the need for public goods and services that private markets fail to provide but without which private markets could not function—transportation or other infrastructure investments, for example;

3. non-existent markets for socially needed goods and services—low-income housing, health care for the indigent, etc.

Without positive government rectifying and transcending these market failures, it is difficult to imagine U.S. society functioning efficiently in any sense of the word—let alone equitably or humanely. While inefficient public administration is hardly commendable—and, as Chapter 3 outlines, the positive state should be anchored in administrative efficacy—the failures of private markets have much more serious consequences for most people. The key task of policymakers should be to determine the proper blend of state and market: what public goals are best met by market mechanisms and what public goals are best accomplished through government action.

Revitalizing positive government is not an end in itself. The goal, of course, is a state that acts in the public interest. As much of the writing on the state in capitalist societies makes clear, active government has often been controlled by capital and has acted in the interests of capital on crucial policy matters (Carnoy 1984, 208–246). Even state institutions aimed at limiting the destructive consequences of private markets—Progressive Era reforms in urban planning and business regulation, for example—have often been controlled by powerful economic interests or have seen their range of action significantly circumscribed by those interests. Today, sophisticated business community leaders understand how positive government can serve their class interests—in a corporate-oriented industrial policy, for example—and thus strongly support the idea of revitalized positive government. Their idea of what government should do as well as how public decisions should be reached, however, is radically different from ours. As Maurice Zeitlin points out, "What they want is state planning of the economy, but planning that is by and for them, inaccessible to elected officials and sheltered from popular demands" (1982, 70). It would be planning in the private interest, socializing risk, and privatizing profits.

Who controls the state, the *accountability* of state action, and the *process* by which public decisions are made are all crucial to whether reinvigorated government institutions will serve the public interest or the interests of the economically powerful. Concomitantly, there is a legitimate concern that positive government can degenerate into statism: inefficient and, more importantly, unaccountable bureaucracy. In the absence of vibrant democratic political movements, combined with institutional mechanisms to facilitate participation and ensure accountability, the state can become a threat to individual freedom as well as a tool of the economically dominant.

Our notion of revitalized government, then, is one that occurs within the context of expanded political participation and a renewed democratic culture. Only in this context can individual freedom be maintained while rendering "the exercise of both property rights and state power accountable" (Bowles and Gintis 1986, 177). As each chapter makes clear, democratizing the *process* of public choice is more important than whether or not elite planners make the correct policy choices. This book advocates increased public participation in revitalized government, not democratic elitism, however well intentioned.

In sum, our somewhat immodest aim is to contribute to the development of a new public philosophy in the United States—one that comprises communitarian values, a state capable of effective action in the public interest, a participatory political culture, and a democratic, accountable process of public choice.* The contributors to this volume address these themes in four key areas of government activity: administration, regulation, economic development, and

---

* The section that follows was co-authored by Carol MacLennan and Marc V. Levine

national security. These are not, of course, all of the important things government does—or can do. Our purpose is not to examine comprehensively all areas of public policy. Instead, by selectively focusing on key areas of government action, we are attempting to restate the case for positive government as well as illuminate the negative consequences of an undemocratic policy process.

John Kushma's chapter on democracy sets the stage for the following chapters with a historical overview of the decline of parties and mass political participation. Kushma shows how the rise of political parties in the early 1800s was essential to the development of a democratic vision. The decline of parties during the Progressive Era and continuing throughout the twentieth century has effectively eroded the key institutional mediator between the people and their government. Kushma argues that a democratic crisis exists, with a growing "party" of non-voters increasingly alienated from the political process, a condition that enhances elite control over policy and lessens government accountability. A crucial step for the revitalization of democracy, argues Kushma, is the reinvigoration of local partisan politics.

Carol MacLennan addresses the problem of the state's administrative apparatus itself, often a major obstacle to the articulation of democratic interests. She shows how a philosophy of public management—an "administrative orthodoxy"—has prevailed over the last century to insure the evolution of bureaucracies dominated by technocratic elites who are insulated from public input and vulnerable to ideological control from the White House. Because the orthodoxy insists that public administration is a politically neutral instrument of public policy-making, it encourages an unhealthy distance between bureaucracies and citizens. Historically, this concept of government has been reinforced by increased centralization of management, periodic drives for economy and efficiency, creation of a politicized civil service system, and pressures to privatize government functions. MacLennan argues that enhancing democracy must involve restructuring public administration itself. Her proposals include civil service reform and the creation of open government methods of decision-making.

Charles Noble examines environmental and workplace regulation. He concludes that new institutions must be established to deal with the serious problem of hazards to public health. Noble explains that current regulatory institutions have failed because they do not confront the "deep structure" of market capitalism, which is the source of hazards. Moreover, as Noble points out, past "regulatory regimes" have been constrained in effectively dealing with environmental hazards because of the inordinate power of corporate interests. He proposes "transitional" reforms to strengthen state regulatory capacity through health and safety investment planning and centralized regulatory institutions. At the same time, however, he calls for greater Congressional involvement and enhanced rights of unions and communities in monitoring hazards and regulatory compliance.

Marc Levine analyzes the growing role of state and local governments in economic development. He demonstrates how political-economic conditions of the 1970s—deindustrialization, the politicization of the business community, and the fiscal distress of local governments—stimulated an "investment climate" approach to economic policy in which private sector elites determined the investment priorities and local policies for economic revitalization. A "growth ideology," based on the notion that the interests of capital are synonymous with the community or public interest, has dominated state and local economic development efforts. The results of this approach to economic development have been urban decline, increased inequality, and decreasing democratic control over local policy-making and public institutions. Levine proposes a democratic alternative to the investment climate approach, one that emphasizes strategic planning and neighborhood participation in economic development.

The final two chapters tackle two crucial substantive issues for post-Reagan government: forging a new direction in national economic planning and rethinking national defense policy. Jeff Faux indicates how the changed global economy threatens to undercut the living standards and economic growth Americans have enjoyed since 1945. Faux argues that Adam Smithian, anti-government models of economic policy are anachronistic in the current environment and that an active planning state is essential to our future well-being. Faux develops specific proposals to enhance the role of the public sector in managing the national economy, all predicated on the notion that explicit public planning is central to full employment and the creation of quality jobs. In a very real sense, Faux resurrects the radical Keynes from the limitations imposed by neo-classical economists.

Marcus Raskin raises the critical question of how democratic government deals with the difficult issues of national security in a nuclear world. He outlines how the rise of the U.S. national security state has threatened democracy at home while creating havoc throughout the world. His chapter is a vivid reminder that conservatives and capitalists also have their version of activist government, but it is neither democratic nor progressive.

References

Blumenthal, S. 1986. *The rise of the counter-establishment: From conservative ideology to political power*. New York: Basic Books.

Bowles, S. and H. Gintis. 1986. *Democracy and capitalism: property, community, and the contradictions of modern social thought*. New York: Basic Books.

Burnham, W. D. 1983. *The current crisis in American politics*. New York: Oxford University Press.

Carnoy, M. 1984. *The state and political theory*. Princeton: Princeton University Press.

Carnoy, M., D. Shearer, and R. Rumberger. 1983. *A New social contract: The economy and government after Reagan*. New York: Harper and Row.

Dickson, D. and D. Noble. 1981. By force of reason: The politics of science and technology policy. Eds. T. Ferguson and J. Rogers, *The hidden election: Politics and economics in the 1980 presidential campaign*. New York: Pantheon Books.

Edsall, T. B. 1984. *The new politics of inequality*. New York: W. W. Norton and Company.

Fogelsong, R. 1986. *Planning the capitalist city: The colonial era to the 1920s.* Princeton: Princeton University Press.

Frieden, K. 1986. Public needs and private wants. *Social Policy* 17(2): 19–30.

Gilder, G. 1981. *Wealth and poverty.* New York: Basic Books.

Gordon, D. 1986. To have and have not: Class warfare is being waged in U.S. society and most people don't even know it. *Washington Post National Weekly Edition.* 10 November.

Graham, O. 1976. *Toward a planned economy.* New York: Oxford University Press.

Hartz, L. 1948. *Economic policy and democratic thought: Pennsylvania, 1776–1860.* Cambridge: Harvard University Press.

Huntington, S. P. 1975. Chapter III—the United States. M. Crozier, S. P. Huntington and J. Watunuki, *The crisis of democracy: Report on the governability of democracies to the Trilateral Commission.* New York: New York University Press.

Huxtable, A. L. 1987. Creeping gigantism in Manhattan. *The New York Times,* 22 March.

Kolko, G. 1977. *The triumph of conservatism.* New York: The Free Press.

Kristol, I. 1983. *Reflections of a neo-conservative.* New York: Basic Books.

Kuttner, R. 1984. *The economic illusion: False choices between prosperity and social justice.* Boston: Houghton, Mifflin and Company.

Leff, M. 1973. Consensus for reform: The mothers' pension movement in the Progressive Era. *Social Service Review* 47(4): 397–417.

Lowi, T. 1979. *The end of liberalism: The second republic of the United States.* 2nd ed. New York: W. W. Norton and Company.

Mollenkopf, J. 1983. *The contested city.* Princeton: Princeton University Press.

Murray, C. 1984. *Losing ground: American social policy, 1950–1980.* New York: Basic Books.

Orloff, A., and T. Skocpol. 1984. Why not equal protection? Explaining the politics of public social spending in Britain, 1900–1911, and the United States, 1880–1920. *American Sociological Review* 49(2): 726–50.

Phillips, K. P. 1982. *Post-conservative America: people, politics, and ideology in a time of crisis.* New York: Random House.

Piven, F. F. and R. A. Cloward. 1981. *The new class war: Reagan's attack on the welfare state and its consequences.* New York: Pantheon.

Reeves, R. 1985. *The Reagan detour.* New York: Simon and Schuster.

Rose, R., and G. Peters. 1978. *Can government go bankrupt?* New York: Basic Books.

Schneider, W. 1987. The new shape of American politics: A primer for the Reagan years and beyond. *The Atlantic* January: 39–61.

Schwarz, J. E. 1983. *America's hidden success: A reassessment of twenty years of public policy.* New York: W. W. Norton and Company.

Skocpol, T., and J. Ikenberry. 1983. The political formation of the American welfare state in historical and comparative perspective. *Comparative Social Research* 6: 126–131.

Steinfels, P. 1979. *The neo-conservatives: The men who are changing America's politics.* New York: Simon and Schuster.

Stokey, R., and E. Zeckhauser. 1978. *A primer in policy analysis.* New York: W. W. Norton and Company.

Whitaker, R. 1987. Neo-conservatism and the state. Eds. R. Miliband, L. Panitch, and J. Saville. *Socialist register 1987.* London: Merlin Press.

Will, G. F. 1983. *Statecraft as soulcraft: What government does.* New York: Simon and Schuster.

Wolfe, A. 1981. *America's impasse: The rise and fall of the politics of growth.* New York: Pantheon.

Zeitlin, M. 1982. Democratic Investment. *Democracy* 2(2): 69–80.

2 Participation and the Democratic Agenda: Theory and Praxis

John J. Kushma

> The most powerful and perhaps the only means that we still possess of interesting men in the welfare of their country is to make them partakers in the government.
>
> —Alexis de Tocqueville

More than a century and a half ago, Alexis de Tocqueville, perhaps the most perceptive foreign analyst of U.S. democracy and the American character, marvelled at the political activism of the American people. He observed,

> It is difficult to say what place is taken up in the life of an inhabitant of the United States by his concern for politics. To take a hand in the regulation of society and to discuss it is his biggest concern and, so to speak, the only pleasure an American knows. If an American were condemned to confine his activity to his own affairs, he would be robbed of one half of his existence; he would feel an immense void in the life which he is accustomed to lead, and his wretchedness would be unbearable. (1945, 1:250)

Tocqueville's observation is best confirmed by the high voter turnout in the decades after the crystallization of the first mass party system in the 1830s. By 1840, voter turnout in presidential elections exceeded 80 percent of the eligible electorate. This high level of political participation was maintained throughout the remainder of the nineteenth century: approximately three-fourths of the eligible voters cast ballots in presidential elections and two-thirds in congressional races.

One need not romanticize the past (nor forget those groups excluded from the franchise in the nineteenth century) to recognize how electoral participation has changed. Despite Americans' continuing interest in politics, slightly more than half of the electorate has bothered to vote in presidential elections and well below half has voted in off-year congressional races during the last twenty-five years. The dramatic decline in voter turnout since the nineteenth century is illustrated by the fact that the *losers* in the presidential canvasses in the last quarter of the nineteenth century—Samuel J. Tilden, Winfield S. Hancock, James G. Blaine, Grover Cleveland, Benjamin Harrison, and William Jennings Bryan— averaged a 16 percent greater proportion of the eligible popular vote than did Ronald Reagan in his "landslide" 1984 victory.

Meanwhile, the chief institutions of electoral politics—political parties— are also in the process of decline. In recent years, the number of Americans who identify strongly with a political party has decreased (Wattenberg 1984). Split-ticket voting has become increasingly prevalent, and independent candidacies proliferate. The thinness of what V. O. Key, Jr., terms the "party in the electorate" is evident in the rate at which House and Senate incumbents were returned to office in 1984 (among the highest ever recorded), despite Reagan's extraordinary popular vote victory. Except for occasional flashes of partisan unity in the House and Senate, the role of party in shaping Congressional behavior is also ebbing. Finally, many of the functions that the parties traditionally performed—from educating the electorate, to enrolling new voters, to selecting candidates, to organizing campaigns, to shaping the public agenda—have increasingly been taken over by other agencies or specialized, essentially closed organizations within the party hierarchy that are not accountable to the party rank and file (Sabato 1981; Blumenthal 1982).

Simultaneous with the precipitous decline in electoral participation and the weakening of political parties over the last quarter century has been a veritable explosion in the number and variety of groups designed to achieve collective political goals (Katz 1981; Smith et al. 1980; Schlozman and Tierney 1986). Although precise figures are lacking, it is probable that this growth is unsurpassed in U.S. history. Many of these groups are more or less traditional in their aims, functioning as interest or pressure groups in the political system or as service groups for their members. On the other hand, many of these newly formed groups represent a distinct concern for what have been termed "post-materialist" values (Inglehart 1977). Such values focus on individual and collective self-development and self-realization rather than on the exclusive satisfaction of material needs.

Even a cursory examination of contemporary political participation reveals a paradox that analysts of U.S. electoral behavior have been hard pressed to explain. Today's electorate, which is subject to fewer legal and geographic barriers, is more educated and more affluent, and presumably possesses more political information than its predecessors, turns out to vote at a considerably lower rate. A U.S. public that actively participates in a variety of collective enterprises from voluntary associations to churches, labor unions, and communitarian, cooperative, and self-help organizations and that still believes in its own efficacy has rejected the ballot as an instrument for the realization of public goals. Almost half of the American people have abandoned the historical bridge between the citizen and the state.

Surveying the decline in electoral turnout through the 1960s and 1970s, Richard A. Brody concludes that "the shrinking level of participation in American national elections confounds our expectations and is at odds with the explanations of turnout offered by available theories of political behavior" (1978, 290). The same paradox is evident if Americans are compared to citizens in other democratic nations. With the exception of Switzerland, which has a lower turnout rate than the United States, all of the other Western European democracies had turnout rates well over 30 percent greater than the rate recorded in U.S. presidential elections during the 1970s. As G. Bingham Powell has recently noted, "Americans seem to be more politically aware and involved than citizens in any other democracy, yet the levels of voter turnout in the United States are consistently far below the democratic average" (1986, 17).

Although the first precipitous decline in turnout dates to the turn of the century, some view today's shrinking level as only a temporary phenomenon. The most recent Census Bureau report on voting in the United States sanguinely concludes that the hemorrhage of voters from the active electorate has been stanched. It confidently asserts that "[a]ssuming no drop in the rates for individual age groups, overall voter participation rates will rise through the rest of this century, as the large baby boom cohorts age and move into older groups, which traditionally have higher voter turnout" (U.S. Bureau of Census 1986, 1). Turnout in 1986 belied that prediction, however, since it dropped to its lowest level since World War II. Even if the Census Bureau's projection ultimately proves accurate (and given the volatility the U.S. political system has manifested over the last twenty years, all projections should be subject to healthy doses of skepticism), turnout will still remain considerably below historical rates and rates in other democracies.

The unresolved paradox of contemporary political participation is only the most visible symptom of a profound and enduring political crisis in the United States. True, people are not taking to the streets to signify their discontent. There are few, if any, overt manifestations of political ill health to compare to the dislocation and genuine fear of the Great Depression. Politics seems to continue as usual, but in fact political alienation is pervasive, public trust in government is staggeringly low, and public cynicism is equally high. Over the past decades, citizens have increasingly come to believe that public officials do not care what they think and government does not respond to public opinion. In their recent study of the public's attitudes toward key institutions, Seymour Martin Lipset and William Schneider document the dimensions of public discontent and distrust and conclude that the United States now suffers "a lower reserve of confidence in the ability of its institutional leaders to deal with the problems of the polity, the society, and the economy than at any time in this century" (1982, 411–12). Democracy is in jeopardy.

Tocqueville would not have been surprised by today's moribund electoral politics or by the depressingly barren public life of the vast majority of U.S. citizens. He predicted that the combination of increasing administrative centralization of government and increasing privatization of human existence could ultimately transform U.S. citizens into colonists in their own land, dependent on yet resentful toward a remote and arbitrary state. In the face of bewilderment and confusion spawned by a government seemingly beyond popular control, Americans would withdraw into ever more circumscribed lives. Even individualism itself, Tocqueville argued, would eventually become impoverished because materialism and unsatisfying politics of self-interest could not compensate Americans for their abandonment of public concerns and communal life. He concluded that under these conditions a political society "may contain good subjects, but it can have no active citizens" (1945, 1:69). Tocqueville's prediction is a remarkably accurate description of contemporary U.S. public life and political culture (Bellah et al. 1985; Merelman, 1984).

U.S. democracy has weathered political crises before. As Samuel Huntington suggests, the gap between democratic ideals and their realization in political institutions has resulted in a creative tension that has inspired recurring eras of political reform (1981). Likewise, periods of widespread discontent with the existing political order have historically been resolved through a series of electoral upheavals wherein the realignment of political groups in a new party system is linked to a new political agenda, a corresponding set of new public policy initiatives, the growth of new political institutions, and ultimately a fundamental reorientation of the political system (Key 1955; Burnham 1970, 1982; Sundquist 1973). These periods of "critical realignment" have occurred more or less regularly from the 1790s to the 1930s, beginning with the overthrow of the Federalists by the Republicans under Thomas Jefferson in 1800 and evident most recently in the Democratic dominance under Franklin D. Roosevelt inaugurated during the Great Depression.[1] Why not simply assume that our contemporary crisis, although clearly more protracted than any other in our nation's history, will be similarly resolved?

Some analysts suggest that our national political crisis has already been resolved or at least is in the process of resolution under the guidance of the political right. After all, U.S. politics has entered a period of conservative dominance, culminating in the "Reagan Revolution," in which the passions and the agenda of the 1960s and 1970s have been abandoned (White 1982). The Republicans have been victorious in four of the last five presidential elections, frequently by impressive margins. A variety of Democratic leaders has proclaimed their party's ideological bankruptcy, called for "new issues" to replace an older set of political concerns, and advocated a turn to the right. The impressive gains that the Democrats made in the 1986 Senate elections seem to confirm this wisdom since these gains were clearly not accompanied by an explicit rejection of the conservativism that has recently characterized national politics. Moreover, Democratic gains in Congress were more than offset by Republican victories in gubernatorial races, and Republican Senate candidates actually polled a higher percentage of the votes cast in Senate races in 1986 than they did in 1980 when they took twelve seats from the Democrats.

Public philosophy seems to have drifted in a conservative direction as well. The ideas of neo-conservatives, spiritually renewed, if not refurbished, traditional conservatives, and big business tend to dominate public discourse and the public agenda (Steinfels 1980; Peele 1984; Edsall 1984). Particularly after the apparent failure of Keynesian economic policies the political right has advocated and the public has tacitly accepted the imposition of fiscal restraints on the public sector, the elimination of a variety of transfer and entitlement programs, and the abandonment or weakening of regulatory programs. A philosophical commitment to reducing the public sphere in favor of the private and opting for market over governmental solutions has come to predominate. These ideas have been advocated by the Republicans under Ronald Reagan, generally acknowledged as the most conservative president of the last half century. They have also been promoted by an impressively large network of newly created right-wing institutions, which the late John Saloma termed "the new conservative labyrinth" (Saloma 1984). Americans have been encouraged to ask less and expect less of government.

Public policy has also careened in a conservative direction. The Reagan administration's systematic onslaught against the welfare state, a move carried out without a majority in the House of Representatives, resulted in a change in public policy perhaps unmatched in half a century. Although major cuts in social programs were confined to the first two years of Reagan's presidency, subsequent years have not seen a return to or an extension of previous social welfare policies designed to redress gross social and economic inequities.

The nation does seem to have moved in a conservative direction, but this move is more illusion than reality. The major changes in public policy during the Reagan administration have come about without a fundamental change in Americans' beliefs or behavior. As Walter Dean Burnham has demonstrated, we have witnessed "a *policy* realignment without *electoral* realignment" (1985, 250). The public is generally opposed to the basic policies of the Reagan administration and the Republican party (Ferguson and Rogers 1986a; Lipset 1986). It should be unnecessary to point out that this reality is at odds with democratic traditions. In short, this erosion of institutions of popular, democratic control is the crisis in U.S. politics.

What makes the resolution of the contemporary crisis problematic is that traditional institutions of democratic mediation between citizens and the state— elections and political parties—are weakening. The decline of electoral participation, the slow decomposition of legislative parties, the lack of coherence between the executive branch and Congress, and the partisan dealignment of the electorate all testify to the weakness of what have traditionally been the predominant agencies of democratic politics. To the extent that fewer voters go to the polls and our political parties continue to deteriorate, we face more than a crisis of political performance. U.S. democracy is undergoing a slow and protracted death. Should an economic collapse or an equally devastating national crisis occur, the weakness of the agencies of democratic governance will be quickly apparent, for it is unlikely that such a crisis would be resolved in a democratic manner.

One entrenched principle of democracy, for example, is the belief that elections ought to ensure public control over governmental leaders and public policy or at least institutionalize the responsiveness of the state to public opinion. Building on inherited British wisdom, the American revolutionary generation viewed elections as an important means for protecting citizens from the arbitrary exercise of power by governmental leaders.

Equally important to the democratic tradition, though less frequently articulated, is the recognition that elections legitimate and strengthen the state and mobilize popular support for the regime. James Wilson, more democratically inclined than the majority of delegates to the Constitutional Convention, nonetheless joined with conservatives in favoring a strong national government; he understood that a strong national government required popular participation. Wilson proclaimed himself in favor of "raising the federal pyramid to a considerable altitude, and for that reason wished to give it as broad a base as possible," through popular elections (Farrand 1911, 1:49). Other delegates reluctantly endorsed the popular election of representatives because they could see no alternative. They knew that Americans would never accept a government that did not secure its legitimacy and power through elections. As the avowedly elitist George Mason admonished his colleagues, "Notwithstanding the oppressions and injustices experienced among us from democracy, the genius of the people is in favor of it, and the genius of the people must be consulted" (Farrand 1911, 1:101).

Despite the widespread antipathy to political parties in the late eighteenth century and the "constitution against parties" drafted by the Constitutional Convention, political parties emerged as those agencies through which Americans would realize the potential for popular control and mobilization of public support (Hofstadter 1969). It is appropriate that during this bicentennial anniversary of the Constitution the American people and government revert to their first principles and recognize that democracy demands an active citizenry. Democracy requires popular participation in an electoral process that ensures the state legitimacy and authority to realize the humane, just, and equitable society the American people desire.

What is likely to occur if the crisis of our democratic institutions is not resolved? Theorists from both the political right and left have made predictions. Conservatives and neo-conservatives have focused on the "governability" problem, the fear that the proliferation of demands spurred by increased public expectations (or actual needs, although conservative theorists tend to dismiss these) will overwhelm the ability of the state to respond adequately. If the state does not accede to legitimate demands, it will promote frustration, cynicism, and lack of trust among citizens and ultimately lead to a legitimacy crisis. On the other hand, if the state lacks sufficient authority to manage these demands in a manner congruent with the national and international economy, economic decline and ultimately severe deprivation and dislocation will result. Hence the prescription of Ronald Reagan—individual moderation, self-reliance, and the abandonment or weakening of a variety of positive governmental programs (Crozier, Huntington, and Watanuki 1975; Brittan 1975; Kristol and Glazer 1976; Rose and Peters 1978).

The left sees the Reagan prescription as a traditional conservative capitulation to the power of capital in the United States, particularly under conditions of economic instability and slow growth. The state, lacking the ability to compel capitalists to invest in a manner beneficial to the entire society, is required to make a variety of concessions to induce investment. This political response serves to narrow democratic alternatives, abandon norms of equity and fairness, and impose repressive constraints on those groups presumed to threaten the business climate (Block 1977). With increased use of repressive techniques, the state becomes increasingly unable to mobilize public support through normal democratic channels. This, in turn, leads to the use of institutions and values whose relationship to democratic traditions is, to say the least, highly irregular. The conduct of foreign policy over the last few decades is perhaps the most obvious example.

As Claus Offe has perceptively argued, it is likely that both conservative and radical predictions are correct. As he suggests, "the polity becomes *repressive* and *unmanageable* at the same time" (1980, 8).[2] The course of American politics over the last quarter century certainly coincides with this judgement. Governmental elites have been unable to manage satisfactorily the myriad conflicts of a post-industrial United States, have frequently bypassed the traditional agencies of democratic governance, and have resorted to a variety of extra-constitutional mechanisms and repressive tactics to achieve their policies.

Offe's analysis suggests the depressing state of American political culture today and explains the recent success of political conservatism. More than two decades ago, during the heyday of the "Great Society," Lloyd Free and Hadley Cantril concluded that the modal political belief system in the United States was "schizoid." Americans, although essentially liberal in favoring policies designed to reduce inequality, provide for social and economic security, and institutionalize political rights, were profoundly conservative in rejecting "big government" (1967). If by "big government" we understand arbitrary government, then this set of apparently conflicting values is quite comprehensible. Americans maintain considerable support for many fundamental values of social democracy but openly question whether the traditional institutional mechanisms of popular control—elections and political parties—are sufficient to ensure that the power granted to the state to realize those values will not be used for other less laudable purposes that threaten their freedom. In an eerie way, contemporary American values echo revolutionary values. Just as eighteenth-century Americans viewed, in Bernard Bailyn's words, the "antinomy of power and liberty . . . as the central fact of politics," so many Americans today have come to see an arbitrary, uncontrolled, and power-hungry state as a threat to their liberties (1970, 56). There is no pathology in the political values of the American people. The pathology lies in the structure of American political institutions.

This analysis also suggests a resolution to the paradox of political participation in the United States and an explanation for the deterioration of political parties. Americans have realized that these traditional agencies of democracy no longer function as effectively to mediate between citizens and the state. Many people have consequently abandoned them or have continued to participate in them in a more or less ritualistic manner. To the extent that they have done so, democracy has been weakened. To the extent that they increasingly continue to do so, democracy is at risk.

The structural weakness of democratic institutions remains evident beneath the surface of contemporary conservative resurgence, which by no means represents a successful response to the crisis of democracy. In an era when Americans no longer trust the state to behave in a manner congruent with their values, less government appears an attractive alternative to arbitrary government. This analysis must inform strategy and tactics on the left. Coalitional politics, the search for a "political formula" to rival that put forth by neo-conservatives, or even a charismatic and skillful presidential candidate with a different agenda and different values may provide a temporary reversal to the current political balance and lead to more progressive governmental policies. However, without a highly developed popular base of electoral support, without a revitalization of the Democratic party or an alternative structure of collective power that operates in accordance with traditional democratic norms, all progressive policies will be just as vulnerable as those weakened by the Reagan administration.

The revival of interest in democracy among leftist theorists testifies to the growing recognition that more is at issue for the left than merely affecting current government policy (Cohen and Rogers 1983; Green 1985; Bowles and Gintis 1986). At issue is democracy itself. This, of course, is precisely what radical groups and theorists argued in the 1960s. Unwilling to accept the facile and fraudulent notions of consensus, interest-group liberalism, bargaining, and incrementalism summed up in the concept of pluralist democracy, a variety of radical critics pointed out the inequities of the political system and its departure from traditional ideas of democracy (Bachrach 1967; Connolly 1969; Kariel 1961; McConnell 1966; McCoy and Playford 1967; Mills 1959; Schattschneider 1960). At the time few Americans were convinced, and the call for a retrieval of democracy fell on deaf ears. The course of U.S. politics after this failure of reform has been sobering.

Two important political changes suggest that a similar call now stands a much better chance of success, even in today's more conservative political climate. First is the disarray of the pluralist framework that had served as the primary paradigm of American academic political science since the 1950s and that was often uncritically employed to legitimate the actual operation of the U.S. political system. Recent studies by Robert A. Dahl and Charles E. Lindblom, who themselves helped to establish the dominance of pluralism as an analytical approach within the academy, are highly critical of the institutional arrangements and inequalities of the U.S. political system (Lindblom 1977; Dahl 1977, 1982). Although neither Dahl nor Lindblom, contrary to many of their critics, functioned as an apologist for the U.S. political system, the pluralist analytical framework did quickly become identified as "pluralist democracy" and acquired normative connotations in public discourse.

Second, and of far greater importance, is that Americans themselves have come to recognize the chasm that separates traditions of democracy from politics today. Millions of Americans who were unconvinced by radicals in the 1960s no longer need convincing, as public opinion polls demonstrate. The language of consensus is no longer part of public discourse, having been replaced by frank recognition of power, special interests, "iron triangles," privilege, and inequality. Dissatisfied, the public has retreated from active participation in politics, an attitude that fails to address the problem.

Yet, there are signs that the "new populism" across the country—citizen action groups, consumer groups, neighborhood associations, the environmental movement—represents a return to democratic traditions (Boyte 1980). Less vocal and strident than the new left of the 1960s, the new populism is also more rooted in real as opposed to visionary communities where practical experience in democracy is available and the concepts of democratic citizenship and equality are more existentially meaningful. The movement's growth has been impressive, and its potential to revitalize the American political system is genuine.

Even in the face of these hopeful signs, however, the decomposition of parties and the decline in electoral turnout continue. Clearly, something more than community-based organizing is needed to reconstruct a democratic political system. The deterioration of the channels linking citizens and the state suggests that the solution must comprehend the larger structures of mediation in U.S. politics. The remainder of this chapter will trace briefly the history of changes in elections and political parties and their relationship to the American state. My purpose is twofold: to illuminate the origins of the current crisis and thereby to generate proposals for its resolution.

The American state was created by a generation of individuals particularly concerned with the moral qualities of citizenship. American revolutionaries were motivated by a political ideology summed up in the concept of republicanism (Bailyn 1967; Wood 1969; Shallhope 1972; Pocock 1975). With roots in ancient ideals of civic humanism and the tradition of English political dissent, republicanism called attention to those conditions that made it possible for republican government to succeed. Most important was the idea of public virtue, the willingness to forego one's personal desires for the greater good of the nation.

Cognizant of the fragile nature of historical republics and their invariable tendency to decline, the revolutionary generation continuously guarded against the encroachment of vices inimical to the public good. In practice, the greatest danger to republican society was considered to be irresponsible power. This power could emanate from a corrupt, tyrannical government or an economy driven not by republican notions of frugality, industry, and communal responsibility but by selfishness, luxury, and idleness. It was an ideology particularly well suited to an agrarian nation where as late as 1800 over 90 percent of all Americans were still working on the land.

Many revolutionaries believed that what ensured Americans' republican character was the economic structure of U.S. society. The agrarian base of self-sufficient freeholders and the rough equality that prevailed among them were believed to provide the requisite popular virtue to sustain the republican experiment. But economic life became increasingly commercialized and eighteenth- and nineteenth-century Americans were faced with the problem of maintaining republican ideals within a changing economy. Their quest for an appropriate republican political economy was an intensely ethical one, and they believed that it was entirely proper, indeed necessary, for the state to assume responsibility for directing the economy in a manner promoting those qualities associated with republican citizenship. As Drew McCoy has noted, the "revolutionaries lived during an age when a consideration of the normative dimension of economic life had not yet been sacrificed to the hubris of those would claim to make economics into a 'non-moral' science" (1980, 6). Indeed, much contemplation about what industrialization would do to America was rooted in these republican norms (Kasson 1976).

The state constructed by the delegates to the Constitutional Convention of 1787 is well known—a weak, decentralized federal state with divided powers designed to protect citizens from arbitrary governmental power. The delegates sought to insulate the state from direct popular control by depending on a wise and virtuous leadership class to govern. To the extent that protecting against unchecked power was uppermost in their minds, they succeeded. There was, however, one serious drawback. The national government found itself unable to govern effectively without mechanisms for securing public support and creating coherence among the various centers of divided power. These mechanisms were political parties.

Within a few short years after the Constitution was ratified, factions developed within Congress over a variety of public policy issues and spread into the electorate. Not the least of these issues was Alexander Hamilton's attempt to institute neo-mercantilist policies to promote the commercialization of economic life and the development of manufacturing. Hamilton was joined in this attempt by the Federalist Party, a narrowly based segment of what passed as the American establishment. Strongly commercial in outlook and disdainful of the notion that common people were capable of governing, the Federalists came to dominate Washington's administration. The Federalists' triumph reflected two features of the new national government: it was highly elitist in composition, and it rested on the votes of an extraordinarily small percentage of the eligible electorate (Chambers 1963; Goodman 1975). New, remote from aspects of daily life, and with the republican aegis of George Washington at its head, the national government attracted little attention from the vast majority of eligible voters. The Federalists never attempted to develop a popular following and depended instead on the deference of segments of the public to local notables and the use of military power when they believed it necessary to maintain order. Very few Federalists in the 1790s ever accepted the legitimacy of partisan competition, for they scarcely believed in popular politics, let alone democracy.

Consistently defeated in Washington's cabinet and in Congress, Thomas Jefferson and James Madison unwittingly became the architects of the first popular political party, the Republican Party, as they sought to move the conflicts within the national government into the electorate at large and mobilize a following against current governmental policy. They opposed the Federalists' anglicization of the United States in economic, political, and cultural terms, which they maintained would destroy the republic, and believed in the Americans' capacity for self-government. Aided in their politicization of the electorate by public reaction to the French Revolution and the repressive Alien and Sedition Acts, which abridged the political rights of citizens, the Republicans succeeded in forging a heterogeneous coalition that by 1800 was strong enough to elect Jefferson to the presidency and secure majorities in Congress. In many states previously inactive voters were mobilized, and voter turnout increased to more than 50 percent by 1800. Although the turnout rate fluctuated erratically for the next few decades, it never returned to the 10 percent level that characterized the first elections under the Constitution (Fischer 1965).

The development of national political competition popularized political life without necessarily democratizing it. One reason for the lack of democratization of politics was the collapse of the Federalists, who remained competitive only in New England. A second and more important reason was the failure of the Republicans to develop a supporting ideology for political parties. Republican leaders viewed their party only as a temporary organization to be disbanded after the Federalist threat to republicanism had been removed (Hofstadter 1969). Party organization was never systematized, control by local elites predominated, and informal procedures remained the rule within the government and among partisan leaders.

Nevertheless, the Republicans' victory in 1800 marked a milestone in the development of democracy and the state. Jefferson himself went so far as to call it the "revolution" of 1800, a revolution he viewed as equally important as the American Revolution itself. It validated the idea that the state ultimately had to rest on a popular base and that the basic contours of public policy would be set by election results. Moreover, as the parties bridged the formal and unworkable separation of powers in the national government, a real, if tenuous, collective responsibility for governing was institutionalized, and a crude means for providing a link between elections and public policy emerged.

The demise of the Federalists as a nationally competitive party temporarily halted constructive party-building. In the absence of organized parties erratic and ad hoc electoral coalitions prevailed, and the link between election returns and public policies became attenuated. The Republicans functioned as loosely organized cadres of local notables, albeit drawn from a wider social base than the Federalists.

The vagaries of this system of partyless politics spurred party-building in the United States. Building on the democratic impulses of the first party system of the 1790s and the hostility to economic privilege that resulted from the first major depression, the Panic of 1819, the importance of government's role in maintaining the republic once again became prominent. The resentment and confusion that attended the four-candidate presidential election of 1824—in which Andrew Jackson, who garnered the largest number of popular votes, was denied the presidency in the House of Representatives—also played a major role in convincing many Americans that the time had come for constructive party-building.

Political movements that sought to preserve the integrity of political institutions gained momentum. They were built on widespread opposition to the informal, private, and elitist practices that regulated nominations and partisan activity as well as public policy-making, the Antimasonic movement's condemnation of all concentrated and irresponsible political privileges, and the Democratic Party's condemnation of economic privilege. Within a decade, these movements had become political parties, and a period of vibrant and effective democratic politics was born.

In many ways, the decade of the 1830s represents the triumph of democracy in the United States. The Democratic Party and its opponents—the Antimasonic Party, the National Republicans, the Workingmen's Parties, and ultimately the Whig Party—collectively democratized politics through a variety of initiatives. Almost all property qualifications for voting were gradually lowered and ultimately abolished in favor of taxpayer qualifications, resulting in adult, white, male suffrage. Electoral units were made smaller and polling places more accessible. More public offices became elective. Restrictions on office-holding were removed, and shorter terms became the norm (McCormick 1966).

By the 1840s, the development of a modern party system was complete. Participation in party politics was widespread. A variety of mechanisms was devised to organize the public down to the smallest electoral unit. Informal nomination practices and the elite-oriented caucus system were replaced by a convention system. An organized partisan press emerged, and the parties played an important role in educating voters. Party platforms became a regular feature of election campaigns and party discipline in the national and state legislatures tightened. In the face of these and other changes voter turnout reached 80 percent of the eligible electorate in 1840 and remained high throughout the remainder of the nineteenth century as intense party competition mobilized the vast majority of eligible voters (McCormick 1975; Shade 1981).

By the late 1830s, the party system was the primary link between citizens and the government. It continued in that role for the rest of the nineteenth century. As Theodore Lowi suggests, parties served a constituent function by institutionalizing, channeling, and socializing conflict over the control of the regime (1975). The parties also performed a policy function, putting forth competing economic and social programs that were mirrored by legislative votes (McCormick 1979). Because of the frequent turnover of representatives in the national and state legislatures, who was elected made a real difference in public policy, a difference that voters could clearly see and on which they could depend. Even the trauma of the Civil War did not significantly alter the structure of democratic politics; parties came to be defined as necessary to the successful operation of the democratic state (Hofstadter 1969; Wallace 1968).

Both economic and social controversies found direct expression in the Democratic and Whig Parties in the antebellum decades. Both parties were distinct coalitions of disparate groups, united in programmatic responses to changes in U.S. society. The Democrats were in many respects traditionalists nostalgic for the agrarian past and suspicious of the economic transformation in which they were participating. Jackson's message in vetoing the recharter of the Second Bank of the United States was that the corruption of the republic could be traced to consolidated national power, the influence of economic privilege, and unchecked economic power. The Democrats' political solution to the country's economic transformation was to sever all connections between the state and the economy.

In endorsing a philosophy of the negative state, the Democrats under Jackson and his successors rejected the constructive management that characterized the earlier philosophy of the revolutionary generation. This philosophy was not a glorification of bourgeois egoism. Rather, as Marvin Meyers notes,

> . . . the movement which helped to clear the path for laissez-faire capitalism and its culture in America, and the public which in its daily life eagerly entered on that path, held nevertheless in their political conscience an ideal of a chaste, republican order, resisting the seductions of risk and novelty, greed and extravagance, rapid motion and complex dealings. (1960, 12)

The Whig coalition, in contrast, comprised groups who welcomed economic modernization in U.S. society. All but abandoning republican themes that linked commercialization, luxury, and speculation with decline, most Whigs eagerly identified progress with economic growth and industrialization, certain that the

United States would be spared the satanic mills of Manchester and other English industrial cities. Because the Whigs tended to view society as an organic unit whose elements were in harmony, they believed economic growth would benefit all citizens and not compromise democracy.

Although the triumph of political democracy (for white males) in the nineteenth century was total, economic democracy was only partial. In ways that remain unclear, republicanism and liberalism became allied in the minds of many, particularly middle-class Americans during the first half of the nineteenth century. These people, Sean Wilentz argues, "did not reject republicanism in favor of liberalism; they associated one with the other" (1982, 55).[3] Although they arrived at similar positions by very different routes, by mid-century both the Democrats and Whigs, and the Republicans after them, were engaged in promoting economic enterprise, a pattern that continued for the rest of the century. Attempts to democratize business enterprise through general incorporation laws and distributional policies, which encouraged vigorous activity by local governments to attract business—policies that then coincided with the scale of economic organization—seemed fitting. Unfortunately, it ultimately turned out to be neither. Institutionalizing market considerations in the place of political values only tended to reduce tremendously the scope of economic policy considerations in the political arena and ultimately left the political system incapable of dealing with the fundamental alterations in society wrought by industrialization and corporate capitalism later in the century.

The political patterns established in the 1830s endured throughout the remainder of the nineteenth century. Even the realignment of political parties in the 1850s (in which the Whigs were replaced by the Republicans) did not alter the prevailing structure of partisan politics. Parties had become the centerpieces of U.S. democratic politics, the agencies of collective political power. Partisan loyalty was extensive. Party activity played a central role in public life for the vast majority of white male Americans.

After a period of constructive building, the political system failed to continue its democratizing course, seeming to freeze in place. As Morton Keller notes, "during the 1870s the character of American politics sharply changed. The passionate, ideologically charged political ambiance of the Reconstruction years gave way to a politics that rested on the perpetuation of party organization rather than the fostering of public policy" (1977, 238). The passion for organization, which Ostrogorski found so prevalent that he made it the fulcrum for his classic condemnation of late nineteenth century U.S. political parties, did indeed become a primary feature of party operation, and patronage and careerism increased in importance (1902). Nevertheless, the vast majority of Americans must have approved of the intense, personal, and highly organized local parties and their leaders, for turnout in national, state, and local elections was considerably higher than it is today. Condemnation of the party system came primarily from disgruntled middle-class and genteel reformers who found themselves increasingly isolated from positions of leadership and who scorned the new "professional" politicians.

The composition of each party's electoral base after the Civil War lent itself to the patronage considerations that reformers found so offensive. Although there were marginal social class differences, each party was a "confessional" organization comprised of groups sharing similar cultural values (Kleppner 1979). Patronage was useful in cementing the elements of coalitions that were highly stable. Estimates suggest that fewer than 5 percent of voters changed parties between elections or split tickets. Parties reached a remarkable level of organizational complexity, with considerable opportunities for citizens to become active in party work. At the base was the precinct or ward club, whose meetings were open to all party members. From this base rose a formidable organizational structure: county, state and ultimately national committees, which transacted ongoing party business, and nominating conventions, which wrote party platforms and selected candidates and party officials.

Americans who did not accept the presumed republican virtues of liberal capitalism found a more compelling reason to criticize the party system: its failure to address important economic issues. During the nineteenth century those who had experienced the most severe dislocations of industrialization and the growth of markets launched criticisms of the new economic order from a traditional ideological strain of American republicanism. These groups included the nascent labor movement in urban areas, various radical agrarian groups, and ultimately even many American-born Socialists like Eugene Debs (Wilentz 1984; Fink 1983; Goodwyn 1976; Palmer 1980; Salvatore 1982). All of these groups organized parties in the late nineteenth century to challenge the dominance of liberal capitalism and to attempt to disrupt the major parties' hegemonic position. Many achieved significant electoral strength in various states after 1876, sometimes garnering as much as 20 percent of the vote in individual elections. Analysts who condemn the partisan culture of the late nineteenth century ignore the fact that this period saw the rise of radical third-party challenges to a degree unknown in subsequent years. During this period of high voter turnout political reformers and radicals had remarkable access to the public.

The long-term decline in commodity prices that began in the 1870s and the depression that began in 1893 eventually led to another political realignment, one with perhaps the most far-reaching consequences for American democracy. Widespread unemployment, strikes, and labor violence punctuated the depression years and threatened profound social upheaval. Contributing to this climate of fear was the unprecedented growth of the Populist Party, which fed on the economic discontent prevalent in agrarian areas.

Populism, emerging out of a process of political organizing in agricultural regions, represented a democratic vision of economic possibilities based on the principles of cooperation, self-respect, and community. It raised the question of whether industrial and corporate capitalism could be brought under democratic control and adjusted to traditional republican ideals of political economy that guaranteed autonomy and freedom. As Henry Demarest Lloyd stated the populists' conviction, "Government exists only by the consent of the governed. Business, property, capital, are also governments and must also rest on the consent of the governed" (Destler 1966, 218). Populism was a radical challenge to the laissez-faire positions staked out by the major parties; it asserted the primacy of democratic political values over industrial capitalism.

Populism emerged out of voluntary organizations, farmers' alliances that spread throughout depressed agricultural areas in the South and Midwest in the 1880s. Building a sense of community, credit cooperatives, and ultimately a movement culture, the alliances coalesced into the National Farmers Alliance and Industrial Union. By 1892 its organizers had visited more than two million farm families in forty-three states. The Alliance Lecture Bureau had thirty-five thousand lecturers, and the National Reform Press Association was comprised of more than one thousand newspapers. In 1892 Alliance veterans founded the People's Party and secured over one million votes in that year's presidential contest.

Although the Alliance and the Populist party sympathized with and courted urban labor, they had no success in forging a coalition. The cultures of the two groups were too disparate to achieve a hasty amalgamation, and the Populists' economic analysis could not easily be conveyed to the urban working class, a class unique in its cultural and religious heritages and just beginning to overcome its internal fragmentation and develop its own organizations and institutions. As Lawrence Goodwyn writes, "few Americans understood better than veteran Alliance lecturers that organizers could not create mass institutions of reform by winning, one at a time, intellectual debates with individual citizens over the fine points of a political platform" (1978, 178). Because the Populist Party soon dissolved, no continuing dialogue was possible between these groups, and any opportunity for collective action was lost.

The depression elections of 1893 and 1894 resulted in a decline of Democratic strength, since that party controlled the presidency. The elections weakened the power of the party's leadership, paving the way for its capture by the forces of "free silver" under the leadership of William Jennings Bryan, who secured the presidential nomination in 1896. The fusion of some Populist groups with the Democrats on this issue was disastrous for the Populists, who lost their political identity and most of their program in this action, and even more disastrous for the Democrats, whose agrarian nostalgia and inflationary economic policies drove urban workers away from the party in extraordinary numbers. Conversely, the elections strengthened the Republicans. New leaders emerged in what had been traditionally Democratic constituencies. They supported William McKinley's politics of "social harmony" in an effort to prevent the Democrats from retaking control. Capitalists, fearful of the political challenges already posed to the ideology of industrial capitalism, provided McKinley's campaign with a war chest of previously unmatched proportions. These actions set the state for the election of 1896.

That election was a landmark in U.S. political history for a number of reasons. The immediate result was a period of Republican domination of the national government, which lasted until the election of Franklin Roosevelt in 1932. The election reduced the Democratic Party to a nonviable electoral option in all sections of the country except the South. More importantly, however, it led to the massive demobilization of the electorate, weakened the parties as mediating institutions, and resulted in an entirely new structure of policy-making institutions.

The demobilization of the American electorate is easily demonstrated (Figure 1.1). From an average rate close to 80 percent during the last quarter of the nineteenth century, turnout began dropping after 1896 to a low of less than 50 percent in 1920. This low figure coincides with female suffrage, but the earlier downward trend is abundantly clear (Burnham 1965; Kleppner 1982). There were many reasons for this decrease in popular participation, as Michael McGerr has demonstrated (1986). What is unmistakable, however, is that the decline of turnout coincided with the decline of political parties and accompanied changes that removed large areas of public policy from the potential influence of party behavior and elections themselves. As many analysts have recognized, the years in which a disproportionate number of working class and poor voters exited from the ranks of the active electorate coincided with the period of the creation of Western European social democratic parties. By the time the high point of American socialism was reached in 1912, when Socialist Party candidate Eugene Debs received 6 percent of the presidential vote, turnout had decreased from 79

Figure 1.   Turnout in Presidential Elections
1876-1984

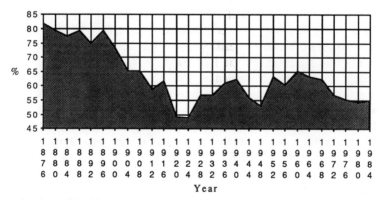

Sources: Burnham 1974, 677; idem 1985, 217.

percent in 1896 to 59 percent. While social democracy was growing throughout the rest of the industrializing world, it was retreating in the United States. The post-1896 American political system insulated capitalist groups from mass political pressures.

The extreme sectional imbalance of party predominance shifted much of the competition between parties to competition within parties. Bourbon Democrats in the South quickly consolidated their hegemony, thereby disfranchising black voters as well as a considerable proportion of working-class and poor whites who had been active in the populist movement (Kousser 1974). Republican Party dominance elsewhere in the country led to the institution of the direct primary as factions fought to control party machinery and define party policies. These changes had unfortunate consequences for party organization because primary elections focussed less on the party itself and more on individual candidates, who came increasingly to rely on extra-party organizations and resources.

The Progressive movement, which flourished from the turn of the twentieth century to the 1920s, coincided with the decline of partisan and electoral politics and was in many ways also responsible for this decline. Denied power in the dominant party by the extreme imbalance of party strength and opposed to the now politically unaccountable power of corporate capital, Progressives were compelled to attack the parties and seek new channels of political expression through which to address the nation's economic problems. Progressive reforms attacked almost all of the constructive party-building that had occurred before the Civil War. The number of offices subject to direct election was reduced, and in urban areas the strong mayor and the commission form of government (which removed the election of the chief executive municipal office entirely from the electoral realm) replaced city councils as the chief agents of policy-making. The importance of local party organization was minimized through nonpartisan municipal elections and the separation of national, state, and local elections. New ballot laws prohibited fusion tickets between parties, thus removing coalition politics as a possible radical response, and set higher standards for a place on the ballot, thus denying reform groups access to the ballot and decreasing the political power of groups that had threatened industrial capitalism (Argersinger 1980). Laws that made ticket-splitting easier also emerged under the Progressives' guidance (Rusk 1970). Personal registration laws, residency requirements, and a variety of other provisions reduced the number of voters as well. Finally, although the Progressives were not directly responsible, the party press, long a staple of parties' roles in political education, was increasingly replaced by a muckraking, middle-class journalism that found partisan corruption a major target (Leonard 1986).

Under this sustained attack parties could no longer maintain their role as the most important channel through which Americans affected government policies. As Martin Shefter concludes, "the central thrust of Progressivism was an attack upon the political party—which since the Jacksonian period had been the central institution of American government—and an effort to create an executive establishment to supplant the party in this pivotal position in the American political system" (1978, 231–2). An entirely new state structure emerged, one that was executive-oriented as opposed to legislative-oriented. The political premium was now on access to administrative agencies, and access shifted from those with electoral support to those with resources. The mass-based political parties of the nineteenth century became less important than versions of corporatist representation—interest groups linked to administrative agencies (McConnell 1966; Weinstein 1968). This change introduced a profound class bias in public access to the state, a bias revealed by the exit of working-class and poor citizens from the active electorate.

The structure of the mediating political institutions changed fundamentally. A panoply of pressure groups emerged: civic leagues, trade and professional associations, manufacturers' organizations, labor lobbies, and a host of others. Lacking a large-scale public base, these institutions campaigned under the banner of rationality, efficiency, and expertise. They quickly gained direct access to newly created governmental agencies. To the extent that party organization in the national and state legislatures was weakened, many of these groups were also very successful in influencing the course of legislative policy as well. They lobbied to replace legislative politics with administrative politics and were responsible for a variety of reforms that significantly enlarged the scope and sphere of public administration. Thus, even more aspects of public policy were removed from party and popular control.

Historians who have examined the Progressive Era frequently disagree about the motives of the individuals engaged in the different Progressive reforms, but they generally agree that the period marked the eclipse of the local community and the informal group, not to mention the local party, as the basic structures of political life in the United States. Early twentieth-century Americans increasingly operated in vastly different, bigger, and more remote organizations, including the new administrative state (Wiebe 1967; Galambos 1970).

Although not all Progressives shared the same goals or the same rhetoric, many of them employed the language of social efficiency and technique, language derived from the business firm, the factory, and the scientific laboratory. Ultimately, that same language came to dominate public discourse and professional political science. "As late as 1905," Daniel Rodgers claims, "the 'state' . . . and philosophical idealism held preeminent place. By 1915 they were all being brushed into the corners by a new concern with governmental technique and political behavior" (1982, 127).

Arthur Bentley's classic book, *The Process of Government*, published in 1908, is characteristic of the new ideology. "The 'idea of the state'," Bentley concludes, "has been very prominent, no doubt, among the intellectual amusements of the past, and at particular places and times it has served to give coherent and pretentious expression to some particular group's activity" (263). But, he argues, it was time for political science to replace political philosophy. In attempting to fashion a tool for scientific political analysis, Bentley introduced an empirical pluralism into American political science. Five years later, Charles A. Beard purported to find the philosophic origins of pluralism in Madison's Federalist, Number 10, which he made the fulcrum for his analysis in *An Economic Interpretation of the Constitution of the United States* (1913). Within a short time a variety of tendentious readings that ripped Madison out of the context of eighteenth-century republican thought provided a foundation for viewing what was an entirely new set of political structures and values as wholly within the philosophical traditions of American democracy (Bourke 1975). The new theory of corporate liberalism that emerged out of this approach, as R. Jeffrey Lustig has brilliantly argued, was democratically deficient in its concepts of citizenship, public authority, and the state. Unlike populist ideology, which spoke in terms of adjusting the economy according to traditional democratic values, the theory of corporate liberalism represented a revision of democratic theory to accommodate the realities of economic power (1982).

In this new ideological framework the devaluation of public participation is evident. After all, if politics is considered the competitive struggle for group advantage, then adding up the relative strengths and weaknesses of various groups in society is all that is necessary. Wise policy is simply the adjustment or brokerage of group pressures, not the result of a process of democratic participation and deliberation. Here is the source of interest group liberalism and the demise of popular participation in political parties as well (Lowi 1979).

No institutions die quickly, including political parties. But they never again saw the organizational strength and public support that they received from the 1830s to the 1890s. To summarize, the reasons for the parties' decline are obvious. First, with public policy less dependent on election outcomes, there was less reason for citizens to invest resources in partisan activity. Second, a shift to functional, corporatist representation minimized the importance of the local community as an arena of shared political values, weakening the solidarity of local parties and ultimately mocking the notion of community itself. Finally, as more and more voters exited from the ranks of the electorate or began to split tickets, party leaders put a greater premium on courting nonpartisan and independent voters, thus minimizing traditional partisan stands in favor of novel programs and policies and thereby contributing to a diminution of partisan ideology.

An examination of the realignment of the 1930s illustrates that political parties have never recovered. Not even the profound disruptions of the Great Depression nor the success of the Roosevelt coalition returned electoral turnout to its nineteenth-century level (see Figure 1.1 on page 30). The realignment was less structured and more protracted than previous realignments in the 1850s and 1890s (Burnham 1970; Sundquist 1973). It had its origins in the 1928 election when the presence of Al Smith as a candidate brought significant numbers of Catholics into the Democratic Party in urban areas. The actual transfer of partisan control of the national government occurred after the presidential election of 1932, without the articulation of an explicit policy agenda by the Democrats. The Democratic New Deal coalition reached its peak of strength in 1936 and suffered deterioration almost immediately in 1938, highlighted, of course, by Roosevelt's attempted intervention in congressional races.

New Deal reforms, which became part and parcel of the welfare state, were consequently enacted with only a temporary electoral base in the Democratic Party and often without even that. Likewise, the executive reorganization that Roosevelt accomplished after his first term was similar to administrative reform during the Progressive Era. Instituted with the support of the liberal wing of the Democratic Party and at times over the opposition of the Party's conservative bloc, Roosevelt's administrative reforms insulated various elements of the New Deal welfare state from electoral pressures and legislative intervention. In many ways the welfare state that emerged in the 1930s was identical in its problem-solving orientation to the regulatory state that the Progressives designed and marked a further retreat from public participation in the governing process.

It is important to recognize, however, that Democratic liberals advocated a strategy of mass mobilization and cultivated local party organizations and alliances with trade unions when it was necessary to expel more conservative party leaders. This undoubtedly was partially responsible for the significant rise in popular participation in elections during and following the Depression (see Figure 1.1 on page 30) and for increasing turnout rates among the poor (Kleppner 1982). Also contributing to this partial remobilization of the electorate was the increased salience of legislative politics during the first years of the New Deal.

For the last quarter century analysts have been searching for another re-alignment to restore order and coherence to American politics. In the face of the deterioration of the Democratic New Deal coalition, analysts have been expecting a fundamental reorganization of the electorate since 1960. For a quarter century they have been disappointed. Although some have pointed to a slow-moving, secular realignment during this period, the weight of the evidence contradicts that conclusion.[4] Since 1960 parties have continued to deteriorate, and turnout has continued to decrease, reaching its low point in the 1986 congressional elections. More importantly, electoral results and public policies have lacked the coherence and continuity that characterized previous periods of relatively stable partisan control following historical electoral realignments.

A brief look at the fate of Great Society policies illustrates this drift. In spite of the landslide victory for Lyndon Johnson and the Democrats in 1964, new social policies and agencies created during the Great Society years lacked enduring electoral and partisan support, best evidenced by Richard Nixon's victory in 1968. Democratic political leaders and liberal reformers then (as now) skillfully employed bureaucratic politics, litigation, and interest group activity to achieve their ends when popular support for legislative initiatives was lacking. But, as Burnham suggests, "the use of elite-insider strategies to pursue liberal ends in the absence of demonstrated popular support for them" incurred a severe cost, the legitimacy problems that ultimately paved the way first to Nixon's and then to Reagan's victories (1982, 300–301). Many of those liberal policies have not survived or live on today in desiccated form, despite the fact that the Democrats have maintained uninterrupted control of the House of Representatives and all but continuous control of the Senate. Continuing legitimacy problems may well cause the conservative policies of the Reagan years, even more lacking in popular support than the Great Society, to suffer a similar fate.

Given these trends, the left must confront massive disenfranchisement and political disaffection before creating and implementing new progressive policies. In short, without a mass base of popular support, all policies will be vulnerable, transitory, and ineffective. Although there are indications that perceptive political leaders are beginning to realize this and are willing to make the effort to build coherent popular movements and organizations, their actions to date have been less than successful.

Attempts to create alternatives to political parties have ended in failure or been less than democratic. The defeat of the Greenhouse Compact in Rhode Island is a revealing example. Designed by the Governor's Strategic Development Commission, the Greenhouse Compact was a comprehensive plan for economic development in Rhode Island. It tackled the problems that currently plague industrialized states, from a poor business climate to a declining manufacturing base. The plan incorporated many items most popular with economic planners: targeted subsidies, investment incentives, and education and training programs. The Greenhouse Compact relied on a "corporatist" approach to policy formation. Government, business, and labor leaders worked together, and the final plan was endorsed by the gubernatorial candidates of both parties, the state's congressional delegation, the AFL-CIO Executive Board, the Chamber of Commerce, corporate leaders, bankers, and the only statewide newspaper. A sophisticated media campaign was undertaken, and hundreds of public meetings were held throughout the state to marshall public support. Although a majority of the state's voters believed that state government should take a leading role in improving the state's economy, the plan went down to a crushing four-to-one defeat in a referendum held in June 1984.

A post-election poll reveals the reasons for the plan's defeat. John Carroll, Mark Hyde, and William Hudson conclude that

> . . . the Commission's corporatist approach to policy-making failed to generate a consensus beyond the boundaries of the interest groups which they had judged immediately relevant to their work. . . . In effect, the corporatist approach was

viewed as an anti-democratic conspiracy of the state's most powerful interests who were seeking private gain at public expense. (1985, 111)

Rhode Island's experience should certainly give pause to those who seek new forms of interest intermediation to replace political parties. There are a number of reasons why "corporatist" or "conciliar" forms of policy-making are unlikely to find public support in the United States. First, corporatist solutions have emerged successfully in those countries with a historical tradition of a strong Social Democratic party in the government (Panitch 1977). In the United States, however, attempts to "impose" a corporatist form of policy-making will invite an understandable popular backlash, just as occurred in Rhode Island. Second, the negotiated settlements that have emerged through corporatist policy-making in Western European countries have become increasingly brittle and subject to attack from groups who believe their interests have not been fairly represented. Managing these conflicts has proved difficult, inviting repressive reactions and actually increasing demands on the state. Third, given contemporary negative evaluations of U.S. politics, labor unions, and big business, the institutionalization of corporatism would likely contribute to an even greater public disaffection with the political process. Finally, corporatism does not effectively deal with the new post-materialist values that are increasingly prevalent in our post-industrial society. Democratic participatory aspirations stemming from these values are unlikely to be satisfied by such a policy-making framework (Schmitter 1981).

Another proposed solution to our political crisis is the "empowerment" movement, which seeks to recognize nongovernmental institutions and social groups in the policy process. "Empowerment" approaches range from giving groups and institutions access to policy-making arenas and administrative agencies to granting them public funds or public service functions and investing them with public authority. In many ways, "empowerment" is an attractive strategy, relying upon strong traditions of voluntarism in U.S. culture and often combined with strategies for decentralization and devolution of policy-making. Although these approaches are attacking our political crisis, they too often oppose state institutions and public life. They therefore fail to address the fundamental problems of government for a number of important reasons.

First, "empowerment" and decentralization do not directly address the question of mediation. That is, although they clearly can reduce demands on the state, they do not necessarily link individuals to the state democratically, particularly when institutions and groups are traditionally viewed as "private" organizations. Rather than function as mechanisms for the upward flow of citizen demands, these strategies frequently serve to encapsulate and deflect problems rather than resolve them. Further, when the membership of "empowerment" organizations is characterized by similarity rather than diversity, no vibrant democratic policies will emerge within them. Restrictive, exclusive associations have been just as prevalent historically as open, voluntary associations. The religious right should serve as a warning.[5]

Proposals for decentralization and "creative federalism" are subject to similar problems. They are sometimes little more than a cover for dumping major policy problems on local and/or state governments, whose political resources are easily overwhelmed by national or multinational corporations. The devolution of public policy-making onto smaller units does provide the opportunity for more extensive citizen participation in the policy-making process, but it also rigs the game in favor of capitalists who hold the trump cards. Decentralization cannot possibly work without a supportive *national* commitment to honor democratic political values over capitalist economic ones. Smaller governmental units simply lack the power to do this themselves.

Tellingly, the proliferation of quasi-political groups and the more prevalent use of federalism have not resulted in increased participation in national elections over the last two decades. Likewise, public trust and confidence in the state have continued to deteriorate. It is difficult to see how a greater use of these strategies, by itself, will lead to renewed public confidence.

The state will not "wither away." Conservative policies designed to restrict its influence are destined to fail. The challenge we face is to strengthen the legitimacy of and public confidence in the state to enable it better to carry out its functions in response to authentically democratic public choice, a program to increase the power of citizens and the state together.

The U.S. left is not alone in attempting to reconstitute a popular base for progressive policies. The electoral bases of social democratic movements in all post-industrial countries show signs of deteriorating as the nature of capitalism changes (Sänkiaho 1984; Esping-Anderson 1985; Paterson and Thomas 1986). What makes the situation somewhat different in the United States, however, is the absence of a coherent, class-conscious, organized electoral base for the welfare state. Much as we can deplore the way that the historical obliviousness to class has retarded the development of the U.S. welfare state, it may be strategically useful at present.

The failure of economic class cleavages to find extensive historical expression in U.S. electoral politics and their clear weakness today suggest that it may be somewhat easier to find a formula in the new populism for electoral coalition-building that can integrate traditional economic concerns with post-materialist values. It should be obvious that the only agency with the potential to radically reconstruct U.S. political and economic systems is the political party.

But how might the movement toward democracy be achieved through a party? Haven't recent reforms designed to strengthen political parties provided sufficient openness and internal democracy? The answer is that the reforms have been made in the wrong places and have addressed the wrong problems (Polsby 1983).

The solution is not simply to find the most appropriate and appealing policies. In many respects political parties are more concerned with and have more policy-making structures than ever (Price 1984, ch. 9). The problem is not how to organize parties more effectively at the national level; today's parties have created truly integrated national organizations, especially the Republicans (Cotter et al. 1984; Schlesinger 1985). Rather, what was traditionally the heart of the vibrant nineteenth-century American political parties—the local party—is dying (Ware 1985). Lacking in organizational vitality and resources, overwhelmed by candidates and their independent committees, robbed of many of its functions by professional consultants, the local party no longer functions as a participatory and deliberative organization. The success of the numerically small Lyndon LaRouche forces in taking over the local Democratic organizations and of the new right in Republican local party organizations is proof.

Progressive Era reforms and many current reforms nominally designed to democratize parties had precisely the opposite effect, if by "democracy" we mean active participation of party members in collective decisions. Local party organizations during the nineteenth century were not thoroughly democratic agencies; they were frequently oligarchic and sometimes involved little mass participation in policy affairs. But they did provide mechanisms for bringing together antagonistic social groups in a forum where collective identities could be forged and collective needs and similarities discovered, aspects of partisan activity missing in today's local parties. "Nineteenth-century partisan culture," Robert Westbrook recognizes, "fostered an active, rich symbolic experience of community, ethno-religious, and class solidarity, while for the modern American voter electoral politics has . . . come to share with other spheres of experience the peculiar features of the culture of consumption: passivity, atomization, and spectatorship" (1983, 151).

It was against the sterility of politics as well as its bureaucratization that the New Left protested so vigorously in the 1960s; its major innovation was "participatory democracy."[6] But, as Jane Mansbridge observes, "what the term meant then was unclear, and it became less clear afterward, as it was applied to virtually every form of organization that brought more people into the decision-making process" (1970, 376n). The New Left's democratic impulse was authentic, but it ignored or dismissed the traditions and culture of most U.S. communities and missed the most promising opportunity to realize a democratic rebirth.

Today, the call for participatory democracy sounds like little more than 1960s nostalgia. Nevertheless, this is where I believe that a program to revitalize democracy and the party system must start. If the New Left's demand for participatory democracy did not succeed in revitalizing American politics, it did spur a host of studies that explore the philosophical roots of the concept among democratic theorists and address its empirical validity. Not surprisingly, predictions that active public participation would result in self-development, the acquisition or enhancement of beliefs and values associated with democratic citizenship, and appropriate political skills were empirically demonstrable (Pateman 1970; Mason 1982). However, because practical implementation of participatory democracy seemed so utopian, it dropped out of currency with much of the left, and because it threatened expertise and professionalism (read "elitism"), it was roundly condemned by conservatives. On the other hand, participatory democracy saw a vibrant rebirth (without all of the rhetorical trappings of the New Left) in the grassroots activism of the new populism of 1970s and 1980s.

Unfortunately, many of the organizations that comprise the new populist movement have ignored or actively avoided electoral and partisan activity, considering alliances beyond the bounds of their local communities threatening to their integrity and authenticity. (The Citizens Party is, of course, a notable exception.) Consequently, there has been no concerted challenge to the dominance of capital, the powerful, entrenched organizations, and the national policies that facilitate the anti-democratic aspects of communal economic and social life on a national scale. The new populism has failed to realize its inherent potential to spark authentic American democracy.

Transforming the new populism into a national political movement with the potential to revitalize American democracy will not be easily accomplished, for the new populists' commitment to the local community is deeply entrenched. Undoubtedly speaking for many of the new populists, Sara Evans and Harry Boyte maintain that "loss of organic connection to the communal sources of social movement can lead to the amorphous and rootless stridency of the late new left on the one hand, or to the bureaucratic stagnation apparent in many contemporary trade unions on the other" (1986, 201). Yet, unless these local new populist movements extend beyond the bounds of their communities, they will ultimately retreat into sectarianism and defensiveness and hence fail to recognize the similarity of interests and ideas they potentially share with millions of other U.S. citizens. Likewise, unless these fragmented movements coalesce and challenge the entrenched interests that corrupt the national polity as well as the local community, the undemocratic structures of power in this country will remain fundamentally unchanged, despite their heroic efforts.

A democratic reinvigoration of local partisan politics would allow community-based democratic movements to employ the traditional channels of democratic mediation in the United States without fear of losing their authenticity. In order for this to happen, the new populist movements together with traditional reform constituencies like organized labor, must actively undertake to change both the structure and operation of local parties.

Recent changes in national party rules, court decisions, and governmental policies have conspired to weaken local parties and political parties in general.

Although some of these changes have emerged from laudable motives, a thorough reform of party organization and operation is needed in order to transform political parties into more authentic agencies of democratic mediation.

Parties have ceased to be deliberative organizations at all levels, particularly with respect to candidate selection, an area in need of tremendous reform. Parties must offer citizens more than simply the opportunity to cast votes in primary elections. Insofar as possible, caucuses and conventions should replace primary elections so that education and conflict resolution can assume their rightful roles in the political process.

Local parties should play a major role in their own revitalization by promoting voter registration and educational programs. Parties should be encouraged to develop a concept of party membership, defined by the payment of nominal dues. Party decisions and activities should be limited to party members. Where party registration is not provided in state law, legislative action will be necessary to restrict participation in party primaries to party registrants. Where primaries are retained in state law, these laws should be amended to provide for party endorsement of candidates. Above all, local parties must be popular democratic organizations with their own autonomy.

Party organizations should be adequately funded by a dues-paying membership, supplemented by federal matching funds in whatever multiples are necessary. (Public opinion polls strongly suggest that abstention from voting is a consequence of the belief that all candidates are so mortgaged to special interests that it matters little who wins.) Qualifications for public funds for parties should be established at the local level so that local community groups can organize themselves into a party for local elections. Up to a certain level tax credits should be given for contributions to parties and eliminated for contributions to political action committees or candidates to help institutionalize collective partisan responsibility. Campaign finance reform has generally weakened parties by focussing on candidates rather than on parties, thereby reinforcing candidate fundraising and organization at the expense of party influence. It has similarly weakened parties vis-à-vis interest groups. This imbalance needs to be redressed.

The Supreme Court's equation of independent expenditures with "free speech" is a major problem that must be confronted (*Buckley v. Valeo*, 1976). Unrestricted, independent expenditures can corrupt the election process, and they have produced some of the most glaring examples of negative campaigns. It is unlikely that the Court will alter its position in the near future. In 1985 it upheld a lower court ruling that declared unconstitutional any limitations on independent expenditures by political action committees in presidential elections (*FEC v. NCPAC*, 1985). The Court's posture has so far prevented effective remedies. Nevertheless, the continuing efforts to address this problem deserve support.

Local elections should be returned to a partisan basis not only to strengthen local party organization but also to provide more linkage between local and national politics. This would put a premium on more human-scale, face-to-face politics and provide more incentives for participating in local party activities. It would also encourage local parties to take more initiative in scheduling policy forums and debates. Much new communications technology, including interactive cable television, provides a fruitful opportunity for local political groups and should be explored as well.

The above recommendations should partially answer some of the concerns that groups comprising the new populist movement have about participating in electoral politics. My goal here is not to suggest a tactical alliance with any existing partisan organization but to offer ideas about how the structure and operation of parties can be altered so that they pose no threat to community groups and in fact enhance the possibilities for democratic politics. The appropriate and effective vehicle for the new populists can be a third party (assuming existing barriers to a place on the ballot and public funding are reduced to an appropriate level), the local Democratic Party, or a caucus within the local Democratic Party. The choice should be dictated by community traditions and prevailing political forces.[7]

Finally, a number of changes in the conduct of elections would facilitate their reemergence as agencies of democratic mediation. Some, discussed briefly below, would be easy to realize. We must begin by recognizing that placing *any* burden on the exercise of the franchise is undemocratic. We do not know exactly the degree to which current registration procedures inhibit participation, but it is clear that they do nothing to encourage citizens to exercise their voting rights. The state already keeps track of citizens in a variety of ways, from federal and state tax lists to the Census. Universal, state-sponsored registration should be encouraged. As a temporary and expedient alternative, election day registration should immediately become law.

Lack of information inhibits participation in elections. The state should assume responsibility for providing information about elections, both partisan and referenda. Something like the Oregon pamphlet system (in which candidates are provided with free space in a publication that is made available to all voters) should be applied to all elections. Free time for candidates and parties on commercial and public radio and television stations should also be allocated.

Finally, to facilitate both individual voting and local party volunteer activity, two-day elections should become the norm. A shift to weekend elections would also provide local and community-based organizations the opportunity to play a more important role in mobilizing citizens.

The above recommendations seem to pale in comparison to the contemporary political crisis. But these practical recommendations to revitalize political parties, simplify voting, facilitate new forms of political organization, and encourage greater citizen participation in electoral politics are in fact radical. They represent a continuation of the historical struggle to realize democracy in the United States. As E. E. Schattschneider recognizes,

Massive nonvoting in the United States makes sense if we think of American government as a political system in which the struggle for democracy is still going on. The struggle is no longer about the *right to vote* but about the *organization of politics*. Nowadays the fight for democracy takes the form of a struggle over theories of organization, over the right to organize and the rights of political organizations, i.e., about the kinds of things that make the vote valuable. (1960, 102)

Politics as usual over the last four decades has resulted in increasing public distrust and disaffection, a continuing deterioration of elections and parties, and the practical disenfranchisement of almost half of the U.S. public. Modern-day political parties, electoral machinery, and election practices mystify what is, contrary to the neo-conservative gospel, a stunningly simple concept—democracy. Populists have always understood this. The Populist Party sought to make the late nineteenth-century economy conform to traditional democratic standards. Modern-day populists should also want to make today's political system conform to the historical democratic traditions and aspirations of their communities and their country. Unless practical democracy is strengthened in the United States, the result can only be Leviathan.

NOTES

1.   There has been considerable criticism of the critical realignment model, particularly given the absence of an expected critical realignment in the 1960s. Although this is not the appropriate place to enter into that extended debate, the critical realignment model, in my opinion, provides the best description of the dynamics of U.S. electoral politics through the 1930s.

2.   The argument of the previous two paragraphs owes much to Offe's theoretical formulation of the problem. Recent theoretical interest in the state has resulted in an outpouring of innovative scholarship and creative formulations. Useful introductions to this literature include Jessop (1982); Benjamin and Elkin (1985); Evans, Rueschemeyer, and Skocpol (1985); and Alford and Friedland (1986).

3.   There was a strain of Lockian liberalism that had coexisted with republican thought since the Revolution (Appleby 1976, 1978, 1982; Hartz 1955). Until recently, historians tended to exaggerate the dominance of liberal thought in the post-Revolutionary years and failed to explain how republican ideology accommodated liberal values. Berthoff (1979) has offered a preliminary assessment of how these ideas merged.

4.   Petrocik (1981), among others, has argued for a secular realignment. Burnham (1982, 1985), on the other hand, presents compelling evidence that the post-1960 period is one of continuing partisan decline and party disaggregation, a view that currently predominates.

5.   Some of these potential problems are treated, unsuccessfully in my judgment, in Berger and Neuhaus (1977).

6.   A representative sampling of contemporary formulations of participatory democracy is available in Benello and Roussopoulous (1971).

7. A successful movement to challenge the current undemocratic political system must ultimately become national in scale. This movement must, of course, develop an effective program of action and a supporting ideology. My argument here is that the idea of democracy itself can be a radical ideology, as indeed it has been historically. A new political party might effectively articulate and demonstrate that argument. On the other hand, it would be difficult for the left to abandon the Democratic Party's historical traditions of social democracy. Yet, unless the Democratic Party revives its commitment to these traditions and reaches out to those Americans currently excluded from the electoral process, it offers little hope for enduring and fundamental change in the political system and the reinvigoration of democracy. Ferguson and Rogers (1986b) provide an excellent analysis of the Democrats' current retreat from their historical social democratic traditions.

Such a movement must also articulate a theory of political economy and ultimately draw some specific lines of economic conflict rather than pursuing the "social harmony" arguments that characterize contemporary political discourse. My argument is that these ideas must emerge from or at least along with reconstructed partisan and political organizations.

References

Alford, R. R., and R. Friedland. 1986. *Powers of theory: Capitalism, the state, and democracy.* Cambridge: Cambridge University Press.

Appleby, J. 1976. Liberalism and the American revolution. *New England Quarterly* 49 (March):3–26.

——— 1978. The social origins of American revolutionary ideology. *Journal of American History* 64 (March):935–58.

——— 1982. What is still American in the philosophy of Thomas Jefferson? *William and Mary Quarterly* 3rd ser., 39 (April):287–309.

Argersinger, P. H. 1980. A place on the ballot: Fusion politics and antifusion laws. *American Historical Review* 85 (April):287–306.

Bachrach, P. 1967. *The theory of democratic elitism: A critique.* Boston: Little, Brown.

Bailyn, B. 1967. *The ideological origins of the American revolution.* Cambridge: Harvard University Press.

——— 1970. *The origins of American politics.* New York: Vintage.

Bellah, R. N., et al. 1985. *Habits of the heart: Individualism and commitment in American life.* Berkeley: University of California Press.

Benello, C. G., and D. Roussopoulos, eds. 1971. *The case for participatory democracy: Some prospects for the radical society.* New York: Grossman.

Benjamin, R., and S. L. Elkin, eds. 1985. *The democratic state.* Lawrence: University Press of Kansas.

Bentley, A. F. 1908. *The process of government: A study of social pressures.* Chicago: The University of Chicago Press.

Berger, P. L., and R. J. Neuhaus. 1977. *To empower people: The role of mediating structures in public policy.* Washington, D.C.: American Enterprise Institute for Public Policy Research.

Berthoff, R. 1979. Independence and attachment, virtue and interest: From republican citizen to free enterpriser, 1787–1837. Eds. R. L. Bushman et al. *Uprooted Americans: Essays to honor Oscar Handlin.* Boston: Little, Brown.

Block, F. 1977. The ruling class does not rule: Notes on the marxist theory of the state. *Socialist Revolution* 7 (May–June):6–28.

Blumenthal, S. 1982. *The permanent campaign.* Rev. ed. New York: Simon and Schuster, Touchstone Books.

Bourke, P. F. 1975. The pluralist reading of James Madison's tenth federalist. *Perspectives in American History* 9:271–295.

Bowles, S., and H. Gintis. 1986. *Democracy and capitalism: Property, community, and the contradictions of modern social thought.* New York: Basic Books.

Boyte, H. C. 1980. *The backyard revolution: Understanding the new citizen movement.* Philadelphia: Temple University Press.

Brittan, S. 1975. The economic contradictions of democracy. *British Journal of Political Science* 5 (April):129–59.

Brody, R. A. 1978. The puzzle of political participation in America. Ed. A. King. *The new American political system.* Washington, D.C.: American Enterprise Institute for Public Policy Research.

Buckley v. Valeo. 1971. 96 S. Ct.. 612; 424 U.S. 1.

Burnham, W. D. 1965. The changing shape of the American political universe. *American Political Science Review* 59 (March): 7-28.

————— 1970. *Critical elections and the mainsprings of American politics.* New York: Norton.

————— 1974. "The United States: The politics of heterogeneity." in R. Rose. *Electoral behavior: A comparative handbook.* New York: Free Press.

————— 1981. "The system of 1896: An analysis." in Paul Kleppner et al. *The evolution of American electoral systems.* Westport, CT: Greenwood Press.

————— 1982. *The current crisis in American politics.* New York: Oxford University Press.

————— 1985. The 1984 election and the future of American politics. Eds. E. Sandoz and C. V. Crabb, Jr *Election 84: Landslide without a mandate?* New York and Scarborough, Ont.: Mentor, New American Library.

Carroll, J., M. Hyde, and W. Hudson. 1985. Economic development policy: Why Rhode Islanders rejected the greenhouse compact. *State Government* 58 (Fall):110–12.

Chambers, W. N. 1963. *Political parties in a new nation: The American experience, 1776–1809.* New York: Oxford University Press.

Cohen, J. and J. Rogers. 1983. *On democracy: Toward a transformation of American society.* New York: Penguin Books.

Connolly, W. E., ed. 1969. *The bias of pluralism.* New York: Atherton.

Cotter, C. P., et al. 1984. *Party organizations in American politics.* New York: Praeger.

Crozier, M. J., S. P. Huntington, and J. Watanuki. 1975. *The crisis of democracy: Report on the governability of democracies to the trilateral commission.* New York: New York University Press.

Dahl, R. A. 1977. On removing certain impediments to democracy in the United States. *Political Science Quarterly* 92 (Spring):1–21.

————— 1982. *Dilemmas of pluralist democracy: Autonomy vs. control.* New Haven and London: Yale University Press.

Destler, C. M. 1966. *American radicalism, 1865–1901.* Chicago: Quadrangle.

Edsall, T. B. 1984. *The new politics of inequality.* New York: Norton.

Esping-Andersen, G. 1985. *Politics against markets: The social democratic road to power.* Princeton: Princeton University Press.

Evans, P. B., D. Rueschemeyer, and T. Skocpol, eds. 1985. *Bringing the state back in.* Cambridge: Cambridge University Press.

Evans, S. M. and H. C. Boyte. 1986. *Free spaces: The sources of democratic change in America.* New York: Harper and Row.

Farrand, M., ed. 1911. *The records of the federal convention of 1787.* 4 vols. New Haven: Yale University Press.

FEC v. NCPAC. 1985. 105 Sup. Ct. 1459.

Ferguson, T., and J. Rogers. 1986a. The myth of America's turn to the right. *Atlantic Monthly.* (May):43–53.

————— 1986b. *Right turn: The decline of the democrats and the future of American politics.* New York: Hill and Wang.

Fink, L. 1983. *Workingmen's democracy: The knights of labor and American politics*. Urbana: University of Illinois Press.

Fischer, D. H. 1965. *The revolution of American conservatism: The federalist party in the era of jeffersonian democracy*. New York: Harper and Row.

Free, L. and H. Cantril. 1967. *The political beliefs of Americans*. New Brunswick, N.J.: Rutgers University Press.

Galambos, L. 1970. The emerging organizational synthesis in modern American history. *Business History Review* 44 (Autumn):279–90.

Goodman, P. 1975. The first American party system. Eds. W. N. Chambers and W. D. Burnham. *The American party systems: Stages of political development*. 2nd ed. New York: Oxford University Press.

Goodwyn, L. 1976. *Democratic promise: The populist movement in America*. New York: Oxford University Press.

———— 1978. *The populist moment: A short history of the agrarian revolt in America*. New York: Oxford University Press.

Green, P. 1985. *Retrieving democracy: In search of civic equality*. Totowa, N.J.: Rowman and Allanheld.

Hartz, L. 1955. *The liberal tradition in America: An interpretation of American political thought since the revolution*. New York: Harcourt, Brace.

Hofstadter, R. 1969. *The idea of a party system: The rise of legitimate opposition in the United States, 1780–1840*. Berkeley, Los Angeles and London: University of California Press.

Huntington, S. P. 1981. *American politics: The promise of disharmony*. Cambridge and London: The Belknap Press of Harvard University Press.

Inglehart, R. 1977. *The silent revolution: Changing values and political styles among western publics*. Princeton: Princeton University Press.

Jessop, B. 1982. *The capitalist state: Marxist theories and methods*. New York and London: New York University Press.

Kariel, H. 1961. *The decline of American pluralism*. Stanford: Stanford University Press.

Kasson, J. F. 1976. *Civilizing the machine: Technology and republican values in America, 1776–1900*. New York: Grossman.

Katz, A. H. 1981. Self-help and mutual aid: An emerging social movement? *Annual Review of Sociology* 7:129–55.

Keller, M. 1977. *Affairs of state: Public life in late nineteenth-century America*. Cambridge: The Belknap Press of Harvard University Press.

Key, V. O. Jr. 1955. A theory of critical elections. *Journal of Politics* 17 (February):3–18.

Kleppner, P. 1979. *The third electoral system, 1853–1892: Parties, voters, and political cultures*. Chapel Hill: The University of North Carolina Press.

———— 1982. *Who voted? The dynamics of electoral turnout, 1870–1980*. New York: Praeger.

Kousser, J. M. 1974. *The shaping of southern politics: Suffrage restriction and the establishment of the one-party south, 1880–1910*. New Haven, CT: Yale University Press.

Kristol, I., and N. Glazer, eds. 1976. *The American commonwealth, 1976*. New York: Basic Books.

Leonard, T. C. 1986. *Power of the press: The birth of American political reporting*. New York: Oxford University Press.

Lindblom, C. E. 1977. *Politics and markets: The world's political-economic systems*. New York: Basic Books.

Lipset, S. M. 1986. Beyond 1984: The anomalies of American politics. *PS* 19 (Spring):222–36.

———— and W. Schneider. 1982. *The confidence gap: Business, labor and government in the public mind*. New York: The Free Press.

Lowi, T. J. 1975. Party, policy, and constitution in America. Eds. W. N. Chambers and W. D. Burnham. *The American party systems: Stages of political development*. 2nd ed. New York: Oxford University Press.

———— 1979. *The end of liberalism: The second republic of the United States*. 2nd ed. New York: W. W. Norton and Co.

Lustig, R. J. 1982. *Corporate liberalism: The origins of modern American political theory, 1890–1920*. Berkeley: University of California Press.

Mansbridge, J. J. 1970. *Beyond adversary democracy*. New York: Basic Books.

Mason, R. M. 1982. *Participatory and workplace democracy: A theoretical development in critique of liberalism*. Carbondale and Edwardsville: Southern Illinois University Press.

McConnell, G. 1966. *Private power and American democracy*. New York: Alfred A. Knopf.

McCormick, R. L. 1979. The party period and public policy: An exploratory hypothesis. *Journal of American History* 66 (September):279–98.

McCormick, R. P. 1966. *The second American party system: Party formation in the jacksonian era*. Chapel Hill: The University of North Carolina Press.

———— 1975. Political development and the second party system. Eds. W. N. Chambers and W. D. Burnham. *The American party systems: Stages of political development*. 2nd ed. New York: Oxford University Press.

McCoy, C. A. and J. Playford, eds. 1967. *Apolitical politics: A critique of behavioralism*. New York: Thomas Y. Crowell.

McCoy, D. R. 1980. *The elusive republic: Political economy in jeffersonian America*. Chapel Hill: The University of North Carolina Press.

McGerr, M. E. 1986. *The decline of popular politics: The American north, 1865–1928*. New York: Oxford University Press.

Merelman, R. M. 1984. *Making something of ourselves: On culture and politics in the United States*. Berkeley: University of California Press.

Meyers, M. 1960. *The jacksonian persuasion: Politics and belief*. Stanford, CA: Stanford University Press.

Mills, C. W. 1959. *The power elite*. New York: Oxford University Press.

Offe, C. 1980. The separation of form and content in liberal democratic politics. *Studies in Political Economy* 3 (Spring):5–16.

Ostrogorski, M. 1902. *Democracy and the organization of political parties*. 2 vols. New York: Macmillan.

Palmer, B. 1980. *"Man over money": The southern populist critique of American capitalism*. Chapel Hill: The University of North Carolina Press.

Panitch, L. 1977. The development of corporatism in liberal democracies. *Comparative Political Studies* 10 (April):61–90.

Pateman, C. 1970. *Participation and democratic theory*. Cambridge: Cambridge University Press.

Paterson, W. E., and A. H. Thomas, eds. 1986. *The future of social democracy: Problems and prospects of social democratic parties in western europe*. New York: Oxford University Press.

Peele, G. 1984. *Revival and reaction: The right in contemporary america*. Oxford: Clarendon Press.

Petrocik, J. R. 1981. *Party coalitions: Realignment and the decline of the new deal party system*. Chicago and London: University of Chicago Press.

Pocock, J. G. A. 1975. *The machiavellian moment: Florentine political thought and the atlantic republican tradition*. Princeton: Princeton University Press.

Polsby, N. W. 1983. *Consequences of party reform*. Oxford: Oxford University Press.

Powell, G. B., Jr. 1986. American voter turnout in comparative perspective. *American Political Science Review* 80 (March):17–43.

Price, D. E. 1984. *Bringing back the parties*. Washington, D.C.: Congressional Quarterly Press.

Rodgers, D. T. 1982. In search of progressivism. *Reviews in American History*. 10 (December):113–32.

Rose, R. and G. Peters. 1978. *Can governments go bankrupt?* New York: Basic Books.

Rusk, J. G. 1970. The effect of Australian ballot reform on split ticket voting, 1876–1908. *American Political Science Review* 64 (December):1220–38.

Sabato, L. J. 1981. *The rise of political consultants: New ways of winning elections*. New York: Basic Books.

Saloma, J. S. III. 1984. *Ominous politics: The new conservative labyrinth*. New York: Hill and Wang.

Salvatore, N. 1982. *Eugene V. Debs: Citizen and socialist*. Urbana: University of Illinois Press.

Sänkiaho, R. 1984. Political remobilization in welfare states. Eds. R. J. Dalton, S. C. Flanagan, and P. A. Beck. *Electoral change in advanced industrial democracies: Realignment or dealignment?* Princeton: Princeton University Press.

Schattschneider, E. E. 1960. *The semi-sovereign people: A realist's view of democracy in America*. New York: Holt, Rinehart and Winston.

Schlesinger, J. A. 1985. The new American political party. *American Political Science Review* 79 (December):1152–69.

Schlozman, K. L., and J. T. Tierney. 1986. *Organized interests and American democracy*. New York: Harper and Row.

Schmitter, P. C. 1981. Interest intermediation and regime governability in contemporary western Europe and north America. Ed. S. Berger. *Organizing interests in western Europe: Pluralism, corporatism, and the transformation of politics*. Cambridge: Cambridge University Press.

Shade, W. G. 1981. Political pluralism and party development: The creation of a modern party system: 1815–1852. in P. Kleppner et al., *The evolution of American electoral systems*. Westport,, CT: Greenwood Press.

Shallhope, R. E. 1972. Toward a republican synthesis: The emergence of an understanding of republicanism in American historiography. *William and Mary Quarterly* 3rd ser., 29 (January):49–80.

Shefter, M. 1978. Party, bureaucracy, and political change in the United States. Eds. L. Maisel and J. Cooper. *Political parties: Development and decay*. Sage Electoral Studies Yearbook, vol. 4. Beverly Hills, CA: Sage Publications.

Smith, D. H., et al., eds. 1980. *Participation in social and political activities: A comprehensive analysis of political involvement, expressive leisure time, and helping behavior*. San Francisco: Jossey-Bass.

Steinfels, P. 1980. *The neoconservatives: The men who are changing America's politics*. New York: Simon and Schuster.

Sundquist, J. L. 1973. *Dynamics of the party system: Alignment and realignment of political parties in the United States*. Washington, D.C.: Brookings Institution.

Tocqueville, A. de. 1945. *Democracy in america*. Ed. P. Bradley. 2 vols. New York: Alfred A. Knopf.

U.S. Bureau of the Census. 1986. *Voting and registration in the election of November 1984*. Current Population Reports, Series P-20, No. 405. Washington, D.C.: Government Printing Office.

Wallace, M. 1968. Changing concepts of party in the United States: New York, 1815–1828. *American Historical Review* 74 (December):453–91.

Ware, A. 1985. *The breakdown of democratic party organization, 1940–1980*. Oxford: Clarendon Press.

Wattenberg, M. P. 1984. *The decline of American political parties, 1952–1980*. Cambridge: Harvard University Press.

Weinstein, J. 1968. *The corporate ideal in the liberal state, 1900–1920*. Boston: Beacon Press.

Westbrook, R. B. 1983. Politics as consumption: Managing the modern election. Eds. R. W. Fox and T. J. J. Lears. *The culture of consumption: Critical essays in American history, 1880–1980*. New York: Pantheon.

White, T. H. 1982. *America in search of itself: The making of the president 1956–1980*. New York: Harper and Row.

Wiebe, R. 1967. *The search for order, 1877–1920*. New York: Hill and Wang.

Wilentz, S. 1982. On class and politics in jacksonian America. *Reviews in American History* 10 (December):45–63.

——— 1984. *Chants democratic: New York city and the rise of the American working class, 1788–1850*. New York: Oxford University Press.

Wood, G. S. 1969. *The creation of the American republic*. Chapel Hill: The University of North Carolina Press.

3   The Democratic Administration of Government

Carol MacLennan

It appears that the public mood currently favors limiting Big Government, in some cases to the point of eliminating the government role altogether in economic and social life. This devaluation of government and its role in guiding social reform, in academia and in media,[1] has been spurred on by Ronald Reagan, who has strangulated regulatory programs, centralized power in a small White House clique of elite decision-makers, and disenfranchised well trained civil service workers. Anti-government ideology looms large and is, indeed, a serious mistake.

U.S. citizens have not always been so suspicious of government. While always maintaining a vision of limited concentration of political power, this society has nevertheless experienced several periods of faith in the public sector—when authority was delegated to public bureaucracies to solve some of the most difficult and important issues of the day. Today, that responsibility, according to many academics and public officials, belongs to the ever elusive "marketplace." Why this shift from the belief that the state has a positive role to play in our society to the belief that the state is a nuisance, or even a danger?

The answer is found in this country's limited history of success of demo-cratically-based public institutions. John Kushma's preceding chapter in this volume illustrates the historical decline of political parties, the critical mediating institution between citizens and government. This essay builds on Kushma's analysis by describing the rise of administrative policies that created technocratic-elite bureaucracies, which in turn have made government more vulnerable to ideological control from the top and more insulated from the people. The resulting split between the policies of public administrators and the democratic values of the citizenry has given rise to the current suspicious attitudes that Americans hold about their government.

The public's traditional distrust of centralized political power has recently been transformed into a strong dislike for "politics" in general. Yet politics is the essence of democratic practice. Without open debate, political parties and other organizations, citizens have little power to run their government. The public today is in a vulnerable position, alienated from the essence of control over the governance of the nation—participatory democracy. This distancing has given rise to a powerful duo of non-democratic institutions in our political system: a dangerously independent centralized power embodied in the presidency served by a technocratic and elite-oriented administrative apparatus of bureaucratic organizations. Simultaneously the primary institution of democratic expression in our political culture (Sundquist 1981)—the Congress—has weakened.

This chapter will address the problem of an inappropriately powerful central authority and a technocratic-dominated administrative apparatus and propose strategies for changing this arrangement in our governmental structure. These strategies amount to steps that can lead us to a democratic administration of government—a goal that has proved to be historically elusive.

The discussion in this chapter and the reforms outlined at the end are based on a framework that runs counter to popular ideas that insist on the denigration of the public sector and find remedies in a glorified private sector. Three important points are implicit. First, politics is a vital and important part of our social and cultural health. If a system of open debate and democratic participation is allowed to flourish, democratic control of political and economic institutions can be exercised. Second, "free market" ideology is not applicable to government activity, organization of bureaucracies, or public management. The public sector is distinct from the private sector, and differing operative rules apply. Third, the sanctified separation of market (that which is economic) from government (that which is political) is inappropriate in U.S. society, where the ideal of democratic control over social life (both political *and* economic) runs deep in the historical and institutional fabric of the culture. These three ideas run counter to the popular disdain for "politics," and the demand that government be simultaneously run like a business and kept out of business matters.

This chapter is intimately linked to the other chapters in this book because of the importance of politics and administrative policies in public institutions. This book as a whole envisions a strengthened public authority that is acutely responsive to the democratic values of U.S. society and simultaneously active in planning for and implementing fundamental social and economic reforms. Such reforms will fail under the current administrative structure of our national government. Their success demands a reformed system of bureaucratic organization that reunites the public with the demanding and complex task of implementing and administering federal initiatives. Without changing the administrative policies and rules determined by laws such as the Civil Service Reform Act (1978), or the centralization of budgetary and regulatory authority in the White House's Office of Management and Budget, or the narrow (but useful) means of citizen access to government provided by the Administrative Procedures Act and Freedom of Information Act, the political and economic reforms suggested here will not succeed.

This chapter advocates reforming the administrative *processes* of government, highlights some of the sources of the current disenchantment with the way government works, shows how this disenchantment is deeply rooted in an ideology of governance, and provides strategies for transition to a democratic administration of government. The remainder of the chapter is divided into three sections: 1) an analysis of the "administrative orthodoxy" that has dominated the political and intellectual debate over creating an effective government; 2) a description of civil service reform and new policies that encourage more open and democratic decision-making—two areas where the first steps toward reform must occur; and 3) an outline of specific strategies for change.

Administrative Failures and the Administrative Orthodoxy

Presidents, publics, and academics alike are acutely aware that even the most far-reaching reforms often come to naught when their implementation is handed over to government bureaucracies. One example of such "administrative failure" is the airbag standard, which has yet to be implemented by the Department of Transportation, despite fifteen years of proof that airbags are an inexpensive method of saving lives in automobile crashes (Tolchin 1984). Other examples include the notorious Superfund instituted by Congress in 1980, which, through the EPA, has been able to clean up no more than a handful of hazardous waste sites, and, in an earlier generation, the War on Poverty, which established a number of new administrative bureaucracies whose mission was to reduce and then eliminate poverty. There are numerous explanations (both popular and academic) for the "administrative failures" of the U.S. system. Academics often claim that "interest group politics" divert technically competent bureaucracies from implementing what would otherwise be rational policies. Popular opinion, of late manifested in presidential political campaigns, tends to be that there is something terribly wrong with the bureaucracies themselves, with either their employees or their organizational structure and procedures. One current version of this belief holds that failure is inherent in the inevitable inefficiency of government (which simply proves that government should not be involved in most spheres of life in the first place) and that things are better left to the marketplace, where efficiency is given priority. Because the problem with government is labeled "administrative," the debate is restricted to questions of internal organization and management. In this context, the issue of democracy in public institutions falls by the wayside. Notions of accountability, open government, and citizen participation are ignored in favor of economy and efficiency.

During this century, presidents have chartered numerous commissions and studies to figure out what can be done to make government more organized, efficient, economical, and better managed. Presidents have historically viewed administrative reform of government as a central concern of the U.S. citizen and his or her democratic interests. But the focus has always been on internal organization and management of the executive branch, not on democratic process.

In 1937, Roosevelt's Brownlow Committee stressed that "the safeguarding of the citizen from narrow minded and dictatorial bureaucratic interference and control is one of the primary obligations of democratic government," and further, that "the forward march of American democracy at this point in history depends more on effective management than upon any other single factor" (March and Olson 1983, 290). Since the 1930s, issues of public administration—the civil service, administrative law, organization of bureaucratic components, and methods of policy implementation—have been at the forefront of every new president's agenda. Presidents Carter and Reagan have pressed commissions into service to "bring the horrible bureaucratic mess under control" (Carter) and identify opportunities for increasing efficiency and reducing the cost of the federal government (Reagan's Private Sector Survey on Cost Control, or the Grace Commission).

In short, for over one hundred years, the administration of government programs has been perceived by presidents, Congresses, public interest groups, and citizens alike as a thorn in the side of historical progress. Problems of administration have gradually come to be identified as the *cause* of social stagnation or economic decline. This view predominates today.

The desire to pursue economy and efficiency in government programs and the belief that these twin goals are essential to democracy has a long history in the United States. They date back to and to some extent have their roots in industrialization in the 1870s, when major debates in Congress erupted over the constitution of the civil service and problems with the "spoils system." Until about 1930, administrative reform was viewed primarily as civil service reform. More often than not, the problems of government were articulated in terms of federal workers, their political affiliations, and the inefficiencies that resulted from a politicized federal bureaucracy. Consequently, civil service legislation (the Pendleton Act of 1883) and various executive actions on personnel issues were the standard solutions to administrative problems.

After the Great Depression, personnel management and administration of government became two separate areas of concern for reformers.[2] Political debate centered less on anxiety about the reemergence of a spoils system, and more about the size, management, and organization of a complex bureaucracy in the executive branch. This shift reflected the influence of the "administration-as-science" tendency in public administration, a theory that had been heavily dominated by the thinking of Frederick Taylor and the school of scientific management. It was an era when administration was virtually equated with management and centralized control. As a result, intellectuals argued that politics and administration could and should be separated. With appropriate safeguards preventing politicized bureaucracies (civil service laws, for example) and ensuring efficient hierarchies, government administration could proceed according to rational laws and principles. Public administration could be devoted to issues of productivity, organizational coherence, efficiency of decision-making—all concerns of "better management."

More recently, with the reaction to the welfare and regulatory policies that proliferated in the federal government during the 1960s and 1970s, the debate over government administration has shifted into a third realm. Beginning in the Carter administration and continuing under Reagan, the debate has focused less on *how* government functions (i.e., efficiently or inefficiently) and more on concerns of *what* government does (e.g., intervenes in the marketplace, subsidizes the poor). Especially during the two terms of the Reagan administration, organizational reform of the federal bureaucracy has become overtly linked with a political movement to curtail the political authority of the state system. Reagan initiatives such as deregulation, cuts in social service personnel and funding, and increases in defense spending are all part of this movement. Economy and efficiency are, as they were in the early 1900s, still the concern of reformers such as Peter Grace, who headed President Reagan's Private Sector Survey on Cost Control. Instead of symbolizing a bureaucracy free from political manipulation by federal employees (1870–1930), or a bureaucracy organized rationally and implementing policies with maximum effectiveness (1930–1975), economy and efficiency represent reduced government function and authority.[3]

Throughout the three epochs of administrative reform briefly outlined above, there has existed in U.S. political culture an "administrative orthodoxy"[4] that holds certain key values and assumptions about how government organizations should work and, more importantly, about what the proper role of government in society should be.

Orthodox values often assume ritualistic and mythical proportions, evidenced by repeated attempts to reorganize government through various administrative reforms (March and Olson 1983; Cohen 1977). While the commissions and their recommendations may have no practical value, they have potent political value. The language of organizational change in the public sector is formulated within a framework that reasserts economy and efficiency.

Orthodoxy functions by establishing procedures that facilitate the efficiency and effectiveness of bureaucratic hierarchies. Emphasis is placed on centralization (rather than decentralization) of authority, development of strong managerial leadership, and meritocratic personnel procedures. These values are prominent in the recent Grace Commission recommendations for cutting and controlling costs. Three major ideas characterize this orthodoxy and can be found throughout scholarly articles, commission reports, and Congressional hearings:[5] 1) the belief that administration is a *politically neutral* instrument of public policy-making; 2) the view that problems of bureaucratic unruliness can be cured through centralizing *managerial control* and strengthening hierarchical decision-making; and 3) the assumption that *business principles* of management are directly applicable to the public management of bureaucratic organizations.

These three core principles of administrative orthodoxy have, over the years, become "common sense" and are therefore assumed to be true within government, among professionals, and among the wider citizenry. Incorporated into congressional testimony, agency reports, government regulations, personnel practices, and presidents' speeches, these beliefs and all of their attendant rituals have become a kind of *folklore of governance*.[6] The term "folklore" here refers to a tradition of customs and sayings that reflect unsupported and specious notions of reality. Hidden, they are extremely powerful influences on what government should do and how. Some insight into each of these beliefs is useful before a critique of more specific administrative policies and proposals for change.

Political Neutrality

Public administration advocates from Woodrow Wilson on believed that it was possible to separate politics—and policy—from the administration of government. They conceived of public administration strategies as rational tools to be applied to organizational and implementation problems in government. As a science administration had certain "laws" that could lead to effective and efficient management. Because science was assumed to be value-free in general, specific policies for civil service, agency management, and decision-making were also considered to be politically neutral. This position led to the views that it is possible and desirable to separate the expertise and non-political judgements of civil servants from the politically biased views of presidential appointees, both in the bureaucratic hierarchy and in the decision-making process; that policy implementation should be isolated from political pressures; and that the civil service can be protected from the political pressures of Congress and the presidency through the appointments process and various rules to insulate federal employees.

The most significant step toward creating a vision of the neutral state was probably passage of the Pendleton Act of 1883. This act established the modern civil service as a system of "meritocracy," rather than one dependent on "spoils." More importantly, the act symbolized new ways of thinking about the role of government in U.S. society, ways of thinking that were heavily influenced by the emergence of industrial capitalism in the late 1800s. On the one hand, a stronger, more active government that would bring a limited order to chaotic social change was clearly needed. On the other hand, belief in a limited government that did not harm the marketplace remained strong. Out of this set of conflicting needs emerged the notion of a professional, politically neutral, but limited government authority.

The Pendleton Act itself grew out of the post-Civil War pressure of rapid industrialization and resultant social movements, such as populism. As the country experienced major economic transformation, widespread pressure for fundamental economic change emerged from agrarian communities and to a lesser degree from the growing working class. As Paul Van Riper, the preeminent historian of the Civil Service, has argued, this era was dominated by a perceived need for collective action against new problems of industrialization (1958). Civil service reform was one example. The Pendleton Act was the only fundamental government reform between 1870 and 1900, an era of rapid change and the merit system of federal employment represented a new way of doing government business.

Three major features of the Pendleton Act provided the foundation of the merit system: 1) establishment of competitive examinations for entrance into public service; 2) security of tenure for employees; and 3) regulations intended to insure neutrality of civil servants. By institutionalizing the merit system, the act laid the foundation for the formation of the modern U.S. state. It distributed offices more systematically and rationally than the spoils system had, avoiding oligarchical tendencies that had combined the business world with the political. It also laid the foundation for developing the technical expertise crucial to the operation of the modern state.

In practice, the Pendleton Act did not mandate sweeping changes, but rather encouraged a slow conversion of government positions to the merit system. This allowed the continued appointment of large numbers of partisan individuals to bureaucratic jobs. Until the Truman administration, presidents had flexibility in deciding which positions would be merit-based and which would be political appointments.

The Pendleton Act was a crucial historical landmark in the evolution of the modern U.S. state.[7] The pre-Act spoils system represented an explicit melding of business and party interests with politics and had achieved scandalous proportions by the 1860s. With the advance of industrial enterprise, the development of new social classes, and the rise of reform movements, demands for collective action against business abuse and control of the political system became more urgent. In government administration the spoils system threatened the evolving concept of democratic politics. Establishing a system of "political neutrality" through various mechanisms (exams, tenure, a bipartisan civil service commission) created the "ideal" of a state independent of direct business and party control.

This concept of political neutrality was the necessary precursor to the formation of the regulatory state in the early 1900s and the welfare state of the 1930s. Early twentieth century laws took the Pendleton Act one step further with an attempt to separate state power from business influence by establishing a limited public authority over the marketplace.

By the end of the nineteenth century it was in the long-term interest of both capitalists and democratically-oriented social groups for government administration to operate independently from special business interests. The state system had by this time assumed an ideological posture compatible with capitalist interests; economic decisions of primary importance to business remained within the private sector. The gradual creation of a technical and more neutral workforce also set the stage for the development of professional expertise and the eventual development of new forms of state action such as welfare programs and social regulation. The independence of administration from politics, however, fueled a growing chasm between citizens and their government—an unforeseen side-effect—and the modern belief that technocratic elites are better able to make public decisions than are ordinary citizens. Implicit in this position is a fundamental distrust of and a corollary reverence for "expertise."

Managerial Control

The idea that government activity could and should be centrally managed has been held up as the ideal form of public administration since the early 1900s— a notion quite compatible with the neutrality of public administration. Further, such management could be achieved through the application of *rational* (and neutral) tools such as budgeting, cost accounting, personnel rules, productivity measures, and the like. Replacing government "managers" with government "executives" indicates this shift in perspective. The view is that clear lines of authority are important, hierarchical organizational structures efficient, and elaborate rules for correct organizational behavior essential to the well managed bureaucracy. What some political scientists call the "administrative presidency" (Nathan 1983) illustrates how attempts toward increasing executive control have succeeded in recent years under the Nixon, Carter, and Reagan administrations. The degree of control currently exercised by the Office of Management and Budget (OMB) in the White House over regulatory affairs, personnel policy, budgeting, and information policy is just an example of the drive for centralized, executive control over government activity.

The origins of managerial control date from the Progressive Era, when presidents and their advisors became intent on achieving centralized control over the executive departments. Not surprisingly, managerial control also coincided with the emergence of public administration professionals and their insistence that government be run by "experts" rather than by political appointees. Beginning with Theodore Roosevelt's administration, debate over government reform included a new distinction between personnel management and government administration and a commitment to applying business principles of economy and efficiency to solve bureaucratic problems. During this era elaborate systems of worker control were established to regularize employment and achieve more managerial control over the workforce. Personnel management procedures were set up that continue to affect federal employees today.

Theodore Roosevelt's reform effort centered on replacing party controls over civil administration with independent executive controls. His campaign for economy and efficiency in government began a major struggle for the reconstitution of institutional power relations in the early twentieth century. Roosevelt was successful in enhancing the powers of the Civil Service Commission and in creating a Commission on Department Methods. These efforts brought about executive control over personnel and administrative affairs that had, until then, rested with Congress. Many of his reforms, however, were not implemented until the Taft and Wilson administrations.

President Taft began his administration by establishing a Commission on Economy and Efficiency. His demand for civil service reform included a comprehensive position-classification and pay plan that began the institutionalization of a codified system of personnel management. (Interestingly, there has been no adjustment of government pay since the 1850s.) One of the more significant outcomes of this commission was the establishment of a bureau of personnel responsible for examining applicants, certifying qualifications, classifying positions, developing efficiency records, promulgating rules governing discipline, arbitrating disputes between employees and supervisors, and inspecting working conditions. Although legislative enactment took several years, this idea of a central personnel agency represented a major step toward incorporating the ideology and principles of business management into the government administrative machinery. The conviction that public service work could be organized and managed smoothly under the guidance of for-profit business principles remains a critical feature of proposals for civil service reform today and indeed, of public expectations of government administration.

The separation of personnel management and government administration during this period is important to understand. This change was prompted by the growing belief that managing workers was essential and that personnel practices should be uniformly established throughout an organization in the interest of both cooperation from workers and enforcement by management. The Bureau of the Budget (predecessor of OMB), created in 1921, brought careful oversight of personnel and personnel costs and led to pressure for standardization of wages and job descriptions. The Classification Act of 1923 established salary ranges, limited raises, and established a separate wage-setting agency, the Personnel Classification Board. By 1934, the height of the Depression, the centralization of personnel functions had increased considerably. The Depression forced consolidation of various boards into the Civil Service Commission.

Business Principles

Notions of efficiency, cost-cutting, size reduction, and productivity measurement have been an integral part of the public administration dialogue for decades. Commissions on reorganizing executive branch operations, their mandates, and the rhetoric surrounding their studies usually have telling names: for example, Reagan's Private Sector Survey on Cost Control and Taft's Commission on Economy and Efficiency. The current interest in "privatizing" government services and functions (Savas 1982) goes as far back as the 1930s, when it was believed that private business could perform government services more cheaply and efficiently than the public sector and that, in fact, government programs and production were harmful to the business community because they damaged the market. There has consequently been a long history of government agencies "contracting-out" for products and services. Privatization is a revival of the older view that government and business activity are essentially the same, except that one is performed privately and the other publicly.

Privatization has more opportunity to alter the government now because administrative and management procedures have been institutionalized through regulations that are enforced by the OMB. Mechanisms such as performance standards for federal workers, reduction in force, and contracting out of government activities to the private sector are beginning noticeably to alter the nature of public work, the dimensions of the workforce, and the character of government. Specifically, these measures have a triple effect: 1) dividing an already deeply divided labor force and deskilling technical and professional work; 2) limiting the ability of government to perform its welfare and regulatory functions; 3) centralizing power over policy matters through administration of the budget at OMB and introduction of new management principles at the Office of Personnel Management. In essence, what are proposed as economic efficiency efforts to enhance the quality and productivity of government are, in fact, means by which basic government functions may be altered, laws circumventing the legislative process rewritten, and enforcement of agency missions neglected.

The push to "privatize" the federal government has slowed down considerably toward the end of Reagan's second term. Arguments in favor of selling off government lands, for instance, have not persuaded Congress. As a result, contracting out government services and functions remains the primary channel through which conservatives seek to introduce principles of business management into the public sector. In fact, contracting out is acceptable to liberals and conservatives alike because they agree on two basic points. First, they believe that capitalist management principles applied to private-sector work can also be applied to government. (This assumes that these management principles do in fact function as intended in private industry and that there is no distinction between private and public sector organizations.) Second, they believe that the policy process can be separated from the administration and implementation of government programs. (This assumes that while policy-making is a political process that rests on value-laden decisions, the implementation of policies can be rational and value-free as a result of economic, efficient procedures.)

To summarize, these three core principles of administrative orthodoxy— political neutrality, managerial control, and business principles of management— all represent particular ideological constructions. By implication, they suggest that administering government is best left to technical experts and that implementing public policy is not of importance, or interest, to the wider public. This is a mistake. The problems of organization, politics, and values that characterize the administration of government are important to people precisely because this administrative orthodoxy has removed government from the people it serves.

Overcoming the Orthodoxy

The administrative orthodoxy described above has left this country with a formidable legacy of anti-democratic philosophical and institutional obstacles. The real problems of government administration lie in overcoming these obstacles and creating new avenues and institutions in which democratic processes can flourish. How can this be accomplished? If the long-range goal, as this book argues, is to create a more democratically based public authority, then the short-term agenda must be to reform existing administrative structures and laws. Major revisions of current administrative practices are necessary to prepare the way for a radical reconstruction of government. The remainder of this chapter is addressed to outlining this short-term agenda.

Two spheres of administrative policy must be addressed before any dramatic change in government process can be considered: civil service policy and decision-management methods. While these may appear to be insignificant targets for reform because they involve the day-to-day operation of government, it is precisely the day-to-day operation of government that makes it so inaccessible to the majority of the population. Administrative practices that idolize technocratic elites, strengthen centralized political control over decisions, and apply business philosophies to public goals are so embedded in our political culture that we fail to see their power, or even their presence.

During the 1970s and 1980s, there have been important changes in civil service and decision-management policies. On the one hand, we have witnessed an increase in centralized political control over federal employees and policy decisions by the president; on the other hand, we have witnessed the rise of a more powerful federal employee union movement and the emergence of a renewed movement for citizen participation in government affairs. Some of the strongest deterrents to change lie in Carter-Reagan era administrative reforms and policies that are the direct products of the administrative orthodoxy. The Civil Service Reform Act, the Paperwork Reduction Act, the A–76 Circular (OMB regulations that encourage and simplify contracting out government functions), and Executive Order 12291 (mandating cost-benefit assessment of regulatory initiatives) are all examples of recent administrative policies that thwart the democratic process.[8] Similarly, the seeds for democratic reform of our national government lie in strengthening both the federal workers' union and citizen participation movements.

In order to counter the anti-democratic tendencies embodied in these and other recent reforms and capitalize on the potential for building national democratic institutions it is essential to develop a program that moves forward on two fronts: 1) reconstruction of the civil service and 2) establishment of a decision-making model that incorporates an "open government" policy allowing for citizen access and participation. The remainder of this section examines the obstacles to and the potential for reform that have emerged from the Carter-Reagan era in these two policy domains.

Reconstruction of the Civil Service

Although the ideal of "political neutrality" was built into the Pendleton Act of 1883, which reconstituted the civil service into a personnel system based upon meritocracy, the fact is that the federal workforce has since become highly politicized. Politicization pressures have not come from the bottom through powerful interest groups, but rather from the top—the White House. While civil servants have been relatively well insulated from the wider public and their interests through various legislative acts and regulations, they have not been protected from the pressures of a strong, ideologically-oriented presidency. According to public administration professionals, Reagan has been uniquely successful in gaining control over the civil service in a manner that was never intended by Progressive Era reformers, who envisioned a technically competent, neutral cadre of federal employees, or by 1970s reformers, who hoped to build a more responsive workforce (Levine 1986; Rosen 1986).

The Civil Service Reform Act (CSRA), passed in 1978, has proved to be an important impetus to the "Reagan revolution." The CSRA was one of the most important reforms of the Carter years and was the most extensive reform of the civil service since the Pendleton Act. It has fundamentally altered the terms of employment for federal workers, has created a competitive rather than cooperative work environment, and has given White House officials broader mandates to control personnel practices.

The CSRA was a hodgepodge of initiatives that accomplished several reforms, the most important of which are summarized below.

1. *Creation of a senior executive service (SES)*. Pressure had been mounting over the previous years for creation of an elite cadre of senior managers who would be more responsive to political officials, more flexible, easier to fire, and more mobile. The CSRA created an incentive-based system of awards and cash bonuses and placed rank in the person rather than the position.

2. *Merit pay for mid-level managers*. Similar to the incentives principle in the SES, a merit pay system was established for individuals in management grade levels (GS 13–15) of the regular civil service with the intention of doing away with automatic promotion and pay increases. Individuals in these grades receive only one-half the annual automatic pay increase that goes to all federal workers and must compete for the second half of the raise.

3. *Performance appraisals for all federal workers.* The CSRA requires annual performance reviews for all workers, to be used in personnel actions. This makes it easier to remove "unproductive" workers and makes all employees more responsive to political managers.

4. *Organizational reform to protect the merit system.* Because of the strong dose of management control over the workforce established by the CSRA, provisions were made to protect worker and union rights, and to protect the merit system from political manipulation. The old Civil Service Commission was split into two organizations: the Office of Personnel Management (OPM), responsible for personnel management, and the Merit Systems Protection Board (MSPB), responsible for hearing appeals and protecting the merit system. Protection for "whistleblowers" was provided through creation of the Office of Special Counsel (OSC) in MSPB, with a specific mandate to protect them from "improper reprisals." While the original Civil Service Commission had been independent of presidential control, the new OPM placed personnel management directly under the president's executive office with the understanding that MSPB and OCS would curb potential abuses.

5. *Statutory recognition of collective bargaining.* Prior to the CSRA, the employee's right to collective bargaining had been recognized through executive order ever since the Kennedy administration. The CSRA codified collective bargaining and formulated procedures for resolving problems (e.g., creation of the Federal Labor Relations Authority, with the statutory mandate to govern federal labor-management relations, and creation of the Federal Services Impasses Panel to resolve impasses in contract negotiations). Finally, the CSRA defined categories of management and union rights. (The potential strengths and limiting weaknesses of this portion of the CSRA will be discussed in greater length when we deal with the role of federal unions in government reform.)

Several years after implementation of the Act, leaders in the field of public administration are claiming that the CSRA has increased politicization of the bureaucracy and disorganization among the workforce (Ingraham and Ban 1984; Levine 1986; and Rosen 1983). In fact, the CSRA has provided the Reagan administration with the vehicle necessary to carry through significant policies affecting the federal workforce. Working directly under the president, the director of OPM, Donald Devine, responded quickly to the conservative White House agenda to "cut back government." Personnel management became a highly politicized activity as OPM wrote new regulations to limit employee rights during RIFs (reductions-in-force or layoffs), eliminate automatic raises for all employees and add a bonus incentive system, and create new incentives to encourage worker competition in the belief that this would increase productivity. Meanwhile, due to lack of resources in staff and funding, MSPB and OSC have been relatively unsuccessful in protecting the merit system and whistleblowers.

The CSRA and its implementation in the early 1980s reflect some basic assumptions about federal employment shared by both the Carter and Reagan administrations. First is the dominant belief that federal or public work is individualized, that workers perform their jobs in isolation and independently from one another. Bonuses are awarded to senior and mid-level managers on the basis of individual competition for recognition. Annual performance appraisals evaluate workers on the basis of whether or not they have successfully fulfilled the goals outlined for them at the beginning of the year. This view of work contradicts reality in the federal sector. Generally, work is accomplished in groups or teams rather than individually. Project completion is highly dependent on factors outside of workers' control, such as internal agency politics, shifts in the mission of offices, Congressional politics, and funding and resource problems. Under these conditions, basing evaluations and bonuses on individual effort is unrealistic. It also creates serious employee morale problems.

A second assumption inherent in the new civil service legislation is that worker productivity is the key problem in the bureaucracy and, further, that it can be improved by a "performance-based incentive system" (PBIS). Proponents of civil service reform in the Carter administration believed that public sector productivity could be measured as they assumed it was in the private sector. These beliefs reflect a basic naïveté about the nature of public work. Work goals, office budgets, and project missions often change, making the tools for measuring accomplishment practically non-existent and the ability to measure individual output impossible.

In sum, changes in federal employment under the Carter administration increased the ability of the Executive Office of the President to control the civil service for political purposes. This shifted the work environment toward competition even though the work itself continued to depend on cooperation and teamwork. The problem is therefore to rebuild a civil service system that will weaken executive control and challenge the administrative orthodoxy, while simultaneously serving the interests of the larger citizenry through a truer form of democratic authority.

The Importance of Public Worker Unions

Most of the CSRA is based on the beliefs that workers are neither competent nor dependable, that managers are both, and that managers should therefore be able to use strong measures to cope with workers (Parker et al. 1984). One aspect of the CSRA—Title VII, which provides statutory support for collective bargaining within the federal workforce—is consequently extremely important to progressive reform of the civil service. (Prior to the CSRA the right to collective bargaining for federal employees was granted by executive order of the president and was therefore always subject to revocation.) Title VII provides the opportunity to build strong unions in the federal sector, although by itself it does not always grant strong authority to the unions. Nevertheless, recognizing the right to collective bargaining and establishing appeals procedures and agencies encourages collective action.

Outside of the Postal Service the union movement in the federal sector has been weak. Various unions have been active since the 1880s in seeking civil service reform, protecting federal employees from patronage, and improving employment practices in government. But the power of these organizations has been minimal, and federal unions have lagged far behind private sector unions in establishing collective bargaining rights. Until the 1960s,, no president had recognized the collective bargaining rights of federal workers. Theodore Roosevelt issued "gag" rules in 1902 and 1906 that forbade federal workers from influencing legislation concerning federal employment before Congress. Franklin Roosevelt, who sponsored the Wagner Act of 1935, wrote two years later that collective bargaining "had its distinct and insurmountable limitations when applied to public personnel management" (Mosher 1968, 177). In 1962 John Kennedy signed an executive order recognizing the collective bargaining rights of federal employees and providing a decentralized system of bargaining in departments and agencies under the general guidance of the Civil Service Commission. The order, however, fell far short of private sector labor rights; it did not provide for any supervisory and appellate agency (comparable to the NLRB), and it upheld the prohibition of federal worker strikes. Until the CSRA in 1978 that executive order remained the main charter under which unions worked. The narrow definition of collective bargaining established in the executive order continued under the 1978 legislation: it accorded more rights to management than to unions, which were not allowed to negotiate over the mission of the agency, its budget, its organization, the assignment of personnel, or office technology.

It is not surprising that the public has resisted the idea of collective action in the public sector. The premise of public management and civil service since the 1880s has been individual merit. Appointment and advancement in public service are not to be tainted by influences of employee associations. As Frederick Mosher, who has written extensively on the problem of democracy and the civil service, points out, the "cause of organized labor in government is both defended and attacked on the grounds of democratic principles" (1968, 177). On the one hand, the right to associate and organize to improve employment conditions is regarded as an inalienable right of citizens. On the other hand, it is believed that public employee unions pose a unique threat to democracy. To some extent, this view is changing. Public employee unions are now recognized by local governments, states, and the federal government (the result of the Kennedy executive order), and as a result membership has grown. However, the paradox still lingers, as most governments (especially the federal government) do not allow the right to strike. When President Reagan fired eleven thousand air traffic controllers in 1981, it was a powerful reminder to federal employees of their limited rights of association.

The CSRA is a double-edged sword for federal employee unions. Because of the various provisions discussed earlier, which have encouraged further politicization and fragmentation of the workforce in executive branch bureaucracies, the unions and their members have suffered setbacks to organization and retention of members.[9] This is especially the result of placing the OPM under White House control, which under Reagan became the mechanism for implementing an anti-government platform. Staffing in domestic agencies was drastically reduced through the budget process, Reagan appointments to the appellate agencies such as Federal Services Impasses Panel and the Merit Systems Protection Board were clearly anti-union, and various regulations were promulgated by OPM that made it easier for managers to lay off workers for political reasons. Rather than increase in response to the Reagan attack, union membership declined seriously during the administration's first term. Reductions-in-force (RIFs) cut back agencies in which membership was high, and the unions were unable to replace those laid off with new members at the same rate. This drop probably reflects the effects of workforce politicization; because of pressures for increased competition between workers and fear of lay-offs, employees were reluctant openly to join unions.

The other side of CSRA's double-edged sword is that while federal unions do not have the right to strike and membership is declining, they do have a tool they can use toward empowerment and effective action—politics.[10] Unlike the private sector workers, federal workers are responsible to their agencies, the president, and Congress. The ability of unions to utilize this complex system to resolve problems in the civil service can be an effective tool. In fact, the two largest (non-postal) federal unions that represent domestic and defense agencies (American Federation of Government Employees and National Treasury Employees Union) have developed sophisticated legislative staffs to work with Congressional committees, representing the concerns of federal employees in response to Reagan administration initiatives. To a large extent, federal unions have matured politically and substantively during Reagan's two terms, even while experiencing a membership crisis.

Federal unions have a role to play in the reconstitution of the civil service. The potential is there with Title VII and with the enhanced political sophistication of the unions' national offices. Federal workers are in a unique position to break down bureaucratic barriers to citizen access and to nourish a more democratic, less centralized and White House-dominated administration of government. This potential, however, is based on moving beyond shop floor issues toward organizational structures that encourage democratic participation in federal bureaucracies and challenge the elitism inherent in the current technocratic workforce. Further, the union movement must be unified, acting as one voice for federal employees.

Open Government Policies

By themselves a reconstructed civil service and strengthened public unions are not sufficient to create a democratic administration of government. There must also be action to open up government decisions to public participation. We must counter the centralization of policy making in the Executive Office of the President with democratic reforms.

There are serious obstacles to such reforms, specifically information policies, executive orders, and legislation that have emerged during the Carter-Reagan era. Over the last decade, the White House has dominated agency decision-making to the exclusion of career employees and citizens. As a result, policies are more subject to ideological pressures than to intelligent public and professional assessment.[11] Decisions that were made at the cabinet level in the past are currently made in the OMB. They are now based on criteria such as efficiency, economy, and centralization of control rather than on substantative issues in a given policy field.

This trend, not unique to the Carter-Reagan period, is the logical result of the administrative orthodoxy. It has its roots in the Progressive Era fascination with public administration and "management." What is uniquely dangerous about the Carter-Reagan reforms is that they gave the President's Executive Office new administrative powers that potentially affect the most important functions of government in hidden ways. Legislative reform is likely to be shaped by administrative mechanisms. Congress may be ignored and the public bypassed.

Three initiatives from the Carter-Reagan period have significantly undermined the democratic authority of the federal government: the Paperwork Reduction Act, the A-76 Circular, and Executive Order 12291. They are symptomatic of a government insulated from public control.

1. The Paperwork Reduction Act (PRA) of 1980 was passed to limit the amount of federal government paperwork required from business and local governments. Under Reagan, the OMB (which administers the act) has used it as a tool to impose quotas on government questionnaires and surveys of industry, limit large-scale data collection projects, slash agency information budgets, and generally restrict public access to information.

The act also affects the production of information. The popular, consumer-oriented *Car Book*, published by the Department of Transportation, disappeared during the Reagan years and the Bureau of Labor Statistics (BLS), a main source of labor-market data, cut back extensively on its surveys and publications. Agencies charged with solving problems (e.g., hazardous wastes) are at a considerable disadvantage because of their limited ability to collect and analyze data. Further, regulatory agencies have lost ground as independent assessors of industry activity, instead becoming dependent on industry-generated data for evaluating policy options—a rather dangerous practice. In the long run, with little information generated through research or available to citizens, we are vulnerable to increased control by OMB over government agencies.

2. The White House goal of privatizing government functions through contracting out government services is being accomplished through the revision of what is known as the A-76 Circular. The debate over privatization is focused on the particulars of this revised OMB document, which contains rules and

methods governing contracting-out. For instance, how one calculates federal employee fringe benefits makes a considerable difference in the labor cost of a given government unit. It is easy to make federal work look considerably more expensive than the cost of contracting it out to a hypothetical private counterpart. A-76 rules are governed by the principle of "cost-effectiveness," which assumes the best public service is the cheapest. No other criteria for evaluating efficiency and effectiveness exist.

A-76 advocates a policy and vision of government relying on the free enterprise system for goods and services. This is not a new idea. Contracting out, especially in research and development, has a long history. The Department of Defense, for example, is notorious for its reliance on outside contractors. What is significant about the Reagan administration's use of A-76 is its application to *all* federal work and its use as a tool for reducing the size of the federal workforce.

Reagan targeted traditionally in-house government services as candidates for contracting-out. For example, libraries in the major executive agencies have been contracted out to private businesses. Offices with ten or fewer employees became automatic targets for "A-76 Review," no matter what their function. Many administrative functions, such as computer services, mailrooms, and printing plants have become private businesses operating within agency offices, where company employees and their supervisors work in government buildings and use government equipment and materials. Many government workers are no longer covered by civil service rules. Administrative activities managed by several private businesses within one agency are obviously inefficient. Each private unit may appear internally efficient, but the overall effect is the disorganization of agency work. Coordination between privately run units and other parts of the agency is managed through a complex set of contracting regulations. This sets up new communications barriers within all agencies that may create greater inefficiencies than previously existed. Public accountability also becomes a problem when workers are no longer supervised by the agency. Employee morale plummets when employees laid off by the government under A-76 are rehired by the contractor to work in the same office and at the same job, but with lower wages and fewer benefits (U.S. House, 1984).

Not surprisingly, A-76 has rallied federal employee unions. More importantly, it has created a federal work environment full of fear, uncertainty, and employee suspicion of political manipulation (Staudohar 1981; Kolderie 1986). In effect, contracting-out has become yet another means of civil service reform, by executive mandate rather than legislative negotiation.

3. Both Presidents Carter and Reagan have used the executive order to achieve political control over traditional agency policy decisions. Executive Order (EO) 12291 epitomizes this technique and demonstrates the move from a politics of "shared power" to one of "administration by decree" (Cooper 1986; Rosenberg 1981).

Issued by Reagan, EO 12291 subjects all pending regulations from executive agencies to a cost-benefit analysis (CBA). Although cost-benefit predates the Reagan White House (existing in earlier forms in the Nixon, Ford, and Carter administrations), it had never before been used as the decision criterion for evaluating pending regulations or for rescinding regulations already promulgated. Reagan's use of CBA as a decision criterion under EO 12291 resulted in eliminating some regulations (such as the airbag rule, Standard 208), delaying others, and cancelling plans for future rule-making. CBA, in effect, became the *sole* criterion for deciding the merits of regulation.

Before Reagan, CBA provided information on one aspect of regulatory pros and cons. It became popular in the late 1970s when the movement for deregulation gathered steam and encouraged cost-consciousness in Washington. In theory, CBA evaluates whether or not regulations are too costly (to industry) for the benefits they provide (to the public). It assumes that all costs and benefits are measurable. In practice, CBA analysts find dollar costs more quantifiable than qualitative benefits. In health and safety regulation, in particular, benefits are difficult to measure—lives saved and health preserved, often years after the costs of altering a product or production process have been incurred. CBA inevitably tips the balance in favor of industry because benefits tend to be either unmeasurable or underestimated. Applying CBA to health and safety programs also contradicts the original Congressional intent. The goal of traffic safety legislation was to save lives and reduce injuries; the Clear Air Act established a mandate to eliminate pollutants from the air. No economic criteria were mentioned.

Because OMB has established it as a principle of executive management and budget review, CBA has become a powerful tool for substantive policy reform through administrative rather than legislative channels. One legal scholar claims that under Reagan, EO's (especially 12291) have been used "as instruments of expediency to circumvent administrative law" (Cooper 1986, 235) and a recalcitrant Congress. By giving OMB power to impede and eliminate the regulatory process, EO 12291 violates the Administrative Procedures Act (APA) of 1946. The APA sets the parameters by which "informal rule-making" occurs as agencies announce their regulatory intentions, elicit public input through hearings and contributions to the docket, and repeatedly request public comment through the rule-making process. EO 12291 applies narrow economic values— economy and efficiency—to policy decisions about non-economic concerns such as health and welfare. By circumventing the opportunity for public comment, OMB becomes a policy-making organization immune from public scrutiny. The APA has traditionally been the instrument of citizen participation in agency decisions, but executive orders imposing narrow economic values may close the door to effective democratic administration of the regulatory state.

Laws, rulings, and administrative practices such as those described above will lead to a narrow and controlled debate on major public policy issues, thereby putting citizen activists at a disadvantage and keeping the public in the dark.

Restricting the production and distribution of information through the Paperwork Reduction Act limits citizen impact on policy-making. Without information citizen groups are unable to monitor government offices or fully exercise their rights to public comment. Privatizing government functions through administrative rulings like the A-76 Circular will quietly erode our notion of "public space," by creating organizations that are not publicly accountable yet perform public functions—a shadow government. Administration by decree—the executive order—insures replacement of democratic values with technocratic and elitist ones. In the short term administrative reforms must address the anti-democratic trends set in motion by these initiatives.

Citizen Participation

As presidents increased administrative and political control over everyday government affairs, a strong grassroots movement advocated more citizen involvement in government decisions. Citizens have organized into numerous local and national public interest groups; the Ralph Nader organizations are examples. Specific issues such as the environment, auto safety, hazardous wastes, nutrition, and other health and safety concerns have been organizational targets. Successful efforts resulted in numerous legislative efforts and several laws that strengthened the political hand of citizens. Just as a more powerful federal union movement is an important force in civil service reform, the citizen participation movement is critical to the reform of administrative procedures.

The call for open government dates back to the early 1800s, when settlers who had moved west of the Appalachians demanded a voice in government via elimination of voting barriers. Until World War II, such demands focused primarily upon extending voting rights (e.g., the Nineteenth Amendment) and civil service reform (e.g., the Pendleton Act) (Kweit & Kweit 1981).

After the war pressure increased for a more participatory (as opposed to representative) type of democracy. In the 1960s and 1970s, the public interest movement pushed for laws that opened up government agencies to public involvement in internal decisions. The first such legislation was the Administrative Procedures Act (APA) of 1946. In 1966 it was reinforced and enhanced by the Freedom of Information Act (FOIA).

The APA granted citizens new rights: adequate notice of new government rules, the right to participate in rule-making through submission of data and testimony, access to information, and the right to appeal and petition. The idea is that *direct* participation in government affairs is more democratic than *indirect* participation fostered by voting and civil service reform. However, the rights granted by the APA are primarily advisory. Citizens can only suggest changes in rules that are pending. Further, their involvement in rule-making occurs at a relatively late date, often well after the agency has made an institutional investment in the details of a particular rule. Citizens must resort to the courts to repeal or stop decisions.

The FOIA gives any person the right to obtain government information without having to justify his or her reason. Agencies can withhold information that falls into specific categories (documents to be kept secret for national security, investigatory records, certain inter-agency memoranda not available through civil discovery), but are not required to do so. The premise underlying the FOIA is that timely access to information and government data is essential for effective oversight and participation by citizens.

The APA and FOIA remain the basic laws enforcing the rights of citizen participation today. Other laws passed during the 1960s and 1970s further increased the information and advisory rights of citizens. The Federal Advisory Committee Act (1972) regulated the establishment of citizen advisory committees by insuring balanced representation, protecting them from special interests, and assuring that they would have adequate staff and funding. The National Environmental Policy Act (1969) mandated the use of environmental impact statements in public projects, creating independent sources of information used in decisions. The Government Sunshine Act (1976) opened government meetings to the public and required advance notification of date, time, and place.

Other, more radical Congressional proposals were never enacted. In 1977, for example, Senators Kennedy and Mathias introduced legislation to establish "intervenor funding" for agencies to pay citizen groups, experts, and individuals to participate in rule-making proceedings. This proposed Public Participation in Federal Agency Proceedings Act never passed, but the idea has remained popular among citizen groups.

Those who have worked with the APA are well aware of its limitations. Two major problems exist (Langton 1982). First, there are no opportunities for citizens to participate in the initial policy formation process or in the early stages of policy decisions. In regulatory agencies, rule-making begins long before the docket is opened for public comment on a pending rule. Because of the research (often highly technical) and planning that goes into development of a regulation (sometimes three to five years), an agency is heavily invested in the successful promulgation of the rule before the public gets involved. Second, there is no requirement that agencies actually respond to citizen input. In fact, submission of testimony, data, and correspondence to the docket can be entirely ignored by agency staff, although many agencies do informally acknowledge negative public testimony. Citizen input is useful to establish a public record that may be important in a later court case. Subsequent legislation (mentioned above) has resolved some APA problems such as lack of information, access to government meetings, and safeguards protecting citizen groups from special interests. But the basic problems remain.

Since Reagan's election, proposals for reforms to improve APA have all but disappeared. Citizen advocates have been on the defensive, fighting the erosion of open government policies as Reagan implemented the Paperwork Reduction Act and EO 12291. Rule-making proceedings have become even more symbolic and less effective forums for citizen participation. Currently, OMB can intervene in early planning stages for future rules to halt further research and development of regulations. In addition, access to information has grown more difficult as government consumer and research publications have declined dramatically (Demac 1984).

The alternative for citizen activists has been an expensive one. The courts have become the primary vehicle for affecting Reagan's regulatory decisions. When the government shut out citizen groups from major decisions involving automotive safety rules for airbags and crashworthy bumpers, citizen advocates (along with insurance companies) successfully appealed to the courts for a reversal.

Meanwhile, in the legislative arena Reagan amendments to the FOIA, which reduced its scope, have consumed citizen attention. The Reagan administration has criticized the act because it supposedly inhibits government performance and costs too much. In 1983 the Attorney General issued new guidelines for FOIA allowing agencies the right to judge whether a request for information was "legitimate" and whether the requestor was "sufficiently qualified to understand the information contained in the documents and to convey the correct meaning to the public" (Claybrook, 1984, xxx). Theoretically, the FOIA makes no such distinctions.

This and other efforts to limit access to government information have made the question of "information policy" a key concern of the public interest movement (Feinberg 1986). This is unfortunate because the focus on information as a form of participation draws attention away from other, more important opportunities for empowering citizens. More important at this point are proposals that enable citizen involvement through funding of travel and research on public issues. Legislation that empowers citizen involvement in policy formation and the early stages of rule-making is also crucial. Such steps are discussed more fully in the last section.

Empowerment is the important question. Current open government laws really do not allow citizens to participate effectively in the formative stages of agency decisions. Under APA and FOIA the public simply reacts in the later stages, more effective at creating a public record than in having a voice. Private associations and their lobbyists, well funded and more able to use government information to their advantage, are more successful in influencing the early direction of federal rules and agency policies. Citizens are a weak force. Advisory rights mandated by the APA and access to information required by FOIA are only a first step toward citizen participation.

Transitional Steps

The power of the administrative orthodoxy over our public philosophy remains strong. To rid ourselves of the burden of "economy and efficiency" solutions to administrative dilemmas and replace them with democratic solutions based on ideas of "effective government" requires work. Traditional mechanisms such as political parties (see Chapter 2) and administrative rules such as APA and FOIA that allow some public access do not work in the 1980s to break down the barriers between government and citizens. The frightening speed at which the Reagan administration has centralized power over the federal workforce and administrative mechanisms is a real obstacle to civil servants, citizen groups, and open government laws.

The long-term goal must be to create new mediating institutions that allow, encourage, and fund citizen involvement in policy-making and implementation. The enormous gulf between the citizenry and the professional staff of government agencies must disappear. Citizens should demand accountability yet recognize the value of an independent and decisive scientific, technical, and professional federal workforce. Civil servants must understand the importance of public involvement in policy planning and development yet be conscious of the need to assume final responsibility for public decisions. These may seem like contradictory goals—that again is the result of the administrative orthodoxy. At the very least, citizen advisory and information rights should be protected and extended, and the rights of federal workers must be acknowledged and expanded. Significant democratic reform, however, demands many more changes in how government does business.

It is naïve to believe that reforms in administration *alone* will lead to a more democratic political system. Open government requires a revitalized party system (Chapter 2) and a Congress willing to assume a policy role in governance (see Chapters 4 and 6) as well as aggressive institutional reforms at the administrative level. Further, administrative, party, and Congressional reform must proceed *simultaneously*. For citizens to take advantage of opportunities to influence government policy without slowing down the bureaucracy, they must be well organized and adequately represented.

Political parties and the Congress are two viable mechanisms for participation, but not as they are currently structured. The power over Congress of special monied interests and their Political Action Committees (PACs) over

Congress must be significantly reduced. Parties must return to local party-building that encourages citizens, rather than national leaders, to set the national party agenda. Although these and other reforms are not the subject of this chapter, the proposed administrative strategies will work only with continuous attention to these issues.

Suggested below are several transitional reforms intended to reverse some of the worst administrative tendencies in the Carter-Reagan era and in the long run to undermine the administrative orthodoxy that has distorted our notion of how government should work. Important short-term goals are civil service reform (which frees government workers from centralized political control); curtailment of OMB and White House administrative powers; and a new Open Government Policy Act. Long-term goals are more elusive, but vitally necessary. We must experiment with new ways to empower citizens that go beyond Congressional and party reforms. Citizens must have access to individual agencies without compromising the need to make timely decisions that benefit the public as a whole. Specific ideas are offered here that address both the short- and long-term goals for administrative reform.

1. *Reverse the direction of the Civil Service Reform Act.* This might be done either through new civil service legislation or by amending the CSRA. Three specific reforms merit immediate attention. First, direct presidential control over civil service policy should be eliminated. The OMB, created by the CSRA and currently reporting directly to the president, has allowed White House manipulation of day-to-day civil service policy. If the federal workforce is to maintain some professional distance from ideological control, it must be independent. Establishing an independent commission that reports directly to Congress will encourage the development of innovative civil service policies that can be monitored more directly and publicly. Questions of public accountability, citizen involvement in policy formation, program effectiveness, and workplace improvement should be the priorities for this new commission. Civil service policy can no longer be viewed simply a mechanism for "management control" of the workforce through restrictive and punitive strategies. The link between an independent, professional, and effective federal workforce and accountability of government to its citizens must be recognized as an integral part of personnel policy in the public sector.

Second, bargaining rights for federal workers should be strengthened. Title VII of the CSRA provides only limited protection for worker rights by recognizing collective bargaining. Organization of work, personnel rules, budgets, and wages are not negotiable items. Federal workers cannot strike. Expanding the scope of bargaining for civil servants to include these items will allow more input into agency policies that organize federal work. Management strategies are currently issued in a "top-down" fashion and reflect the orthodoxy of economy and efficiency. Federal workers, through their unions, can contribute to restructuring federal work toward democratic (rather than business) goals of effectiveness.

Third, merit pay strategies for federal employees should be eliminated. Merit pay fosters competition instead of cooperation among individual employees and is counter-productive in the federal sector. The CSRA was premised on the false ideas that federal work is individualized and that improving individual worker productivity through pay incentives would solve problems of government effectiveness. Evaluating the performance of whole office divisions in accomplishing their goals would be more appropriate. Workers too need to evaluate the success of their programs and document the types of problems they encounter. This documentation should be publicly available. In this way policies established by OMB to limit the production of information, the collection of data, or regulatory initiatives can be monitored from an informed perspective.

2. *Limit the powers of OMB*. Congress must stop the drift toward a highly centralized system of administrative control in the White House if open government policies are to become reality. Several steps can be taken. First, policymaking must be recognized as a democratic process rather than a formalized presidential system of control. Second, Congress should reassert its responsibility for policy oversight.

OMB is a vital target for reform. Its cost-benefit requirement (EO 12291) is a good example of how presidential oversight and extensive requirements for application of cost-benefit procedures can substantively alter policies. EO 12291 likely violates the constitutional separation of powers and the APA (Rosenberg 1981). Overseeing agency policies is the job of Congressional committees, although the APA gives agencies authority over informal rule-making. In effect, with administrative policy-making centralized in the White House, we have shifted to a less participatory, less open system of law-making. Congress must reassert its policy role by legislatively limiting OMB administrative powers. OMB circulars and executive orders that establish procedures for presidential administrative oversight must be approved by Congress after public hearings and Congressional review.

OMB activities should be restricted to coordinating budget issues, management strategies, and administrative problems among agencies. In essence, OMB should be solely an advisory organization, not a political instrument of the president, as was intended by the Budget Act of 1921, which established OMB's predecessor, the Bureau of the Budget. Congress has already reasserted some of its budget powers by establishing the Congressional Budget Office and enacting the Budget and Impoundment Act of 1974. Similar actions must be taken with respect to OMB's administrative strategies such as the A-76 Circular and EO 12291.

3. *Maximize citizen participation through an Open Government Policy Act*. Laws that encourage and formalize citizen participation in agency decision making need to be consolidated. Further, this legislation must create new mechanisms for citizen access that go beyond participation in public hearings, written comments on pending rules, and access to agency information. Past legislation never

encouraged agencies to listen to citizens or to respond to their proposals. Information access policies never enabled citizens to *use* information effectively.

Three general areas require our initial attention: information, citizen boards, and funds for participation.

FOIA-type requirements must be strengthened to insure citizen access to government data, reports, and so on. But this is not enough. Government agencies must be required to report data and other information directly to consumer, labor, and community groups who are served or affected by that agency's activities. A series of citizen research centers might be established around the country to help individuals and organizations prepare for participation in rule-making and policy decisions. Public interest organizations (many of them located in Washington D.C.) currently serve as citizen lobbying groups. They raise funds by seeking donations and foundation grants and hire professional staff to interpret government information and publicize government decisions. Citizen research centers would allow the public interest movement to diversify and stretch across the country. Local community groups could utilize the research services and professional staff of these centers in much the same way as farmers utilize the Agricultural Extension Service or small business people use the Small Business Administration.

The role and powers of citizen boards should also be expanded. Under the Advisory Committee Act, advisory committees have become formalities, especially under Reagan. Citizen boards should be appointed for both advisory and review purposes for each major activity of a given agency. They should report directly to Congress on their activities, recommendations, and reviews of agency progress and problems. Citizen boards might also have local task forces that involve communities, workers, or specific groups of consumers in their work.

Finally, the problem of funding citizen participation must be addressed. A separate budget for citizen participation, controlled by Congress, must be established. Legislation proposed in the 1970s made the mistake of giving agencies control over funds for citizen participation, resulting in an uneven system favoring special interests. A citizen participation budget could fund citizen research centers and local programs that support other information policies such as worker right-to-know laws.

Conclusion

The transitional reforms in civil service and administrative policies outlined above begin the process necessary to mend the relationship between our citizens and their government. For most of the twentieth century the administrative orthodoxy has emphasized development of a national state characterized by anti-democratic practices. Beliefs in a highly centralized management structure for public agencies, in the application of business principles of economy and efficiency to public work, and in the idea that administrative policies are inherently non-political have damaged the ability of the federal government to function effectively. We have created a government premised on administration by technocratic experts politically controlled by the White House and on the systematic exclusion of citizens from public decision-making. Civil service and administrative initiatives of the Carter and Reagan administrations have only exacerbated the problem. We are left with a national state characterized by a sense of deep mistrust between government officials and citizens and between government workers and their politically appointed superiors.

Steps must be taken to rebuild trust in government, engage the citizenry in public decisions, revitalize the public workforce, and reverse the faulty reasoning of the administrative orthodoxy. Federal employee unions and citizen organizations are important players in this process. Legislation from an active, policy-conscious Congress is essential for building a democratic administrative structure in the executive branch. The tasks are not easy ones. The civil service system must be again reformulated. Strict limitations must be placed and enforced on the OMB, and bold moves must be made in comprehensive legislation that opens up government policy-making and rulemaking to citizens.

To a large extent, the ability of the U.S. government to move into the twenty-first century as a viable democratic institution is predicated on its ability to solve its own problems of administration. Reforms that enhance rather than thwart democracy are central to effective government. And effective government is achieved not singularly through strict measures of economizing and control, but rather through building strong ties, based on mutual respect and dependence, between citizens and the government.

NOTES

1. See, especially, the economic literature on public choice, recently elevated to national importance because its main proponent, James Buchanan, was awarded the Nobel Price. For discussions from a public choice perspective that refer to topics in public administration, civil service, and others covered by this chapter, see Bennett and DiLorenzo (1983), Bennett and Johnson (1981), and Savas (1982).

2. This distinction between personnel management and public administration had been advocated by intellectuals in the newly founded field of "public administration" in the 1920s and in the writings of Woodrow Wilson. It took ten to fifteen years, however, for this theoretical construction to take root in the everyday practice of government business.

3. The symbols of economy and efficiency during the 1980s specifically represent reduced government authority vis-à-vis the business community and enhanced government authority in the area of defense.

4. March and Olson (1983) develop the notion of "administrative orthodoxy" in their discussion of government reorganization efforts and demonstrate how the rhetoric of economy and efficiency

becomes the official language of government reform (see the numerous helpful references in their essay). This chapter extends and develops the concept of "administrative orthodoxy" to describe the ideology of governance in U.S. political culture. Further, I use the notion to explain how a "folklore" of myths and rituals has become operational in legislation, rules, and everyday practices of the federal government.

5.   There have been public administration scholars who do not subscribe to some of these principles. See, for instance, Thayer (1981), Mosher (1968), Goodsell (1983), and Appleby (1949).

6.   More accurately, some public administration scholars have attempted to refute the ideas that comprise this folklore. Simon (1946) wrote a classic article, labelling them "proverbs of administration." Yet much of the folklore remains with us today, institutionalized in recent Carter-Reagan reforms. See Beam (1978) and Huddleston (1981).

7.   For an important statement of this topic, see Skowronek (1982). His argument, which informs this essay, is that the early twentieth-century tension between political democracy and capitalism was resolved by reconstituting a system of state authority in which "a new government framework for maintaining democracy and the private economy in the industrial age took shape around administrative capacities." (17).

8.   No analysis has been written yet on the A–76 or the effects of the Paperwork Reduction Act. Hearing transcripts and government reports are useful: U.S. House of Representatives (1984) and U.S. Office of Management and Budget (1979). More has been written on the changes in OMB: U.S. House of Representatives (1981), Tomkin (1985), Rosenberg (1981), Eads and Fix (1984, especially chapter 6), and Demac (1984).

9.   It is important to note that under Title VII of the CSRA federal employee unions do not have a closed shop. Unions can win exclusive bargaining rights in an agency, but the workers of that agency can elect voluntarily to join the union or not. In practice, this means that unions must represent all employees in grievances and other procedures (which can be costly) yet can collect dues only from those who choose to pay. This seriously weakens the right of federal employees to organize.

10.   This point has been effectively made by Mosher (1968), who argues that the weapons of "politics" open up an entire domain for union action never used by private sector unions.

11.   Public administration professionals (scholars and practitioners) have recently acknowledged alarm about the Reagan administration tendency toward ideological management practices. See especially Goldenberg (1984), Newland (1984), and Levine (1986).

References

Appleby, P. 1949. *Policy and administration*. University, AL: University of Alabama Press.

Beam, D. 1978. Public administration is alive and well—and living in the White House. *Public Administration Review* 38(1):72–77.

Bennett, J. T., and M. H. Johnson. 1981. *Better government at half the price: Private production of public services*. Ottawa, IL: Caroline House Publishers.

Bennett, J. T., and T. J. DiLorenzo. 1983. Public employee unions, privatization, and the new federalism. *Government Union Review* 4 (Winter):59–73.

Claybrook, J., and the Staff of Public Citizen. 1984. *Retreat from safety: Reagan's attack on America's health*. New York: Pantheon.

Cohen, M. 1977. Religious revivalism and the administrative centralization movement. *Administration and Society* 9(2):219–32.

Cooper, P. J. 1986. By order of the president: Administration by executive order and proclamation. *Administration and Society* 18(2):233–62.

Demac, D. 1984. *Keeping America uninformed*. New York: The Pilgrim Press.

Eads, G. C., and M. Fix. 1984. *Relief or reform: Reagan's regulatory dilemma*. Washington, D.C.: The Urban Institute Press.

Feinberg, L. E. 1986. Managing the freedom of information act and federal information policy. *Public Administration Review*. 46(6):615–21.

Goldenberg, E. N. 1984. The permanent government in an era of retrenchment and redirection. Eds. L. M. Salamon and M. S. Lund. *The Reagan presidency and the governing of America*. Washington, D.C.: Urban Institute Press.

Goodsell, C. 1983. *The case for bureaucracy: A public administration polemic*. 2nd ed. Chatham, N.J.: Chatham House.

Huddleston, M. W. 1981–1982. The Carter civil service reforms: Some implications for political theory and public administration. *Political Science Quarterly*. 96(4):607–21.

Ingraham, P., and C. Ban, eds. 1984. *Legislating bureaucratic change: The Civil Service Reform Act of 1978*. Albany, N.Y.: State University of New York Press.

Kolderie, T. 1986. The two different concepts of privatization. *Public Administration Review*. 46(4):285–91.

Kweit, J. G., and R. W. Kweit. 1981. *Implementing citizen participation in a bureaucratic society*. New York: Praeger.

Langton, S. 1982. The evolution of federal citizen involvement policy. *Policy Studies Review*. 1(2):369–78.

Levine, C. 1986. The federal government in the year 2000: Administrative legacies of the Reagan years. *Public Administration Review*. 46(3):195–206.

March, J., and J. Olson. 1983. Organizing political life: What administrative reorganization tells us about government. *American Political Science Review*. 77(2):281–96.

Mosher, F. 1968. *Democracy and the public service*. New York: Oxford.

Nathan, R. P. 1983. *The administrative presidency*. New York: John Wiley & Sons.

Newland, C. A. 1984. Executive office policy apparatus: Enforcing the Reagan agenda. Eds. L. M. Salamon and M. S. Lund. *The Reagan presidency and the governing of America*. Washington, D.C.: The Urban Institute Press.

Parker, D., S. Schurman, and R. Montgomery eds. 1984. Labor-management relations under CSRA: Provisions and effects. Eds. P. Ingraham and C. Ban. *Legislating bureaucratic change*. Albany, NY: State University of New York Press.

Peterson, J. 1984. Citizen participation in science policy. Ed. J. Peterson. *Citizen participation in science policy*. Amherst, MA: University of Massachusetts Press.

Rosen, B. 1983. Effective continuity of U.S. government operations in jeopardy. *Public Administration Review* 43(September/October):383–91.

Rosen, B. 1986. Crises in the U.S. civil service. *Public Administration Review*. 46(3):207–14.

Rosenberg, M. 1981. Beyond the limits of executive power: Presidential control of agency rulemaking under executive order 12291. *Michigan Law Review*. 80(1):193–258.

Salamon, L. M. 1981. The question of goals. Ed. P. Szanton. *Federal reorganization: What have we learned?* Chatham, NJ: Chatham House.

Savas, E. S. 1982. *Privatizing the public sector: How to shrink government*. Chatham, NJ: Chatham House.

Simon, H. A. 1946. The proverbs of administration. *Public Administration Review* 6(1):53–67.

Skowronek, S. 1982. *Building a new American state: The expansion of national administrative capacities, 1877–1920*. Cambridge: Cambridge University Press.

Staudohar, P. D. 1981. Contracting out in federal employment. *Government Union Review* 2(Spring):3–10.

Sundquist, J. L. 1981. *The decline and resurgence of congress.* Washington D.C.: Brookings Institution.

Thayer, F. 1981. *An end to hierarchy; An end to competition.* 2nd ed. New York: Franklin Watts, Inc.

Tolchin, S. J. 1984. Airbags and regulatory delay. *Issues in Science and Technology.* (Fall):66–83.

Tomkin, S. L. 1985. Playing politics in OMB: Civil servants join the game. *Presidential Studies Quarterly.* 15(1):158–70.

Van Riper, P. P. 1958. *History of the United States civil service.* Evanston, IL: Row, Peterson, and Co.

U.S. House of Representatives, Subcommittee on Oversight and Investigations, Committee on Energy and Commerce. 1981. Role of OMB in regulation. Serial No. 97–70. Hearings, June 18, 1981. Washington D.C.: U.S. Government Printing Office.

U.S. House of Representatives, Subcommittee on Human Resources of the Committee on Post Office and Civil Service. 1984. Implementation of circular A–76 Serial no. 98–57. Sept. 20 and 25, Washington D.C.: U.S. Government Printing Office.

U.S. Office of Management and Budget, Executive Office of the President. 1979. Paperwork and red tape: New perspectives, new directions, a report to the president and the congress. September, Washington D.C.: U.S. Government Printing Office.

4   Rebuilding the Regulatory State: Prospects for Environmental and Worker Protection

Charles Noble

The last two decades have seen an unprecedented growth in the scope of federal responsibility for workplace and environmental protection. Between 1970 and 1980 Congress passed major new legislation, including the Clean Air (1970; amended 1977) and Water (1972; amended 1977) Acts, the Occupational Safety and Health Act (1970), the Toxic Substances Control Act (1976), the Resource Conservation and Recovery Act (1976), and the Comprehensive Environmental Response, Compensation and Liability Act, or "Superfund" (1980), mandating the regulation and, in some cases, the elimination of hazards from the air, water, land, and workplace. Many of these laws contain lofty protective goals and expansive citizen rights to health and safety. The Occupational Safety and Health Act assures "so far as possible every working man and woman in the Nation safe and healthful working conditions" (PL91-596, Sec 2[B]). The Clean Air Act requires that air quality standards be set to protect the health of the most physically vulnerable populations, including the elderly and children, maintain air visibility, and protect buildings, crops, and water. The Clean Water Act requires the Environmental Protection Agency to eliminate all discharges of pollutants into navigable waters and to make the waterways "fishable and swimmable."

To implement these goals and rights, two new agencies—the Environmental Protection Agency (EPA) and the Occupational Safety and Health Administration (OSHA)—were created and given the authority to regulate many of the physical, chemical, and biological hazards that threaten people and the environment. These agencies, in turn, have established elaborate programs to monitor and control pollutants, toxic substances, and hazardous wastes.

Despite these policy initiatives, the goals of workplace and environmental protection appear to be receding. To be sure, some progress has been made since the 1960s. Both the EPA and OSHA have issued standards. Some firms have been fined significant sums for violating agency rules. Worker exposure to some hazards, including asbestos, lead, and cotton dust, have been lowered (Office of Technology Assessment 1985, 268). Some air pollutants have been reduced (Council on Environmental Quality 1981, 23). Still, the workplace and the environment remain imperilled. If anything, the biochemical threat posed by industrialism appears to be growing larger.

The public's health is threatened in many ways. Millions of blue-collar workers risk their lives and health at work, exposed to thousands of untested chemicals, including many suspected carcinogens (Office of Technology Assessment 1985, ch.3). Chemical dumpsites grow in volume annually, but no more than 10 percent of this accumulating waste is properly disposed of (Rosenbaum 1985, 183). Every year, a substantial majority of Americans is exposed to moderately or severely polluted air for significant periods (Rosenbaum 1985, 110). New hazards also loom, even as long established problems remain uncontrolled. Remedial action is lacking for acid rain—the corrosive precipitation, caused by sulfur and nitrogen compounds, that makes lakes ecologically sterile and disrupts forest ecosystems—and for the warming in the earth's atmosphere caused by carbon dioxide emissions, commonly known as the greenhouse effect (Conservation Foundation 1984, 3, 101–3). The nation's waters are also endangered. More than ten thousand major lakes have serious pollution problems. Toxins and heavy metals can be found in significant amounts in the surface waters in three-quarters of the states. Synthetic organic compounds are present in the drinking water of many major urban areas. The ground water is polluted by a frightening variety of contaminants, from toxic waste disposal, to agricultural runoff, and acid mine drainage (Rosenbaum 1985, 20–1, 143–44, 147).

Many experts believe that unless they are addressed quickly and decisively, these hazards will create a biochemical threat far into the future, across generations, perhaps threatening the very biological foundations of human life. Clearly, imaginative and effective action is needed if we are to bring these hazards under control. With few exceptions, however, regulatory policy has failed to respond to this challenge.

This chapter analyzes the reasons for this failure and offers an agenda for restructuring the health and safety regulatory process so that it might solve the problems identified above more effectively. I will argue that to be successful, regulatory reform must build new sorts of institutions, rather than simply revitalize existing agencies. I base this conclusion on two observations. First, that the existing economic system shapes the environment in which regulatory agencies act, and, as a rule, discourages effective regulation. Second, that different kinds of regulatory arrangements respond more or less adequately to economic obstacles. Based on these observations, I argue that current regulatory institutions do not have the capacity to implement the goals established for them by Congress. In short, there is a fundamental mismatch between the design of our regulatory institutions and the economic environment in which they intervene.

This approach, and the conclusions that emerge from it, are unique. It is worth pausing for a moment to consider how dramatically this analysis differs from conventional wisdom in this matter. Put as simply as possible, the two most common explanations of regulatory policy do not call the regulatory institutions themselves into question or consider their ability to respond effectively to constraints imposed by the economic environment.

One, a narrowly political view popular within the public interest community, argues that the problems faced by the EPA and OSHA are, for the most part, problems of enforcement brought about by the mobilization of corporate and conservative opposition to Great Society liberalism and the "social" regulatory state (Claybrook and the Staff of Public Citizen 1984; Pertschuk 1982; Tolchin and Tolchin 1983). Seen from this vantage point, health and safety policy has been undermined by an unfortunate, but remediable shift in the balance of power between right and left. According to this view, social regulatory institutions need not be restructured, but they must be reempowered by a renewed commitment of political will, money, time, and energy to worker and environmental protection.

A second explanation focuses on the specific types of policies adopted by the EPA and OSHA (Schultze 1977; Bardach and Kagan 1982). According to this view, Congress' and the regulators' decision to rely on what are called "command-and-control" methods of regulation (principally detailed standards and penalty-based inspections) has led these agencies to adopt inefficient, excessively costly, and counter-productive methods to implement health and safety goals. Since they are "adversarial" rather than "cooperative," these methods can do little to reduce hazards permanently. They do, however, antagonize industry unnecessarily, discourage voluntary compliance, and stimulate political opposition.

These explanations identify pieces of the problem but do not satisfactorily account for the long-term trajectory of regulatory policy; therefore they do not offer an adequate guide to political action in this area. Undoubtedly, the Reagan administration's ideological antipathy to government regulation and the special position its corporate benefactors enjoy in policy-making circles have undermined the state's will to regulate. Presumably, the next Democratic administration will undo some of the damage done by Reagan. But even this ignores how the social regulatory state enables business groups to play such a large role in the policy-making process. If it is to provide the basis for restructuring the regulatory state, the critique of command-and-control regulation must explain how the structure of the economy undermines the capacity of agencies to implement command-and-control policies and suggest how alternative regulatory strategies might deal with these economic constraints.

In short, a comprehensive and progressive set of regulatory reform proposals must begin by identifying those changes in the relationship between the state and the economy that are preconditions for effective workplace and environmental protection. The following sections do this by 1) considering how the U.S. economy frustrates efforts to deal with the problem of health, safety, and the environment; 2) examining the degree to which existing regulatory institutions respond effectively to these economic constraints; and 3) proposing a set of institutional reforms that will increase the likelihood that regulatory agencies can act to protect workers and the environment.

Economic Structure and Political Action

How does the structure of the U.S. economy shape health and safety regulation? The key to answering this question lies first in recognizing how profit-seeking production in markets generates hazards,[1] and, second, how market capitalism constrains governmental efforts to control private, profit-seeking firms. We must recognize how different economic and political arrangements shape the formation and articulation of political demands, the degree to which some interests will mobilize effectively and others will not, and the unequal distribution of politically effective resources to different interests.

"Pluralists," who tend to dominate the policy sciences in the United States, hold almost the opposite view, focusing almost exclusively on the impact of public opinion, the attitudes of public officials, and group pressure on public officials (Jones 1975; Wilson 1980, 364–82). Pluralists believe that policies are the result of partisan political competition and the intellectual orientation of policy-makers. Policy success and policy failure, therefore, are caused by a combination of political force and good and bad judgements about what policy instruments are appropriate to which problems.

The pluralist view is not without merit, but it is severely flawed. The success or failure of government programs clearly rests on more than the balance of political forces in the government's environment. It clearly matters whether government is well or poorly organized and whether social structure and political culture encourage or discourage organized support for regulatory programs. But the pluralist view takes these things for granted. It tends to deemphasize the impact of governmental organization on regulatory capacity, and it does not investigate the factors that shape how people see their interests, the demands that they make on government, and the ability of groups to form and act effectively in the political arena. To deal adequately with these issues, it is necessary to shift the discussion to a more systemic level and look closely at how social structures and institutions shape the environments in which citizens and regulators act.

An alternative approach, commonly called "structuralism," focuses on some of these issues (Poulantzas 1973; Aglietta 1979). Structuralists argue that capitalist states are incapable of seriously reforming corporate behavior. According to this view, "deep" structural features of the political economy, principally private control of the means of production and the separation of the state from the economy, preclude anything but symbolic reforms: the economic "imperatives" of the system require that corporate managers and investors retain the right to dispose of labor and capital as they see fit.

There is much to be said in defense of this view. There is no question that private control over capital creates powerful obstacles to changing corporate practices. But there are analytic pitfalls here as well. To begin with, this view is overstated. Structural constraints determine the outer limits of reform—the possibility of changing the system itself—but do not necessarily preclude attempts to reconstruct specific aspects of the system. Even these outer limits are not permanently inscribed; they are subject to change if appropriate political strategies are pursued. In addition, structuralists rarely investigate the impact of different forms of government on the state's regulatory capacity. This follows from their assumption that capitalist states are by their very nature incapable of effectively controlling private firms.

A new "institutionalism" does look at government organization (Evans, Rueschemeyer, and Skocpol 1985; Skowronek 1982). Institutionalists stress the importance of well ordered, rationalized bureaucratic structures to the success of government policy and the impact that "state actors" and "state interests" have on what government does. Several of their conclusions will be affirmed below. But this view does not fully explain how the institutional organization of the economy shapes the policy environment or the generation of political demands in society. Thus, institutionalism tends to exaggerate the autonomy of public officials and deemphasizes the importance of economic structure and interest conflicts to regulatory policy.

A compelling analysis of the problems of workers and environmental protection, as well as any proposals to address them, must tackle the reciprocal relationship between the institutional organization of the state and economy on the one hand and the formation and mobilization of political demands on the other. It must clearly specify how forces at these two levels interact to create incentives and disincentives to collective action on the part of different interests in society and to autonomous action on the part of public officials. Only then can we provide a compelling account of the determinants of regulatory policy and indicate the preconditions for effective regulation. The next section explores how the institutional organization of the economy shapes and constrains the mobilization of political interests and the regulatory environment of public officials.

The Deep Structure of American Capitalism

Consider the impact of economic structures on the generation of health, safety, and environmental hazards. The processes of investment and technical change are central to productive activity in all modern industrial societies. But different modes of production rely on different mechanisms for deciding what is produced and how it is produced. As a result, health and safety hazards are created and distributed in different ways. In state socialist societies political decisions determine the allocation of environmental risk and protection by establishing production quotas and allocating labor among jobs and occupations. In contrast, in industrial capitalist societies profit-seeking investors initiate production by commiting capital to various uses. Corporate managers, in turn, organize and reorganize production and the labor process to make both as profitable as possible.

Without effective regulation in industrial capitalist societies, it is unlikely that investment, production, and the labor process will be organized with due regard for health and safety hazards. Rather, firms will try to "externalize" these costs and let "third parties" (workers, residents, or government) pay them. There are some countervailing economic interests that make firms' voluntary efforts to prevent indoor and outdoor pollution economically rational. But these are limited and depend on the degree to which firms can be confident in their ability to recapture investments made in protection.

In the case of occupational safety and health, for example, accidents and injuries interrupt production, hurt skilled workers, lower productivity, and force employers to pay increased medical bills. Thus, accidents and injuries can cut into profits by raising the cost of production or lowering total output. But the costs of prevention are also high, and firms have few guarantees that they can capture the future benefits of present investments in health and safety. Without effective regulatory programs, firms are likely to try to avoid these investments, compensating for whatever disruption might result from accidents by further intensifying work and augmenting market shares by introducing new technologies whose long-term effects are unknown. In the case of health hazards, where the effects of exposure to toxic substances take many years to show up and where it is often difficult to establish the precise etiology of a disease, market incentives to control pollution are even weaker.

A similar dynamic occurs in the case of toxic wastes, where the market actively encourages the uncontrolled development and distribution of potentially hazardous chemicals, with little advance thought to their disposal. Currently, about 120,000 firms produce and distribute chemicals in the United States. But few chemicals have been tested for toxicity. To date, of the 55,000 chemicals widely used, only 1,500 to 2,000 have been tested sufficiently to determine carcinogenicity, and we have reason to believe that between 600 and 800 of these are carcinogens. Despite the dangers, few chemicals have been disposed of properly.

The proliferation of hazardous work, unsafe products and production processes, and industrial pollution have stimulated demands for reform, and there are currently statutes and agencies charged with dealing with these problems. But economic structures also shape the ability of these agencies to function effectively in three important ways.

First, economic structures create resource inequalities that systematically benefit those who own and manage corporate enterprises. The pursuit of political activity requires access to leisure time, money, and information. People without these resources, such as the poor and workers, find it difficult to form and sustain the organizations necessary if they are collectively to act and effectively to press demands for government control of business activities. Corporate managers and the rich, on the other hand, find it comparatively easy to pursue their interests through organized political action and block efforts to redistribute power and wealth through state action.

Second, public policy is constrained by the impact of capitalist economic structures on the formation and articulation of political demands (Cohen and Rogers 1983, 47–81). The concentration of productive assets in the hands of private firms and investors leaves most people dependent on private employers for jobs and income. If people in this position conclude that their economic interests are dependent on sustaining business profitability, as they often do, they will be led, quite "rationally," to limit their demands to those compatible with business interests. People who work for others are thus encouraged to use their political power to promote a "healthy" business climate. Public officials are likewise discouraged from taking aggressive actions that might antagonize businesses and employers.

Third, the ability of government to impose costly regulations on private firms is constrained by government's own dependence on the process of capitalist investment. Government's capacity to act in domestic or international affairs depends on its ability to raise revenues through taxation. This ability, in turn, depends on a healthy economy, and a healthy economy depends on the level of private investment. Additionally, because people tend to vote their pocketbooks, the political fortunes of elected leaders also depend on the level of economic activity. When jobs and incomes are insecure, politicians find it difficult to get reelected, and administrations are driven from office. In order to maintain state power and secure their own political fortunes, public officials are likely to try to maintain business confidence in their actions. Even if they are sympathetic to worker and consumer interests, they will tend to avoid policies that threaten capitalist profitability and promote policies that serve business interests (Block 1977, 16–19; Lindblom 1977, 170–88). This creates a powerful disincentive to adopt or implement strict health and safety statutes.

In these three ways capitalist economic structures create incentives and disincentives to various forms of political action as well as barriers to, and opportunities for, imposing controls on business. People are encouraged to eschew radical programs that shift the social costs of health and safety onto firms. Instead, they are encouraged to choose political strategies that emphasize short-term material gain, including job security, higher wages, shorter hours, and changes in the most immediate conditions of work. When costly programs and reforms are adopted, public officials fear that business will mobilize to oppose

them, finding support among those who fear for their jobs and liveli-
hoods.

These constraints imposed by capitalist economic structures are not inevitable. They can be altered by institutions that encourage collective action by
workers and consumers and insulate public officials from business opposition.
The next section considers how this may be accomplished.

Political Responses

As we have seen, deep structural forces based in private ownership of the
means of production and workers' economic dependence combine to limit the
degree to which public policies can challenge private property rights and corporate
profitability. Such constraints exist in all capitalist democracies, but some states
are nevertheless more successful than others at regulating private capital. Well
organized, independent labor and social democratic political parties can strongly
influence the degree to which social policy attempts and succeeds at imposing
controls on business. Support for regulation by an industrial sector with an
economic interest in reform can also be decisive (Ferguson 1983; Kemp 1985).

The state's ability to regulate business effectively is also shaped by how
government institutions themselves are organized. This section considers how
governmental organization shapes policy, focusing on the degree of fragmentation
among national and local authorities, the separation of powers among the executive, legislative, and judicial branches, and the particular arrangements through
which agencies intervene into markets.

The Constitutional Design

A growing literature on the development of the modern state suggests that
the centralization or fragmentation of government authority is a major determinant
of the state's capacity to shape the society in which it acts (Alford and Friedland
1985, ch.8). Centralized government makes it possible for private interests or,
for that matter, public officials, to use government to reshape society. Alter-
natively, checks and balances created by jurisdictional divisions undermine the
ability of government to act coherently and decisively.

A significant degree of centralized state power also appears to be a necessary
if not sufficient condition if non-capitalist interests are to use the state as an ally
against the opposition of propertied interests. Centralized power need not give
nonpropertied interests the advantage; capitalists can also use a centralized state
to their benefit. But where state power is fragmented, those who enjoy private
economic power are more likely to prevail than those (workers or consumers)
whose principal power derives from their ability to influence the state.

Fragmentation disadvantages workers and consumers because it creates three sorts of biases that benefit propertied interests, particularly corporations. It creates many opportunities to veto positive initiatives, therefore making it easier to prevent the state from challenging the market as a means of allocating resources than to marshall state power to alter market outcomes. Fragmentation also works against those who enter into politics with few initial resources, such as unorganized workers or consumers. All other things being equal, it is more expensive to influence a government divided into many powers than a single, centralized authority. Finally, fragmentation benefits those interests that depend on money for influence as opposed to those that depend on numbers. By its very nature, money is easily coordinated and targetted, and those with money are more likely to succeed in influencing a divided public authority than those who are only numerous or popular.

The United States, of course, is famous for its fragmentation of public authority. Both the separation of powers among legislative, executive, and judicial institutions and the division of authority among federal and state governments make for a divided and decentralized state. Most important, the existence of fifty-one political jurisdictions encourages the formation of institutional interests defined by geography rather than class. The representation of these interests in Congress and the pivotal role played by state governments in implementing national policies create powerful centrifugal forces that generally undermine public authority. National authority is even further limited by the division of the federal government into executive, legislative, and judicial branches. Predictably, these divisions have created major obstacles for those who would use the state to regulate private capital, as we shall see below.

Fragmentation does not always result in stalemate and stasis. Competition among institutions for preeminence has occasionally led to reform. For example, competition between Congress and the executive for electoral support helped fuel the dramatic extension of social regulatory power in the 1960s and 1970s (Jones 1975, ch.7; Noble 1986, ch.3). The judiciary's ability to assert its own independent authority has also helped to extend the scope of some laws. In the case of the Clean Air Act, for example, the court has forced the EPA and Congress to take seriously the statute's commitment to protecting still-clean air (Melnick 1983, ch.4). As a rule, however, fragmented power works to the benefit of those with private power.

Regulatory Regimes

Different forms of public authority can also be distinguished according to less fundamental features than these constitutional arrangements. Within a given legal system, regulatory agencies can intervene in markets in very different ways, and these second-order statutory, administrative, and political arrangements profoundly shape the degree to which government can impose social controls on private firms. I will call these second-order institutional arrangements "regulatory regimes" and use this concept to analyze how changes in health and safety regulation have affected regulatory policy.

In using the concept of regulatory regime, I mean to suggest three things. First, the regulatory state has tended to grow in waves, or phases, and regulatory policies adopted during the same wave tend to obey similar dynamics. Second, there is a certain inner-relatedness, or logical coherence, to the goals, means, and justifications of a given set of regulatory policies. Third, major changes in regulatory policy usually involve changes in all of these nominally distinct aspects of regulation.[2] In the case of health, safety, and environmental policy, the two main regulatory regimes can be identified according to seven criteria: where authority is vested, who controls investment, how issues are defined, the scope of agency authority, access for protected interests, access for propertied interests, and the institutional locus of participation.

The earlier theoretical discussion suggests that each of these criteria should matter to the success of worker and environmental protection policies. Given how the deep structures of U.S. capitalism shape the regulatory environment, we can expect that regulatory regimes that encourage effective health and safety regulations would have the following characteristics: vesting authority in national agencies with responsibility for economy-wide regulation; encouraging people to see their interests in environmental protection as part of a larger political struggle; facilitating access by protected interests to policy makers; and restricting business access to public officials. In contrast, regulatory regimes that discourage effective health and safety regulations would have the following characteristics: vesting authority in local officials and disaggregating regulatory authority by industry or sector; encouraging people to treat health and safety as a cost of production; restricting the access of protected interests to policy-makers; and providing easy access to the opponents of regulation.

Changes in regulatory policy in the 1960s and 1970s—from what I will call the New Deal Regulatory Regime (NDRR) to the Public Interest Regulatory Regime (PIRR)—constitute a shift of major proportions, although they did not fully reorganize the pre-existing institutional arrangements.

The New Deal Regulatory Regime

Under the NDRR health and safety regulatory agencies were underdeveloped. Federal authority was limited in scope, and federal regulatory agencies had few compulsory powers and no effective control over the level and kind of private capital investment in environmental protection. Public authority was fragmented among federal and state officials, and federal regulatory agencies targetted specific industries and sectors rather than regulating the entire economy. Health and safety policies were subordinated to policies promoting industrial

Figure 4.1. The New Deal and Public Interest Regulatory Regimes

	NDRR	PIRR
1. Where authority is vested	State	National
2. Who controls investment	Private	Private
3. How issue is defined	Economics	Procedures
4. Scope of agency authority	Sectoral	National
5. Access for protected interests	Limited	Extensive
6. Access for propertied interests	Extensive	Extensive
7. Institutional locus of participation	Party	Bureaucracy

NDRR: New Deal Regulatory Regime; PIRR: Public Interest Regulatory Regime

development and economic growth. For the most part, health and safety problems were seen as economic issues and thus measured by the income loss caused by accidents and injuries or the property damage done by pollution.

Procedurally, regulatory agencies enjoyed a good deal of administrative discretion, legitimated by the expertise of agency officials and the supposed independence of the agencies. However, regulatory officials used this discretion to provide access to regulated interests while limiting the access of protected interests. The courts went along, defining "standing to sue" agencies narrowly so that propertied interests enjoyed privileged access to judicial review of agency rules and decisions. To the extent that protected interests did participate in regulatory policy-making, they did so indirectly, through party-political channels. The major political parties, however, did not even include worker and environmental protection on their issue agendas. Predictably, the regulated interests became the dominant political forces in this regulatory regime.

The Public Interest Regulatory Regime

The "public interest" reform movements of the 1960s and 1970s—including the various Ralph Nader-inspired projects, environmental and consumer organizations, and "good government" advocates such as Common Cause—were intent on using government to rein in corporate power and rejected many of the defining characteristics and ideological assumptions of the NDRR. Public interest reformers were particularly critical of the New Deal tendency to place a higher value on economic growth than on the "quality of life," including the preservation of the natural environment and the health and safety of workers and consumers. They were also critical of the willingness of New Deal liberals to accept a narrowly truncated form of interest group pluralism in the place of more direct, participatory democracy. They believed that regulatory agencies had been captured by the business interests they were supposed to regulate, and they promoted institutional reforms to facilitate citizen participation in regulatory decision-making.

These ideas followed from a view of the proper relationship between the state and society that was in many respects radically different from the one that informed the growth of the regulatory state during the New Deal. In the 1930s Roosevelt had sought to strengthen federal authority to deal with economic collapse. New Deal policies sought to promote economic growth through fiscal management and income maintenance programs for the working and middle classes. To accomplish these ends, reformers enlarged the executive bureaucracy and centralized state power. But unlike the Populist and Progressive movements that preceded it or the public interest movement that followed, the New Deal rarely addressed the problem of corporate power directly.[3] It was, instead, "reform from above," resting on business-government partnerships and corporatist mechanisms rather than more direct forms of democratic participation. Although always justified in terms of the public interest, laws that regulated banking, communications, and transportation did not augment public participation in corporate decision-making or, for that matter, public participation in agency rule-making. Instead, regulations restructured and rationalized markets to promote economic growth and industrial recovery.

In contrast, public interest reform of the 1960s and 1970s reflected a dramatically different theory of the proper relationship between the state and society. Government was to be used to democratize both the state and capitalism not to rehabilitate a failing economy. Where the New Deal had subordinated political reform to economic growth and security, the public interest movement sought to restructure public and private decision-making processes to encourage public participation in both spheres. Popular participation, they believed, would result in the redistribution of political influence and power away from business and toward the public.

Following from their interest in the political process itself, public interest reformers sought a variety of procedural changes to expand the public's right to take part in the administrative process. The goal was always to expand access to the bureaucracy and facilitate the participation of those who were previously unrepresented. Removing barriers that restricted the range of interests and values that were taken into account in rule-making was a special concern.

In order to open up the regulatory process, reformers adopted three related strategies. First, they sought statutory limits on agency discretion. These, they hoped, could facilitate suits by public interest lawyers challenging pro-industry agency decisions. Second, reformers sought heightened judicial review of agency action and they pressed Congress to create new mechanisms that would enable citizens to use judicial review to promote their interests. These included authorization of citizen suits to force agencies to act and provisions for private suits against polluters when agencies failed to act. Reformers also urged reviewing courts to liberalize judicial requirements of "standing to sue." Third, the public interest movement pressed for administrative reforms facilitating participation.

These included rights to information about corporate conduct and agency deliberations, "sunshine" laws requiring open administrative hearings, and the application of the principle of the Freedom of Information Act to the private sector.
At the same time, the public interest movement urged procedural reforms that
lowered the economic costs of participation, including "intervenor" funding—
government grants to "interested citizens" who wished to participate but could
not afford to do so—and government payment of legal fees in suits resulting in
the enforcement of federal statutes.

The movement's conviction that increased citizen participation would contribute to both the independence and quality of regulatory decision-making was
distinctive and innovative. The Progressives had sought to concentrate public
authority in a professional civil service and to staff regulatory agencies with
experts. New Deal reformers, more at home with party politics, sought a greater
role for partisan political leadership. They wanted to restructure the executive
branch and the Supreme Court so that a party-driven government (in the parlia-
mentary sense) could organize regulatory administration. New Deal reformers
did not value direct citizen participation, and their proposals reflected this indifference. Public interest reformers, in contrast, took every opportunity to build
democratic participation into government.

The public interest movement's belief in the virtues of citizen participation
rested on two foundations. First, participation was considered practical: rank-
and-file input into agency hearings would improve decision-making by contributing to a more complete record; taking the experience of people affected by
regulations into account would make for smarter policy; and citizen participation
in enforcement would reduce the administrative burden of monitoring and inspecting corporate practices. Second, participation would promote democratic
accountability. Given access to public officials, people would be able to coun-
terpose their superior numbers to the concentrated wealth and power of regulated
interests. By participating in regulatory decision-making, people would grow
politically, become better citizens, and hold leaders accountable.

To a remarkable degree, the public interest movement managed to impress
these views on Congress and the White House. Regulatory goals changed dramatically. The PIRR imposed social criteria, derived from the emphasis on
"quality of life," on market decisions. These values transformed the way that
worker and environmental protection was viewed: protection became an end in
and of itself. New administrative arrangements were created. The Clean Air and
Water Acts gave the EPA vast authority to reduce pollution. In combination,
the Toxic Substances Control Act, the Resource Conservation and Recovery Act,
and the Comprehensive Environmental Response, Compensation and Liability
Act created an extensive control system for hazardous wastes and made government the primary manager of all dangerous chemical substances in use or
planned for production. OSHA was given extensive authority to set workplace

safety and health standards and to enforce these standards through penalty-based inspections. OSHA and the EPA were both allowed to use informal rule-making procedures that promised to expedite standard-setting.

Reformers also attempted to insulate these agencies from corporate influence by demanding unusually detailed statutory mandates, including legislatively determined timetables. The 1970 Clean Air Act required the EPA to set automobile standards to reduce hydrocarbon and carbon monoxide emissions by 90 percent by 1975 and nitrogen oxide by 90 percent by 1976. The 1972 Federal Water Pollution Control Act Amendments required that major waterways be fishable and swimmable by 1983 and that water pollution be completely eliminated by 1985. The 1977 amendments required industry-by-industry standards for pretreatment of sixty-five toxic substances produced by twenty-two industries.

These and other statutes, as well as judicial rulings, led to the creation of many of the mechanisms advocated by public interest reformers. Provisions for intervenor funding, public notice, and public involvement were common in environmental statutes. Both the Clean Air and Clean Water Acts allowed citizens to sue the EPA for non-performance of non-discretionary responsibilities and the regulated entities for violations of law and EPA rules, orders, and permits. The government in the Sunshine Act required agencies to conduct open hearings. The Freedom of Information Act amended the Administrative Procedures Act to require agencies to make written information in their possession available to the public. The federal courts heightened judicial scrutiny of regulatory agencies and strengthened these new procedural rights, insisting on the enforcement of procedural requirements to promote participation and fair consideration of all interests with a stake in regulatory policies (Stewart 1975, 1723–56).

The Collapse of Social Regulation

Both the deep structure and the constitutional design of U.S. capitalism create formidable obstacles to effective government and challenge those who seek to use public authority to regulate the market. Public interest reformers addressed some of these problems, but they failed to fully confront how economic and political structures discourage social reform. Nor did they establish the political preconditions for the successful regulation of business.

Three problems stand out. First, the PIRR does not directly address how the deep structure discourages public efforts to control the behavior of private firms. Second, while some progress was made in centralizing the state, government remains fragmented by jurisdiction and branch, thereby undermining the state's capacity to impose social criteria on the market. Third, the opportunities to participate provided by the PIRR cannot sustain the existing public interest movement. The next section explores each of these problems and its impact on regulatory policy since the early 1970s.

Deep Structure, Private Power, and Regulatory Policy

Despite their antipathy to corporate power, public interest reformers did little to attack its propertied basis. They eschewed both the nationalization of industry and central direction of investment through the tax and banking systems. Instead, they grafted the new federal regulatory powers onto the existing system of private ownership. As a result, the new apparatus developed without any way to influence the general process of capitalist investment directly, or investment in health and safety.

This respect for private property rights and the maintenance of private control of investment has had several consequences. Significantly, Government has had to respond after the fact to the harmful effects of private initiatives; public officials cannot force firms to anticipate health and safety problems when planning future production. An agency can order a firm to regulate a particular substance, but it cannot tell that firm to develop a substitute for it. As a result, regulators often face a difficult choice: order a firm to suspend a particular activity or allow some "reasonable" level of pollution in order to sustain production. Since industry currently depends on many hazardous substances, firms claim that stringent regulations will cause economic dislocation. While not always effective, this threat has discouraged regulatory agencies from acting quickly and decisively.

By retaining private control over investment and production, firms have also been able to retain control of information about the health and safety effects of their products and processes, information that is necessary if government is to deal effectively with hazards. Companies guard this information as proprietary trade secrets and these claims are often respected. As a result, agencies must rely on corporate managers to monitor and report on their own activities.

Private control over investment has also left government vulnerable to the "disciplining" effects of the market. By the late 1960s, this country's Western trading partners had fully recovered from the devastation of World War II, and many Western European and Japanese industries were highly competitive in international markets. In contrast, many U.S. firms had failed to maintain the competitive edge established in the 1950s, and their market shares were vulnerable to low-priced, high quality exports. At the same time, labor costs, which rose significantly during the Johnson and Nixon administrations, began taking a toll on corporate profits. In the 1970s profits were further threatened by rising energy and regulatory costs (Bowles, Gordon, and Weisskopf 1983, ch.4).

In this economic environment the costs of government intervention became an easy and obvious target for corporate efforts to improve their profit positions. International competition made it difficult for firms to pass on higher costs in the form of higher prices, and few U.S. businesses could exert any control over energy prices. But regulatory and labor costs could be controlled by concerted political activity, and companies undertook a massive campaign to lower both.

Beginning in earnest during the 1973–1975 recession, corporate America mobilized to stop public interest reform in general and health and safety regulation in particular, claiming that regulation's impact on corporate profits undermined the climate for investment. "Stagflation" in the 1970s and sluggish growth in the 1980s reinforced their claims, and under both Republican and Democratic administrations the White House has created and manipulated an oversight program to send, in the words of David Stockman, "long term signals . . . to corporate investment planners" (Noble 1986, 153).

Ironically, the PIRR facilitated this attack on social regulation. Although the protective goals of the PIRR are hard to reconcile with corporate interests, the new administrative structure is not. Because federal agencies were made the final arbiters of corporate practices and control over these agencies was lodged in the executive branch, business groups with access to the White House have been able to lobby relatively efficiently. By focusing their efforts on the White House and the Office of Management and Budget (OMB) they have been able to influence the entire regulatory structure. Detailed legislative mandates—the public interest movements' strategy to preclude the possibility that administrative discretion could be used to the advantage of industry interests—have not prevented this corporate strategy from succeeding. Through adroit use of appointment, budget, and OMB oversight powers, the White House has been able to exercise significant control over the health and safety agencies (Eads and Fix 1984; Noble 1986, ch.6).

The Impact of Fragmentation

The rapid proliferation of potentially toxic substances requires a herculean effort if public health is to be protected. Research is needed to establish the nature and scope of the risks that we face; chemicals in use or planned for use must be registered and tested; identified carcinogens must be removed from use; toxic materials must be isolated, contained, and disposed of carefully; potential polluters must be monitored and when necessary punished for violating health standards. Moreover, given the complexity of health and environmental hazards, regulators must be able to cast their net widely and coordinate a host of specialized research and standard-setting programs.

Despite efforts by reformers to centralize public authority, however, government's capacity to regulate has been undermined by institutional fragmentation. As noted above, the constitutional design hampers action of this sort by fragmenting public authority and discouraging quick and coordinated action. The separation of powers encourages competition among the branches that can lead to heightened Congressional and judicial oversight of agency actions. Often, Congress or the courts delay or block agency actions or force time-consuming and in some cases counter-productive revisions. Quick, decisive, and coordinated action is also frustrated by federalism. National officials who must secure the cooperation of state authorities cannot act as quickly as they otherwise might. Moreover, states often disagree with national goals; they disagree among themselves as well, creating not one but fifty-one policies. In this context regulation is delayed, and government sends mixed, ineffectual messages to those whom it seeks to regulate.

Public interest reformers tried to address some of these problems. They were particularly concerned about removing state officials' control over health and safety regulation. Air, water, and workplace pollution legislation prior to the late 1960s had vested authority for standard-setting and enforcement in the states. Despite mounting evidence of the health hazards caused by uncontrolled industrial growth, states, with few exceptions, resisted strict environmental controls. In response, OSHA and the EPA were given the right to set national standards that preempted state-level rules. In the case of occupational safety and health, OSHA can allow states to retain existing programs or start new ones if it considers these adequate to fulfill the purposes of the law. In the cases of air and water pollution, implementation rests entirely, by design, on state efforts. With regard to air pollution, states have the responsibility to determine how much of the total pollution load within a given airshed is attributable to each polluter and how much each polluter must reduce its emissions. State and local officials enjoy a good deal of discretion in making these decisions, including which emission controls are economically and technically feasible. In the case of water pollution, states grant and enforce permits for effluent dischargers, initiate requests for federal funds to construct municipal waste treatment plants, and supervise the administration of these grant programs. Obviously states retained significant authority over the implementation of major health and safety statutes.

In practice, state authority has undermined the enforcement of federal laws. Although state-level agencies have made significant progress in improving their administrative and technical capacity to regulate (Conservation Foundation 1984, 445–6), they still lack the political will to enforce regulations because they compete with one another for industry and jobs. Sixteen years after the passage of the Clean Air Act, for example, fewer than thirty states have completely approved implementation plans to achieve national ambient air quality standards. State enforcement of water pollution control legislation is equally compromised. States have abused their administrative discretion to interpret economic and technical feasibility, frequently forgiving firms for "temporarily" violating emissions standards (Rosenbaum 1985, 122)[4]

Public interest reformers never addressed the impact of the separation of powers on regulatory policy. In fact, their interest in using Congressional and judicial oversight of regulatory agencies to increase the range of interests represented in the policy-making process exacerbated the problem. Instead of stream-lining and rationalizing the administrative process, they complicated it, hoping that more involvement by Congress and the courts would mean more democracy.

In some instances oversight *has* led to a more representative regulatory process, or at least to stricter regulation. The federal courts, for example, forced a reluctant EPA to come up with a way to prevent the "significant deterioration" of air quality in areas that already met Clean Air Act quality standards. The federal courts also required the EPA to draw up "transportation control plans" for cities with high levels of carbon monoxide and ozone (Melnick 1983, ch.9). And the courts have also extended the right to participate in regulatory decision-making to public interest groups, the poor, consumers, and environmentalists.

But increased oversight has cut both ways, serving to benefit the regulated as well. In the late 1970s, Congressional hostility to strict regulation undercut the ability of health and safety agencies to mount aggressive programs. The same federal courts that forced the EPA to protect already clean air have also delayed agency rule-making by forcing the EPA to adopt elaborate administrative pro-cedures to facilitate judicial review and the fair representation of all interests. The federal courts have routinely delayed compliance schedules for regulated firms and refused to uphold fines unless it can be demonstrated that it is eco-nomically and technically feasible to comply with the violated standards. In the case of OSHA, the federal courts have allowed the Occupational Safety and Health Review Commission (OSHRC) to expand its authority to review the feasibility of OSHA standards, despite a clear legislative intent to limit OSHRC to reviewing fines and abatement orders (Berger and Riskin 1978, 324–32).

State Structures and the Movement for Reform

While the public interest movement did not address the impact of deep economic structures on regulatory policy and only partly confronted the impact of fragmentation, it did directly address the impact that state structures would have on the mobilization of a reform movement. As noted above, this is the one area where public interest reformers can claim to have broken new ground in both the theory of the state and the politics of social policy. Nevertheless, the opportunities provided by the PIRR have not been sufficient either to sustain a political movement to democratize the state or to impose non-economic criteria on the market. Even on its home ground, then, the movement must be judged at least a partial failure.

Two basic problems with public interest reformers' strategy emerged im-mediately. First, this strategy assumed the existence of a mass-based movement interested in serious social reform. Second, it assumed that procedural reforms would be sufficient to allow this purported movement to exercise political power.

The public interest movement was thin, however. Public opinion in support of worker, consumer, and environmental protection is quite different from broadly based, well organized, collective action to elect public officials committed to a program and then hold them accountable once elected. This mass-based movement would require a greater degree of political consciousness and organization than is apparent among the supporters of public interest reform.

It is not clear that most people who endorsed health, safety, and environmental regulation, including activists themselves, fully understood the political and economic implications of imposing non-economic values on private, profit-seeking firms in a highly competitive international economy. If successful, programs to shift the social costs of production from workers and consumers to firms are redistributional in nature and are likely to cause profits to fall. To be sure, increased costs would be reflected in higher consumer prices or firms would develop new, more efficient production technologies. But as long as U.S. firms must compete in world markets, there are serious limits to how far prices can rise to reflect the internalization of increased social costs. Thus, social regulation is likely to threaten profits either directly, by reducing the difference between revenues and costs, or indirectly, because higher prices lower market shares. Unfortunately, these substantive issues are rarely raised explicitly by those who would reform corporate practices.

The movement's organizational infrastructure was similarly underdeveloped. No central clearinghouse coordinated the diverse, issue-specific movements; no executive committee directed the many local, state, regional, and national groups and movements that sprang up. For some time, Ralph Nader served as an unofficial spokesman. But his personal leadership, however skilled, could not substitute for organizational depth. In addition, public interest groups were often top-heavy with young lawyers moving through the movement on their way to more established careers. While some stayed and many provided important services, insufficient effort went into building permanent leadership or a mass base of active members. These problems were exacerbated as the public interest movement increasingly focused its energies on lobbying and lawsuits.

In this political context, the strategy of making procedural reforms had complex and cross-cutting effects. For the most part, well trained, professional middle-class activists were the beneficiaries. This strategy also overstated the importance of participating in formal administrative processes: notice and comment hearings generally come far too late in the administrative process to have much impact on decisions. Most important, this administrative strategy failed to create the kinds of political opportunities that would build a broader, mass-based movement. While the public interest movement sought to provide information and access, this still left most without the time, money, and organizational clout that determine whether people will be able to use information and access to their advantage. In fact, the PIRR lodged regulatory decision-making in distant administrative bureaucracies, where grassroots movements would have little influence, instead of pursuing the kinds of popular mobilizations that worked for the civil rights, anti-war, and student movements in the 1960s and laid the political and cultural foundations for the public interest movements themselves.

Finally, the public interest movement's efforts to promote citizen participation were at odds with efforts to build the stronger state power needed to control health and safety hazards. "Opening up" government to citizen participation also undermined the ability of public officials to act quickly, plan comprehensively, and resolve disputes legitimately. Corporations, trade associations, and conservative lobbying groups proved equally if not more adept at manipulating the new administrative apparatus, blocking strict regulation through participatory channels.

It is, of course, difficult to create a mass movement from above, by crafting government institutions to encourage political activity, but other changes might have proved more salutary. Popular control of the bureaucracy in a modern state probably rests on the ability of strong, programmatic, political parties to organize the legislature and through it to direct and check executive agencies. To accomplish this, reformers would have had to change direction and make ideological and institutional changes to facilitate the transition from diffuse movements to an organized party-political force.

Health and Safety Policy

In combination, these institutional weaknesses have hampered regulatory policy in two ways. Agencies have been unable to set forward-looking standards expeditiously and they have not been able to enforce the standards they do set.

Agencies' failure to set standards is particularly troubling. Not one of the principal social regulatory agencies has moved expeditiously to deal with even a significant percentage of the hazards it was established to control. OSHA, for example, has set only fifteen major health standards, despite the fact that there are over two thousand known or suspected carcinogens in the workplace. Moreover, it has taken OSHA an average of three years to develop each standard (Noble 1986, ch.7).

The EPA's record is equally dismal. The Clean Air Act, for example, orders the EPA to set national air quality standards for seven named substances—the criteria pollutants—and gives the agency the discretionary authority to identify and regulate additional hazardous air pollutants that "endanger public health." But the agency has regulated only four additional substances in sixteen years. The Clean Water Act gives the EPA the authority to set pollution control standards to protect the nation's surface, ground, and drinking water. The agency initially failed to meet the statutory deadline for pretreatment standards for industrial dischargers into municipal water systems. After standards were finally issued, they were withdrawn in response to industry court challenges. EPA standard-setting activity in the area of toxic substances and hazardous wastes is even more limited. Both the Toxic Substances Control Act and Resources Conservation and Recovery Act programs are years behind statutory deadlines and chemical production and toxic waste disposal remain largely unregulated.

The standards that do exist tend to be limited to controlling the most obvious and well established hazards. Neither the EPA nor OSHA has geared its rule-making to anticipating the creation and distribution of *new* hazards. Instead, both agencies try to force firms to clean up after the fact—usually by retrofitting existing plant and equipment—rather than force industry to take the health and safety effects of technical change into account in research and development.

Enforcement has also been slowed by lawsuits brought by polluters. Firms have the right to challenge almost every aspect of the regulatory process, and they often invite penalties in the hope that ensuing litigation will lead to time-consuming delays. Even if the ultimate outcome does not favor a particular firm, money can be saved during the time spent out of compliance. The implementation of water pollution control standards, for example, is all but subverted in this kind of litigation. Similarly, whenever OSHA has attempted to levy stiff fines, firms have pursued all of the avenues open to them to protest, including appeals to the OSHRC and the federal courts. These appeals delay enforcement, and, since agencies must consume scarce resources fighting them, appeals discourage the agencies from penalizing firms.

The White House has also provided a forum for industry appeals of agency enforcement efforts and has thereby helped to vitiate these programs. Generally, firms have treated agency rules as guidelines to be met at their convenience, and they have been quick to take their complaints to public officials when regulators differ from this approach. Public officials have often responded sympathetically: The White House, in particular, has consistently pressed the social regulatory agencies to develop less punitive, more conciliatory enforcement programs. The Reagan administration took this approach to its limit by sharply cutting back on agency enforcement staff and resources and urging the agencies to negotiate voluntary compliance agreements with firms (Eads and Fix 1984, chs. 7 and 9).

Rebuilding the Regulatory State

The analysis presented to this point has focused on the institutional constraints that limit the ability of regulatory agencies to provide effective worker and environmental protection. Some of these constraints are more deeply rooted than others and are therefore more difficult to challenge. Limits on effective state action imposed by private ownership of the means of production, or the separation of powers, will prove more intractable in the short run than constraints that arise from the institutional arrangements of the PIRR, such as the federalization of environmental programs. The analysis of institutional constraints also suggests that there are serious flaws in the public interest movement's reform strategy. Most important, the emphasis on administrative rather than party-political participation has not empowered those whom the PIRR was intended to serve.

Thus, in deciding to reconstruct the regulatory state, reformers must also decide how much of the existing political and economic system they wish to alter. Few health and safety advocates are prepared at this time to suggest fundamental changes in the Constitution or in the mode of production. Nonetheless, it is important to recognize how both vitally shape what any existing regulatory arrangement can accomplish.

It is possible to strengthen the regulatory state within the parameters established by a capitalist economy and a liberal, federal constitution. At a minimum, this would involve a wholesale restructuring of the institutions of the regulatory regime. For those who find an agenda of this sort too reformist, this restructuring can be organized, and presented, as a series of "goals" or "transitional" reforms that lead to, or at least do not preclude, wider, more fundamental changes in the future. However these changes are presented, though, reformers must make clear that they seek to change institutions and not simply policies.

What would such a regulatory regime look like? In the next section, I consider the principal alternatives that have been discussed in the literature and propose an agenda based on the analysis presented in this chapter.

Neo-liberalism

Although neo-liberals make some compelling points about the limits of Great Society reforms, this approach does not contribute to solving the problems outlined above. The heart of neo-liberalism is its emphasis on economic efficiency, the rationalization of administrative structures, and the need to reprivatize functions that neo-liberals believe are better handled by the market (Breyer 1982). All three issues are important: the costs of regulation are real and must be addressed; the U.S. state is not a particularly effective decision-making apparatus; the Great Society reformers did ignore the role that private action could play in promoting public goals.

But neo-liberal solutions to these problems are not helpful, at least to those who would make worker and environmental protection more effective and democratic. To date, neo-liberals have preferred administrative to legislative venues for dealing with cost considerations. Although they have dissented from particular oversight decisions made by OMB and the White House's economic advisors, they have not challenged the legitimacy, or desirability, of the oversight process itself. This process, however, obscures rather than clarifies the political issues underlying the cost debate. In this way, it hinders rather than helps the effort to make public decisions about environmental risk and protection.

Similarly, the neo-liberal effort to bring order and rationality to health and safety regulation by imposing centralized executive oversight on administrative agencies undermines the effort to democratize the regulatory process. It substitutes administrative decisions for legislatively-determined choices about acceptable risks and cloaks these decisions in technical language. Neo-liberalism limits rather than broadens the possibility of informed public debate about protection.

The neo-liberal concept of private action is also questionable. It relies too heavily on markets and does not take full advantage of intermediate social organizations, such as health and safety committees or community boards, that exist *between* the market and the state. Some neo-liberals do propose to devolve decision-making power to organizations of this sort. One proposal, for example, is to let unions bargain with employers over health and safety standards (Bacow 1980). But this solution is naïve; under conditions of economic uncertainty, unions are likely to bargain away protection for higher wages. This has happened before, and this outcome probably is an inescapable result of the way in which current political and economic structures interact. Workers need legislatively-determined rights to health and safety to guide standard-setting agencies. If these standards are to be qualified by economic concerns, it should be done in an appropriate legislative arena where the range of relevant considerations can be taken into account and elected officials can be held accountable for their decisions.

Liberal Corporatism

Liberal corporatism, or "neo-corporatism," refers to a policy-making approach modelled on the political-institutional arrangements popular in Western European countries such as Austria, West Germany, Sweden, and to a lesser extent, Great Britain (Schmitter and Lehmbruch 1979). Under this scheme health and safety policy is set by administrative bodies that include, on a compulsory basis, representatives of the most important business and labor organizations. Standard-setting is tripartite: union and business leaders bargain with government officials over appropriate levels of pollution. Typically, standards are considered part of a more general, comprehensive government policy toward health, safety, and the environment rather than attempts to come to terms with crisis situations one at a time.

Although popular participation under liberal corporatist arrangements varies considerably by country, workers and residents are generally involved in health and safety policy-making in two ways: through officially sanctioned organizations like unions and through plant committees and community-level boards and councils. The kind of direct participation advocated by public interest reformers in the United States is rare in this type of system. For the most part, citizens only promote the implementation of centrally determined programs.

Advocates of liberal corporatism argue that it yields a policy-making process that is at once less adversarial than and as strict as the U.S. model. Thus, they argue, a neo-corporatist regulatory process would be more efficient than the existing approach because it would lead to equally strong standards, albeit set with less conflict. Moreover, because business and labor groups are guaranteed a role in the standard-setting process and participate through central organizations that can discipline recalcitrant individual members, decisions are more likely to be accepted and enforced (Badaracco 1985; Vogel 1986).

The evidence does suggest that liberal corporatism addresses some of the problems created by the approach. Scientific decisions, for example, are much less politicized in neo-corporatist systems. Business and labor groups, guaranteed a place in the policy-making apparatus and tightly integrated into informal policy-making networks, are more willing to defer to government experts and accept their findings. Except in West Germany, liberal corporatist systems rely on a strong national state and deemphasize participation by local governments in policy-making. In addition, citizens are generally more involved than they are here through membership in intermediate organizations.

Liberal corporatism is not, however, a panacea for those who would reform regulation in the United States. Three problems stand out. First, because standards policy is negotiated, the level of risk and protection reflects rather directly the balance of power between business and labor. In Sweden, for example, where the labor movement is very strong, occupational safety and health standards are stronger than those in the United States (Noble 1986, 233). Second, environmentalists are rarely granted access to tripartite bodies. In West Germany the environmental movement has enjoyed greater influence over the policy agenda than it does in other advanced industrial societies because of the power of the Green Party. But even there, it does not have the kind of privileged access to regulatory decision-making enjoyed by organized labor. Third, liberal corporatism substitutes one kind of participatory mechanism for another, and reformers should be aware of the tradeoffs involved. Citizens gain access to implementation through intermediate organizations, but they do not as a rule have the kinds of participatory rights that U.S. citizens have. Under liberal corporatism, there are few formal mechanisms for individual citizen participation in the administrative process. Citizen-driven judicial review of the sort that occurs here is unknown in Western Europe. As a result, opportunities for action-forcing law suits are absent.

In sum, substituting a neo-corporatist, "bargaining" regime in place of the PIRR in the United States is likely to result in the loss of existing participatory rights without the benefit of stronger standards or more effective participation in implementation. In the United States liberal corporatism would produce stronger standards and more effective citizen involvement in enforcement only if organized labor could play a more powerful political role and environmental groups could gain privileged access to social regulatory agencies. If these two things do not occur, bargaining will simply mean federal agency concessions to industry and the states in an effort to encourage them to comply with existing rules and programs.

Public Interest Reform

Some reformers suggest that the PIRR has failed because it has not been taken seriously (Claybrook 1984; Pertschuk 1982). According to this view, political reaction has led to the underfunding of health and safety agencies and the appointment of regulators who have no interest in regulating. The solution to the problems outlined above is not a new regime but more aggressive regulation. Renewed political commitment—presumably under the aegis of liberal Democrats—will lead to effective and democratic standard-setting and enforcement. This is essentially the position of the public interest movement today.

Public interest reformers also propose to deepen and extend the PIRR's logic. Several supplementary reforms could be adopted further to democratize the administrative process. Ralph Nader and the consumer movement lobbied unsuccessfully in the 1970s for a Consumer Protection Agency to represent consumer interests before regulatory agencies; this proposal could be revived. Loopholes in the Freedom of Information Act could be closed, and intervenor funding could be revived and expanded. Right-to-know laws could also be expanded to give citizens even more information about how firms and agencies handle and regulate harmful substances.

Standard-setting and enforcement could also be expedited. OMB's power to intervene in and delay the regulatory process might be limited legislatively. Agencies could be encouraged to develop standards in groups rather than individually. For example, OSHA's original proposal to develop carcinogen standards by category rather than individually could be revived. OSHA and EPA enforcement procedures could be expedited by limiting the avenues through which firms can appeal permit decisions and seek variances.

These proposals make sense, but they do not confront the core problems of the PIRR. Some of these changes would, in fact, reproduce these problems in different forms. Although OMB oversight can and should be restricted, it is impossible to preclude White House intervention into the regulatory process without substantially reorganizing the structure of the regulatory apparatus. As long as executive agencies are subject to White House appointment and budgetary decisions, they will be subject to White House influence. In addition, while bigger budgets will help the enforcement effort, most experts believe that no government inspectorate, whatever its size, can secure compliance with agency rules on its own. Enforcement will have to be delegated to intermediate organizations like worker and community health and safety committees with statutory powers and rights. Finally, the relationship between citizen participation and administrative regulation remains problematic under the PIRR. Efforts to increase citizen participation in administrative standard-setting and enforcement activities will continue to limit the agencies' ability to act decisively.

A Seven-Point Agenda

As the earlier analysis of constraints indicated and as this review of alternative regulatory reform proposals suggests it will be difficult to rebuild the regulatory state so that it is simultaneously more effective and more democratic. Reformers must create institutions that strengthen state power and at the same time provide people with significant opportunities to determine what this expanded state power does. Institutions are needed to establish comprehensive protective goals, translate those goals into standards, transfer control of resources sufficient to enforce these standards from the private to the public sphere, and allow free and informed deliberation about how much risk people want to assume in the course of their lives and work. The following seven-point agenda highlights changes that should move us in these directions.

1. *Initiate health and safety investment planning.* Public authority over private capital spending targets for pollution abatement in particular should be expanded. Government should also undertake long-term research to develop materials that can substitute for hazardous substances now in use and direct investment to producing these alternatives.

This kind of investment planning will help address the constraints on policy imposed by the deep structure of the economy. Greater public control over private investment need not result in the nationalization of industry or finance. Taxation and credit policies may prove more subtle but equally effective in affecting the level and composition of investment and the impact of production on health and safety. It is impossible to assert public values over the private sphere without concurrently giving public authorities more control over the private decisions that create so many of the hazards that society faces.

2. *Centralize existing regulatory institutions.* The federal government should preempt all state-level standard-setting and planning programs that provide less protection than equivalent federal programs or that do not comply with Congressional mandates.

The federal government needs greater control over pollution abatement programs. As long as the states are allowed to exercise discretion when they implement federal standards and guidelines, they will depart from them. Competition among states for industry and jobs, differing local political cultures, and organizational complexity all insure this. If federal regulatory policies are to be implemented, states must either be forced to conform to federal policy or be sidestepped entirely by an expanded federal standard-setting and enforcement apparatus.

3. *Establish a Department of Worker and Environmental Protection.* Mechanisms must be established to encourage the various regulatory agencies to coordinate their research and standards policies. Existing health and safety agencies should be combined into a cabinet-level Department of Worker and Environmental Protection with standard-setting responsibilities.

The case for inter-agency coordination is clear. Few pollution problems are confined to one medium. Toxic and hazardous substances migrate from the workplace into the air, from the air to the water, and from the water to the land. Moreover, pollution from different sources combines to aggravate health hazards. Regulatory policy should adapt to this reality by providing a single forum in which comprehensive control policies can be designed.

OMB does this today but in an environment hostile to protective regulation. For the most part, its deliberations are secret—hidden from Congress as well as from the public—and its decision-making criteria are narrowly economic. A cabinet-level Department of Worker and Environmental Protection would politicize these issues and make it easier for the legislature to oversee policy implementation.

4. *Create a Science Court to develop criteria for rule-making.* Congress should establish an independent, professionally staffed commission or academy to collect and assess scientific information on health and safety hazards. This body should be responsible for summarizing existing knowledge and contracting for research where that knowledge is inadequate. There are agencies in a position to attempt this today. OSHA is supposed to listen to the recommendations of the National Institute for Occupational Safety and Health (NIOSH). The National Academy of Sciences (NAS) has investigated the scientific issues underlying EPA regulation in the hope of influencing that agency's decisions. But NIOSH is too easily ignored by OSHA, and the NAS studies too wide a variety of subjects to focus its full energies on environmental protection.

In their place a single, well respected institution is needed, specializing in the whole range of health and safety concerns. It is imperative that regulatory decisions be based on the best available evidence and that conflicts over health and safety goals be separated from disputes over evidence about hazards and risks. To be sure, disputes over goals can translate into theoretical and methodological controversies. But there should be a concerted effort to distinguish good from bad science. This information need not be binding on regulators. Congress and the regulatory agencies should be free to disregard these recommendations. But they should be forced to justify departures from them.

5. *Coordinate protective and economic policies.* A major effort to protect workers and the environment from health and safety hazards is likely to be very expensive. For example, a comprehensive program to regulate the 2415 known

or suspected workplace carcinogens could entail as much as \$526 billion in capital and recurring costs (Noble 1986, 19). Long-term environmental protection programs are likely to be equally costly. Clearly these costs will affect rates of economic growth, capital investment, and productivity.

Information about these costs and alternative ways of absorbing them should be an integral part of any public deliberation about health and safety goals. Attention to the economic consequences of protection need not deter society from regulating health and safety. To the contrary, a reasoned debate about alternative resource uses should help reinforce support for protection and diminish the impact of corporate-sponsored scare campaigns.

Once protective goals are set, policy-makers can develop economic programs that adapt to them. Growth policies can be adjusted to anticipate and compensate for the diversion of capital from production to consumption.[5] Industrial policies can take sectoral and industry impacts into account by developing research, tax, and credit policies to encourage modernization and technological innovation. Government can provide for the retraining of workers displaced by strict protective policies.

The issue of job loss is particularly important. Beyond job training, government must provide general employment guarantees if it is to guard the interests of individual workers threatened by collective decisions about health and safety. Moreover, a publicly guaranteed right to a decent job will help create an environment in which unions and communities can freely deliberate decisions about worker and environmental protection.

6. *Encourage greater legislative deliberation about acceptable risk.* Congress should be forced to debate a national risk reduction plan, including the formal designation of national health and safety priorities, such as the reduction of acid rain or the prevention of occupational cancers. Legislative deliberation on and approval of the budget of the Department of Worker and Environmental Protection would encourage this. Congressional committee jurisdictions should also be rationalized; the many committees with jurisdiction in these areas should coordinate their efforts to facilitate comprehensive planning.

Greater legislative participation in regulatory affairs may seem misguided or quixotic. While elections help to shape the outer contours of policy, they do not usually provide clear guidelines for detailed questions of public policy. Moreover, Congress rarely acquits itself honorably when called upon to resolve conflicts between the public's interest in controlling corporate behavior and corporations' interests in profits. Nonetheless, Congressional debate may be the only way to provide an authoritative resolution to questions such as the level of acceptable risk.

7. *Maximize local representation and participation.* While the above proposals seek to nationalize regulatory policy-making, local communities, worker organizations, and unions must have additional rights to know about hazards,

to veto the handling, disposal, or shipment of hazardous materials, and to participate in the implementation of regulatory policies.

Community right-to-know laws are essential to the democratic deliberation of health and safety policies. Firms doing business in a particular locality or moving goods from one place to another should be required to make public all available information on the potential hazardousness of materials used or transported. Unions and employees should have similar rights to know about the materials used and handled at work. Some of these rights already exist. A number of states and localities have community and worker right-to-know laws, and OSHA has a national version—the "hazard communication" policy. Coverage, however, is uneven, and the laws are difficult to enforce. A comprehensive national policy should correct these faults and assure compliance.

Local communities and unions should also have the right to block the disposal, shipment, or use of toxic substances. Clearly, it is possible to object to this proposal on practical grounds; it will create obstacles to long-term, comprehensive national planning of both environmental protection and energy development and disrupt the market-based location of industrial activities. Protected by national standards, few communities would voluntarily agree to accept others' hazardous wastes; guaranteed a right to a decent job, few workers are likely to agree to handle hazardous substances. Still, given the severity of these hazards and the possibility that majorities will unfairly abuse dependent minorities by forcing them to accept higher levels of risks, a democratic health and safety policy requires absolute rights of this sort.[6]

These practical problems can be addressed in three ways. First, other reforms designed to encourage a vigorous national debate about acceptable risk and the costs of protection should help to build a sense of community obligation to implement democratically-determined policies. Second, if there is, in fact, a strong public commitment to protection, national policies are likely to be backed by the resources necessary to minimize the use of toxic materials and facilitate the disposal of hazardous wastes. Finally, within a framework of full information, national standards, and job security, workers and communities that are willing to accept above-average risks should be allowed to do so in return for compensation.

It is also important that citizens actively participate in the implementation of regulatory policies. Employees should participate in workplace decisions affecting occupational safety and health and OSHA activities. Community and union boards should enjoy privileged access to the Department of Environmental and Worker Protection. Community groups should monitor corporate pollution and compliance with agency rules. All those affected should be guaranteed access to expertise.

Participation of this sort would have numerous benefits. People would be acquainted with health and safety issues and be more likely to take part in the political deliberations that determine basic policy. Participation should also ease the burden on federal agencies of inspecting and monitoring corporate compliance. Finally, this experience could spill over into other political arenas, facilitating other kinds of democratic collective action.

These proposals for increasing citizen participation in the determination of worker and environmental protection policies differ from the PIRR's provisions for participation in several ways. Most significantly, this approach focuses citizen participation on determining a small number of key regulatory decisions about risk and protection and attempts to channel this participation into party-political and legislative arenas. While citizens can participate in all aspects of implementation, this approach does not give individuals and groups rights to determine or challenge the routine decisions of regulators (except for the veto rights spelled out above). Moreover, these proposals do not indiscriminately open up the administrative process to all groups affected by regulation. Only workers and communities are afforded easy access to policy-makers. Finally, this approach attempts to depoliticize the scientific aspects of the regulatory process and focus citizen input where it is most appropriate, on fundamental choices about our priorities.

Conclusion

None of these institutional changes will, of course, guarantee stricter regulation and more health and safety. A democratic society might decide to accept very high levels of risk in order to enjoy the material benefits of unrestrained economic growth. It is conceivable that once fully informed of the hazards they face and free to choose protection, people will nevertheless decide that they want goods and services that can only be produced and consumed under hazardous conditions. It is even possible that many people will come to value danger in and of itself.

However, these institutional changes should accomplish two critical goals. First, they should make it difficult to distribute health and safety risks unfairly— disproportionately to economically dependent groups. In accomplishing this, these reforms take us one major step forward toward a more equitable society. Second, and perhaps most important, these institutional changes should facilitate the kind of democratic deliberation that is itself the foundation of a legitimate and effective regulatory process.

NOTES

1.   I do not wish to imply that all health and safety hazards result from private, profit-seeking activity or that only capitalist societies have pollution problems. On the contrary, both government

and consumers pollute, and industrial socialist societies experience many of the same problems. Nonetheless, because of the overwhelming importance of private business in the United States, the lion's share of U.S. pollution is caused by capitalist firms. Moreover, other economic activities are shaped by capitalist dynamics. Thus, this analysis applies both to the activities of these private firms and to the more general problem of pollution control in a capitalist democracy.

2.   The concept of regulatory regime is relatively new. For two quite interesting but different formulations, see Aglietta (1979) and Hoberg (1986).

3.   Among the most often cited examples of New Deal radicalism, only the Wagner Act made a concerted effort to empower non-capitalist interests. But even this reform promoted bureaucratic statism by tying the representation of worker interests directly to the political will and organizational capacity of the National Labor Relations Board.

4.   Federalism can benefit progressive forces when state governments are more eager to protect workers and the environment than the White House is, as has been the case during the Reagan administration. The recent battle over amendments to the Federal Insecticide, Fungicide and Rodenticide Act has found environmentalists supporting state-level discretion in the implementation of the act. Still, the general point stands: the disaggregation of popular power inherent in federalism undermines the possibility of using state power to control business. Recent efforts to use the states to block Reagan's deregulation campaign are best understood as a defensive holding action rather than as a long-term strategy for worker or environmental protection.

5.   It is, of course, reasonable to view health and safety expenditures as investments in production rather than consumption. But the conventional literature uses this dichotomy, and I adopt it for convenience here.

6.   In the best of all possible worlds, where dependent relations among different classes were eliminated, these veto rights would be replaced by a system in which democratic deliberation of the criteria for siting and transporting hazardous substances and activities is guaranteed.

References

Aglietta, M. 1979. *A theory of capitalist regulation*. London: New Left Books.

Alford, R. R., and R. Friedland. 1985. *Powers of theory*. Cambridge: Cambridge University Press.

Bacow, S. 1980. *Bargaining for job safety and health*. Cambridge, MA: Massachusetts Institute of Technology Press.

Badaracco, J. L., Jr. 1985. *Loading the dice*. Boston: Harvard Business School Press.

Bardach, E., and R. A. Kagan. 1982. *Going by the book: The problem of regulatory unreasonableness*. Philadelphia: Temple University Press.

Berger, J. L., and S. D. Riskin. 1978. Economic and technological feasibility in regulating toxic substances under the occupational safety and health act. *Ecology Law Quarterly* 7:285–358.

Block, F. 1977. The ruling class does not rule: Notes on the marxist theory of the state. *Socialist Revolution* 7.

Bowles, S., D. M. Gordon, and T. E. Weisskopf. 1983. *Beyond the wasteland*. Garden City, NY: Anchor Press/Doubleday.

Breyer, S. 1982. *Regulation and its reform*. Cambridge, MA: Harvard University Press.

Claybrook, J., and the Staff of Public Citizen. 1984. *Retreat from safety*. New York: Pantheon.

Cohen, J., and J. Rogers. 1983. *On democracy*. New York: Penguin.

Conservation Foundation. 1984. *State of the environment*. Washington, D.C.: The Conservation Foundation.

Council on Environmental Quality. 1981. *Environmental quality*. Washington, D.C.: Government Printing Office.

Eads, G. C., and M. Fix. 1984. *The Reagan regulatory strategy*. Washington, D.C.: The Urban Institute.

Evans, P. B., D. Rueschemeyer, and T. Skocpol, eds. 1985. *Bringing the state back in*. Cambridge: Cambridge University Press.

Ferguson, T. 1983. Party realignment and American industrial structure: The investment theory of political parties in historical perspective. Ed. P. Zarembka. *Research in political economy*. Vol 6, Greenwich, CT.: JAI Press. pp. 1–82.

Hoberg, G., Jr. 1986. The regulatory state: Political structure and public policy. Dissertation proposal. Cambridge, MA: Massachusetts Institute of Technology.

Jones, C. O. 1975. *Clean air*. Pittsburgh: University of Pittsburgh Press.

Kemp, K. A. 1985. Political parties, industrial structures and political support for regulation. Ed. R. Eyestone. *Public policy formation*. Greenwich, CT: JAI Press. pp. 151–184.

Lindblom, C. E. 1977. *Politics and markets*. New York: Basic Books.

Melnick, R. S. 1983. *Regulation and the courts*. Washington, D.C.: The Brookings Institution.

Noble, C. 1986. *Liberalism at work: The rise and fall of OSHA*. Philadelphia: Temple University Press.

Office of Technology Assessment. 1985. *Preventing illness and injury in the workplace*. Washington, D.C.: Government Printing Office.

Pertschuk, M. 1982. *Revolt against regulation*. Berkeley: University of California Press.

Poulantzas, N. 1973. *Political power and social classes*. London: New Left Books.

Rosenbaum, W. A. 1985. *Environmental politics and policy*. Washington, D.C.: Congressional Quarterly Press.

Schmitter, P. C., and G. Lehmbruch, eds. 1979. *Trends toward corporatist intermediation*. Beverly Hills: Sage.

Schultze, C. L. 1977. *The public use of private interest*. Washington, D.C.: The Brookings Institution.

Skowronek, S. 1982. *Building a new American state: The expansion of national administrative capacities*. Cambridge: Cambridge University Press.

Stewart, R. B. 1975. The reformation of American administrative law. *Harvard Law Review* 88 (June):1667–1711.

Tolchin, S. J., and M. Tolchin. 1983. *Dismantling America*. New York: Oxford University Press.

Vig, N. J. and M. E. Kraft, eds. 1984. *Environmental policy in the 1980s*. Washington, D.C.: Congressional Quarterly Press.

Vogel, D. 1986. *National styles of regulation*. Ithaca, NY: Cornell University Press.

Wilson, J. Q., ed. 1980. *The politics of regulation*. New York: Basic Books.

5 Economic Development in States and Cities: Toward Democratic and Strategic Planning in State and Local Government

Marc V. Levine

Throughout American history state and city governments have shaped the contours of local economic life. During the nineteenth century, for example, state and city governments actively influenced their jurisdictions' economies in actions ranging from the elaborate "public profit" enterprises of mid-century Pennsylvania to the frenetic inter-state and inter-city competition for railroads later on (Hartz 1948; Glaab and Brown 1983, 112–34). The "city practical" movement of the early 1900s sought to apply the development tools of urban planning to the task of nurturing "efficient" local economies. After World War II the federal government provided the funds for city governments to promote real estate and commercial development in the name of urban renewal (Fogelsong 1986, 199–237; Mollenkopf 1983, 139–79).

Since the early 1970s, however, economic development has become *the* central policy area for state and local governments: the "priority that supports all other priorities," in the words of New York Governor Mario Cuomo (School-man 1986, 40). Facing deindustrialization, rapidly changing production technologies, and the loss of quality jobs, virtually all cities and states have turned to "economic development" to bolster their sagging economies.

Typically, cities and states have pursued three main approaches in their economic policies. First, they have engaged in ad hoc, "beggar thy neighbor" bidding wars, attempting to put together attractive incentives packages to lure footloose capital. The 1985 competition for General Motors' Saturn plant, a process that eventually involved over 120 cities and states and saw seven governors play "Let's make a deal" with GM officials on national television, was perhaps the clearest recent example of this approach.

Second, states and particularly urban governments have established formal public-private "partnerships" to revitalize their economies. While partnership arrangements have varied from locale to locale, they generally have involved "creative" public financing to "leverage" private investment, the use of public powers such as eminent domain to expedite private development, and public-private joint ventures such as downtown hotels, shopping malls, and waterfront redevelopment. New institutional arrangements—quasi-public economic development corporations—have been established in numerous states and cities to implement the programs of these public-private partnerships.

Finally, increasing numbers of states and cities have adopted the corporate technique of "strategic planning" in an effort to develop comprehensive economic development plans. By one estimate, twenty-five states and over thirty cities have developed "strategic plans," broadly conceived as coordinated efforts to bring together public and private resources to improve the "competitive advantage" of a state or local economy over other jurisdictions (Swanstrom 1986). While the federal government remains unable to implement a coherent industrial policy to help rebuild the national economy, states such as Massachusetts, New York, and Michigan have put elements of state-level industrial policies into place as the centerpieces of their economic development strategies (Goldstein 1986; Epstein 1987).

There are important differences among these approaches to economic development. However, all share—and are limited by—two main premises. First, conventional economic development hinges on the assumption that increasing private investment will, by itself, provide quality employment and economic opportunities for state and city residents. Second, in order to leverage this private investment, the primary economic development role of state and local government is to provide a "good business climate" and help private businesses maximize their profits. As an influential handbook on economic development puts it, "The philosophy behind state economic development programs is simple: public sector and private sector can work together to achieve their common economic development goals when public policies help private firms minimize their costs and maximize their profits" (National Association of State Development Agencies 1983, 4). In short, state and local economic development represents the quintessential expression of "trickle down" theory: "profit-led" economic growth is touted as the key to improving the employment prospects of local residents.

Conventional economic development has been virtually *defined* as public leveraging of private investment. No matter what the specific state or local strategy—from the crudest smokestack chasing to the most sophisticated strategic planning—there is little *active* planning of how best to deploy public resources to create good jobs or support equitable patterns of growth. In almost all cases investment priorities and development strategies are determined by private sector elites or are constrained by notions of what is acceptable to them. The public role does not involve systematic planning on a wide range of options but tends to be limited to providing the financial and legal lubricants—public subsidies, loan guarantees, tax gimmicks—to "make the deals go" (Goodman 1979).

The socio-economic consequences of this approach to economic development have been profound. There is little evidence that low-income communities or distressed areas have significantly benefited from improved investment climates, and compelling signs exist that conditions have worsened as states and cities have courted corporate investment. The bidding war among state governments has resulted in a "race to the bottom," lowering the living standards of millions of working Americans. Research on the results of business-oriented urban redevelopment programs suggests that neighborhood distress, shrinking numbers of quality jobs, displacement of low-income residents, declining public services, and growing inequality have been the logical consequences of the conventional approach to economic development (Fainstein et. al. 1983; Hartman 1984; Levine 1987; Swanstrom 1985; Peltz 1983; Tabb 1982).

It is no accident that this "investment climate" approach has dominated contemporary state and local economic policies. Economic development has been politically controlled by a mobilized and well organized business community seeking fundamentally to reorient local priorities around business interests. Armed with the omnipresent and credible threat of disinvestment, business has been able to impose its policy agenda on local government, generally with little effective opposition. Moreover, state and local economic policy-making has been increasingly conducted by quasi-public development institutions, insulated from public control. As a result, vital decisions affecting the allocation of substantial public resources and the economic future of entire communities are often made in institutions with limited public access and vague lines of accountability. In such policy-making bodies the equation of economic development with profit maximization is assured.

The central argument of this chapter is that the time has come for a fundamental reorientation in the economic development policies of state and local governments. The basic problems of state and local economies—the need for quality jobs, investment in distressed areas, and adequate public services—cannot be solved merely by responding to the agenda of a mobilized business community; strategic planning by local governments is essential. Moreover, effective alternatives to the business climate approach will emerge only if the *politics* of economic development are democratized and mechanisms are established through which citizens can fully participate in planning their communities' economic future.

International economic conditions and the considerable power of mobile capital certainly constrain the policy flexibility of state and local governments. Problems of state and local economic development are unsolvable without fundamental, structural changes in national political economy. Within these "limits," however, there is much that state and local governments can do to improve their economic policy-making capacities, develop rational, genuinely strategic economic development plans, and democratize the economic agenda-setting process.

This chapter is divided into four main sections. The first briefly outlines the structural conditions that, by the mid-1970s, pushed most cities and states into the investment climate approach to economic development. The second and third explore the historical development and current substance of the economic development strategies pursued by state and municipal governments. The last section provides an examination of alternative economic development programs, based on democratic planning and strategic investments rather than elite control and corporate giveaways.

The Political-Economic Context of State and Local Economic Development

The "improve the business climate" economic development agenda of most states and cities took shape in the 1970s in response to three well documented economic and political trends: deindustrialization, the politicization of the American business community, and the realities of local fiscal crises.

Deindustrialization refers to the precipitous decline in manufacturing as a percentage of total employment and output in the American economy. Between 1950 and 1985 the percentage of Americans employed in manufacturing declined from 34 to 20 percent. The portion of the Gross National Product originating in manufacturing declined from nearly 30 percent in 1951 to about 21 percent in 1985 (Data Resources, Inc. 1983, 12). Basic industries such as steel, automobiles, and machine tools contracted markedly. By the mid-1980s, even American manufacturers of high-tech products such as fiber optics, industrial robots, and semiconductor chips were in economic difficulty. By 1986 *Business Week* reported with alarm that in "industry after industry, manufacturers are closing up shop or curtailing their operations and becoming marketing organizations for other producers, mostly foreign" (*Business Week* 1986, 56).

Several factors account for deindustrialization. They include: 1) the declining competitiveness of domestic manufacturers in an increasingly global economy; 2) the investment strategies of U.S.-based multinational corporations, seeking to lower their production costs by closing plants in the United States while concomitantly "outsourcing" and "off-shoring" production in low-wage countries; 3) the "paper entrepreneurialism" of corporate managers, seeking profits through mergers, takeovers, and financial legerdemain, instead of improvements in the productive capacity of American industry; and 4) the impact of new production technologies—mainly robotization and the general application of computerized manufacturing—which enhance manufacturer productivity, but also displace production workers (Bluestone and Harrison 1982; Reich 1983; Congress of the United States, Office of Technology Assessment 1986; Shaiken 1985; U.S. House of Representatives, Committee on Energy and Commerce 1983).

The impact of deindustrialization has been staggering. In the Midwest-Northeast manufacturing belt for every 100 jobs created during the 1970s, 111 were lost due to plant closings and relocations. According to the Congressional Office of Technology Assessment, 11.5 million American workers lost their jobs between 1979 and 1984 because of plant shutdowns and relocations, rising productivity, or shrinking output. Moreover, masked in these aggregate figures is the fact that between 1979 and 1985 the jobs *created* in this country were in industries that, on average, pay 40 percent less than the industries in which jobs were lost (AFL-CIO 1986, 6). During this period, 44 percent of these new jobs paid "poverty-level wages," more than twice the rate of low-wage job creation that existed in the 1960s and 1970s (Bluestone and Harrison 1986). In short, by the late 1970s the evidence that communities were losing their base of "good jobs" was compelling.

Decline in basic industries—with ripple effects to suppliers and tertiary economic activities—has meant significant unemployment and economic hardship. For example, estimates are that every dollar lost through decreased auto and steel production causes almost two dollars additional decline in regional income. As Tables 5.1 and 5.2 suggest, states and cities in the Northeast-Midwest industrial belt have experienced sharp declines in their manufacturing employment since the early 1970s. Moreover, between 1970 and 1984, notwithstanding the growth of urban-based service sector jobs, overall employment declined significantly in Frostbelt cities such as New York (5.3 percent), Detroit (11.9 percent), Cleveland (14 percent), Pittsburgh (6.8 percent), and St. Louis (6 percent) (U.S. Bureau of the Census 1972, 1986). Smaller, specialized manufacturing cities— such as Saginaw, Flint, Youngstown, and Johnstown—saw their economies virtually decimated by the decline in the specific manufacturing sectors—mainly steel and autos—on which they disproportionately depended.

It was in this context of decline that states and cities turned to economic development as a means of reviving their sagging economies. The kinds of strategies pursued by state and local governments, however, were shaped by two other political-economic developments in the 1970s. First, as Thomas Edsall brilliantly documents, during the 1970s "the political wing of the nation's corporate sector staged one of the most remarkable campaigns in pursuit of political power in recent history" (1984, 107). This "campaign" operated on a number of levels: the use of corporate financial power to influence electoral politics and

Table 5.1.   The Erosion of American Manufacturing: Some State Examples, 1972–1984

State	Manufacturing Employment (000)		Change (%)
	1972	1984	
Illinois	1306.0	985.5	− 32.2
Michigan	1076.2	945.8	− 12.1
New York	1679.3	1330.2	− 20.8
Ohio	1346.3	1125.1	− 16.4
Pennsylvania	1417.5	1119.8	− 21.0

Sources: U.S. Bureau of the Census, *State and Metropolitan Area Data Book, 1986* (Washington, D.C., 1986) and U.S. Bureau of the Census, *County and City Data Book, 1972* (Washington, D.C., 1972).

Table 5.2.   The Deindustrialization of Frostbelt Cities: Some Examples

City	Manufacturing Employment (000)		Change (%)
	1972	**1982**	
Baltimore	90.6	59.3	−34.5
Chicago	430.6	277.0	−35.7
Cleveland	131.2	92.5	−29.6
Detroit	180.4	105.4	−41.4
Milwaukee	106.3	77.9	−26.7
Pittsburgh	62.3	52.3	−16.0

Sources: U.S. Bureau of the Census, *State and Metropolitan Area Data Book, 1986* (Washington, D.C., 1986) and U.S. Bureau of the Census, *County and City Data Book, 1972* (Washington, D.C., 1972).

the national legislative process; the underwriting of think tanks that developed policy analyses supportive of business interests; and the sophisticated use of advocacy advertising to help promote a pro-business political culture (Blumenthal 1986, 32–55). At the state and local levels the politicized business community launched what Barry Bluestone and Bennett Harrison call an "assault on the social wage" (1982, 180). Consciously using the threat of capital mobility, corporate managers demanded pro-business local policies—low business taxes, reduced social spending, and "flexible" regulation—as a condition of investment. As Bluestone and Harrison point out, corporate demands focused on

> . . . the whole panoply of government policies that provide social insurance, welfare and food stamps, and minimum wages. These shelters from the insecurity that comes from being totally dependent on the demands of capital represent the spoils of past political victories won by workers and their unions. The social wage is costly to business, and increasingly they want out. *That* is what the corporate demand for a good business climate is all about. (181)

In short, the deindustrialization of the Northeast-Midwest manufacturing belt in the 1970s had a clear *political* dimension. As John Mollenkopf argues, the purposeful corporate disinvestment from older, historically industrial cities— and the concomitant inter-city competition for investment it engendered—"enforced a market discipline over the liberalism of the older cities" (1983, 253). By shifting investment away from "contested cities" toward cities with conservative, pro-business political climates such as those in the Sunbelt, capital mobility pushed *all* cities to adopt "pro-business" budgetary and economic development strategies as a way of proving their political worthiness to footloose capital (242–53).

A final factor shaping the economic development strategies of states and particularly cities was the emergence of local "fiscal crises" in the 1970s. Rooted in a complex array of political and economic factors, the threat of public bankruptcy had profound consequences for the distribution of political power and the content of public policy in states and cities (Tabb 1982). In many ways the 1975 New York City fiscal crisis was a watershed, a symbolic event, "the first act in a new age of reaction," as one writer puts it (Zevin 1977, 11). Whatever the causes of the New York crisis, it underscored the degree to which local governments are limited by the power of capital—and sent a message to state and city governments around the country. The need to maintain access to credit markets, essential for local governments to support their capital projects, meant that in the aftermath of the New York crisis local public policy was "weighted toward the concerns of creditors—and against the democratic impulse" (Shefter 1985, 233). In New York this meant massive retrenchment—budget cuts, declines in public and social services—and an increased emphasis on economic development policies designed to improve the city's business climate. The ultimate authority over the municipal budget was taken out of normal political institutions and placed in a corporate-dominated Financial Control Board (FCB).

In combination with deindustrialization and the demands of a mobilized business community the threat and reality of fiscal crisis had two significant public policy consequences for states and cities. First, fiscal distress legitimated increased control by capital over state and local policy. If states or cities insisted on policies of profligate spending and neglect of business interests, their bond ratings would drop and they would be unable to raise funds on capital markets. The New York solution explicitly recognized an incompatibility between capitalism and local democracy by placing budgetary authority in the FCB and sent an important signal to jurisdictions around the country to get their "fiscal houses" in order in a manner acceptable to capital.

Second, concern with averting fiscal crisis and expanding their revenue base prompted local governments to elevate pro-business economic development to the highest policy priority. Martin Shefter argues that "patterns of public expenditure and public policy in New York have been more favorable to business since 1975 than they had been prior to the fiscal crisis" with billions spent encouraging downtown business development and billions of dollars in tax abatements offered, while social and public services declined (1985, 142). In Baltimore, to take another example, between 1974 and 1984, while real municipal expenditures overall declined by 20 percent, city spending on economic development increased by 400 percent, a figure that does not include millions of dollars in off-budget items and tax gimmicks designed to promote business expansion (Levine 1986a, 12). By pressuring local governments to reorder their budgetary priorities, fiscal crises helped promote an approach to economic development that redistributed public resources from poor and working people in states and cities to the politicized business community threatening disinvestment and public bankruptcy.

In sum, by the mid 1970s three trends—deindustrialization, the politicization of corporate America, and local fiscal distress—had come together to prod state and city governments into action on economic development. States and cities, unfortunately, did not approach economic development with a tabula rasa, seeking systematically and democratically to adopt strategies that would maximize quality job creation and equitable patterns of growth. Facing a hemorrhaging of jobs, imminent fiscal disaster, and a mobilized business community bent on reordering public policy priorities, states and cities began doing what seems logical: pursuing economic policies to promote business investment in their jurisdictions.

The Entrepreneurial City: Patterns of Urban Economic Development[1]

Since the early 1970s most U.S. cities have adopted an entrepreneurial approach to economic development. They have forged elaborate partnerships with private developers and investors, while competing with other cities over who could create the best business climate for mobile capital (Judd and Ready 1986).

This urban entrepreneurialism is based on what several analysts have called the "growth ideology" (Molotch 1976; Swanstrom 1985, 11–34). In brief, this ideology assumes that public policies that increase returns to private capital objectively advance the interests of the city as a whole and reflect a community consensus on economic development. "Developmental policies," argues Paul E. Peterson, "strengthen the local economy, enhance the local tax base, and generate additional resources that can be used for the community's welfare. They are praised by the many and opposed only by those few whose partial interests stand in conflict with community interests." Such "growth policies" supposedly stand in contrast to "redistributive policies," which, again according to Peterson, "negatively affect the local economy" and generate intense political conflict (1981, 131–32).

The growth ideology, in short, assumes an urban environment in which the interests of capital are synonymous with the community interest. It assumes that 1) the benefits of pro-capital growth policies do not disproportionately accrue to developers, corporate elites, and upper-income residents; 2) there is consensus on issues of economic development rather than geographic, racial, and class divisions reflecting conflicting perspectives on economic development; and 3) there are limited social costs to pro-capital development policies. There is, as I explore shortly, almost no evidence to support any of these assumptions. They continue, nevertheless, to drive the economic development strategies of most cities.

The Content of Urban Economic Development
Policy: the Corporate Center Strategy

Invariably, the centerpiece of urban entrepreneurialism has been downtown redevelopment. Through public-private joint ventures and a wide array of public subsidies and incentives given to private developers, older, historically industrial cities have attempted to restructure their downtowns from decaying manufacturing, shipping, and retail districts into modern "corporate centers" of offices, up-scale commercial establishments and residences, hotels, and other tourism and convention facilities. Conscious decisions have been made to displace low-income residents, while cities have oriented their economic development strategies to attract young corporate managers, educated professionals, and well heeled conventioneers and tourists (Hill 1983, 105; Louv 1983, 230). In popular and scholarly publications this type of downtown redevelopment has been touted as the linchpin of economic revitalization in several Frostbelt cities: Boston, New York, Baltimore, and Philadelphia, to name a few (Frieden and Sagalyn 1986; Ganz 1986; Peirce, Guskind, and Gardner 1983; Stevens 1985).

Proponents of corporate center urban economic development maintain that the strategy offers four main public benefits:

1. *Symbolic enhancement of the local business climate.* Flashy downtown redevelopment, proponents argue, is an important symbol to potential investors of a dynamic "city on the move," a city with good profit opportunities. Downtown boosters claim that such symbolism, along with ample public subsidies and incentives, is crucial if cities are to leverage private investment and stimulate growth (Frieden and Sagalyn 1986, 44).

2. *Direct job creation and tax base broadening.* Jobs created in downtown offices, retailing, and hotels, it is argued, may help offset declining manufacturing employment; and the entry-level skill requirements of many of these service jobs may actually expand employment opportunities for low-income residents (Ganz 1986, 41; Swanstrom 1986, 128). Moreover, increased development and rising property values downtown create a broader city tax base through which quality public services presumably can be sustained (Judd 1984, 378–80).

3. *Ripple effects.* Once a critical mass of downtown investment is leveraged, proponents suggest it will spill over into surrounding neighborhoods, stimulating economic growth throughout the city. This is, of course, an urban variant of "trickle down" economic theory.

4. *Spearheading economic adjustment.* Global trends in the 1960s and 1970s rapidly undermined the industrial base on which many urban economies had been built. At the same time, however, as the national economy shifted toward services, the downtown real estate of many older cities was viewed by corporate decision-makers as potentially "functional" for the location of corporate headquarters and related services: investment banking, management consulting, accounting, advertising, and law. Because of the "agglomeration tendencies" of the advanced

services sector, downtowns became increasingly attractive for the central location of corporate offices, as well as the housing, retail, and entertainment facilities to accommodate the professionals who would be working in them (Kasarda 1985, 36–43; Stanback and Noyelle 1982).

In view of these trends neo-conservative analysts such as John D. Kasarda have argued that cities should not squander public funds attempting to rebuild inexorably declining manufacturing bases. Rather, they should adapt to "new economic realities and exploit their emerging competitive strengths" in corporate services, tourism, retailing, and entertainment (1982, 71). In short, the ultimate benefit of corporate center redevelopment would be its role in facilitating the necessary adjustment of older cities to post-industrial urban realities.

The Politics of Urban Economic Development: the Dynamics of Public-Private Partnerships

Typically, cities have planned and implemented this corporate center approach to economic development through public-private partnerships. Formal, ongoing collaboration between city governments and private developers began, of course, in the 1950s with the urban renewal program. Committees of leading corporate executives—such as the Allegheny Conference in Pittsburgh, the Blyth-Zellerbach Committee in San Francisco, or the Greater Baltimore Committee— joined growth-oriented mayors to promote numerous downtown revitalization projects, many of them underwritten with federal funds (Stewman and Tarr 1982; Lyall 1982; Mollenkopf 1983; Hartman 1984). Virtually autonomous "redevelopment authorities"—modeled after the independent authorities erected in New York by Robert Moses—were formed to exercise vast public powers of land assemblage and resource allocation outside the regular channels of municipal governance. Redevelopment authority heads such as Ed Logue in Boston or Justin Herman in San Francisco were notorious for using enormous public financial and land use powers with minimal oversight to implement the redevelopment aims of their cities' corporate communities.

In the 1970s cities built on these earlier patterns of public-private cooperation by dramatically expanding the scope of partnership activity and increasing the public resources available to underwrite private investment. Pushed hard by boosterish, entrepreneurial mayors such as William Donald Schaefer in Baltimore and Kevin White in Boston, modern public-private partnerships functioned to promote corporate center economic development in three main ways.

First, partnerships provided a political framework in which public powers could be used to coordinate private investment and development, maximizing profits from urban land use. According to the Committee for Economic Development, a strong advocate of public-private collaboration, "An important attribute of public-private partnerships is that they provide a means for reducing uncertainty. . . . Collaboration may be essential to the revitalization of downtown commercial centers. Small, uncoordinated, and fragmented investments are rarely sufficient to reverse the cumulative effects of economic decline" (1982, 36–40).

The power of eminent domain—which enabled city governments expeditiously to condemn, clear, and assemble land for development—became particularly useful to private developers looking for coordinated, predictable land use patterns and promising profit opportunities.

Second, the concept of public-private partnership facilitated the extensive provision of public subsidies, loans, and loan guarantees, as well as intricate manipulation of tax policy in support of private investment and development. Increasingly, with the widespread acceptance of the "growth ideology," the public role in these partnerships became to provide financial incentives or fill gaps in capital markets in order to stimulate private investment and development (National Council on Urban Economic Development 1978a; U.S. Conference of Mayors 1984). Occasionally, in some joint projects, there have been shared public-private risks and direct public benefits in the form of equity holdings; Hartford's downtown redevelopment, for example, has apparently involved this kind of partnership (Clavel 1985, 30–46). Independent public investments, however—promising social benefits, perhaps, but no direct support for private developers—have not been part of the conventional public-private partnership model. Public enterprise exceeds the limits set by the "growth ideology."

Third, public-private partnerships have been institutionalized in numerous cities in powerful and nearly autonomous quasi-public economic development corporations (National Council on Urban Economic Development 1978b). These new bodies have become crucial actors in local economic development policy, serving as formal institutional mechanisms in which public-private "deal making" can take place, outside the scrutiny of normal political arenas. In some cities these corporations wield extraordinary powers historically reserved for institutions of representative government. They can condemn and assemble land parcels, issue tax-exempt bonds, establish "tax-increment" districts for development, receive and administer grants and loans from other levels of government, and offer investment inducements such as tax abatements—all outside the control of normal urban political institutions (Hill 1983, 103; Levine 1986b, 17–20).

Quasi-public development corporations offer several advantages to cities interested in rapidly allocating municipal resources to private developers and investors with minimal public oversight. As the National Council on Urban Economic Development (NCUED) argues, such bodies offer the following "advantages" for partnership activity:

- structural independence from city government;
- expansion of public powers because such institutions are not constrained by city charters;
- privacy of negotiations: "negotiations for the sale or lease of public property can occur without constant public scrutiny or bidding procedures";
- coordination of public and private resources;

- continuous access to public officials by private developers. (1978a, 3)

While NCUED recognizes a certain "public accountability" problem with these development entities, it nevertheless warns that "too much public control . . . may discourage effective private participation" (1978b, 3). Quasi-public development institutions were thus *designed* to limit popular control over urban economic development.

The Baltimore experience is instructive in this regard. In the 1970s, Baltimore set up an elaborate network of quasi-public entities to expedite the planning, funding, and implementation of the city's ambitious downtown redevelopment program. The "quasis" were dubbed the "Shadow Government" because they purposefully operated outside the constraints of the city charter in their economic development activities. "Major aspects of the city government," wrote one critic in 1980, "are being run increasingly by men and women whose names never appear on the ballot, whose decisions are not public, and whose actions are obscured through a string of corporations that operate outside the established system of government" (Smith 1980a, 1).

Twenty-four quasi-public corporations were set up in Baltimore. The most important, however, was a development bank called the "Trustees." Operated with virtually complete autonomy by two individuals—"trustees" appointed by the mayor—the bank's purpose was creatively to package public funds (Urban Development Action Grants, Community Development Block Grants, city bonds) in loans and loan guarantees to provide the "gap financing" necessary to make redevelopment deals go. The bank was explicitly designed to "remove government action from the political arena" and cut development deals quickly, confidentially, and profitably (U.S. Conference of Mayors 1984; Smith 1980a; Levine 1986b, 18).

Between 1976 and 1986 the Trustees disbursed or guaranteed over $500 million in 239 economic development projects, creating, in the words of one careful analysis, "a steady market for Baltimore's businessmen" (Smith 1980b, 1; Smith 1986). Creative financing by the Trustees included such innovations as city-created tax shelters for developers and the reallocation of money raised for one purpose (bonds floated for low-income mortgage assistance) to another (a middle- and upper-income townhouse project), all without public scrutiny or debate.

The Trustees operation—commended by the U.S. Conference of Mayors in a study subtitled "How your city can make use of Baltimore's approach to creative financing for economic development"—was explicitly anti-democratic in its approach to economic development. The Trustees were legally required to obtain approval for all their actions from the city's Board of Estimates. However, as one trustee said, "If we need to spend a dime, we spend a dime . . . I avoid the Board of Estimates like the plague" (Smith 1985, 1). Another trustee was even more direct in revealing the political logic of the Trustees' contribution to

Baltimore's economic development: "The Trustees have the responsibility of determining priorities for the community, deciding what projects come above something else. This is, in my view, far better than what happens in most cities, where operations are based on who gets there first and who yells the loudest" (U.S. Conference of Mayors 1984, 70).

In short, public-private partnerships appear to be anything but genuine partnerships. Planning is either done by developers or constrained by notions of what would be acceptable to them, while the public contribution consists of smoothing the way for profit opportunities through the use of municipal legal powers and financial resources.

Public-Private Partnerships in Action: the Rouse
  Company and the Redevelopment of U.S.
  Downtowns

No trend better exemplifies the policies and politics of public-private collaboration than the "Rouse-ification" of downtowns across the United States. With its "festival marketplaces" in Boston (Faneuil Hall Marketplace), New York (South Street Seaport), Baltimore (Harborplace), Milwaukee (Grand Avenue Mall), Philadelphia (The Gallery at Market East), and St. Louis (Union Station), to name a few, the Rouse Company has become the leading downtown developer in the country. Rouse projects, with their distinctive architecture and innovative linkage of entertainment and retailing, have been credited with changing the image of center cities, stimulating spinoff downtown redevelopment, and rekindling investor confidence in downtown—all factors that have made mayors, anxious to promote growth and claim political credit for it, line up to coax Rouse into their cities (Gunts 1985a, 16A–17A).

A hallmark of Rouse's urban operations has been its insistence that projects occur within a public-private partnership framework. As company chairman Mathias DeVito says, "We won't do a project that a city wants us to do unless we see that the city government is terribly committed to it, and ready to be our partners in it to make it work" (Gunts 1985b, 13B).

The "city as a partner" means two things for the Rouse company:

1. *Land assemblage and project coordination.* Says DeVito: "Building a shopping center, we can go out to the suburbs and buy a tract of land. But in order for an urban project to be done there has to be condemnation, relocation of tenants, building of parking structures, changes in streets—all the things that a developer can't do" (Gunts 1985b, 13B).

2. *Financial support.* The Rouse Company requires municipal financial involvement, in part to make its projects "economically feasible" and in part to encourage cities "to think of themselves as entrepreneurs and partners in the redevelopment process" (Gunts 1985b, 13B). For example, the $70 million Grand

Avenue Mall in Milwaukee was funded in three ways: 1) $15 million from a consortium of local firms assembled by the Milwaukee Redevelopment Corporation; 2) $35 million from the city of Milwaukee (including a $12.6 million Urban Development Action Grant); and 3) $20 million from Rouse (Gunts 1985b, 13B).

Aside from assisting in financing, the partnership dimension of Rouse-style development comes in handy in marketing their projects. According to one analyst, "Rouse officials cleverly use their connections with cities in their marketing efforts to make their private projects seem also like civic ventures that people ought to patronize out of civic duty" (Gunts 1985a, 17A).

Nothing more clearly illustrates the skewed priorities of public-private partnerships. There is little evidence that public officials systematically weigh how best to deploy public resources to maximize public benefits—i.e., was the $35 million allocated by Milwaukee to underwrite Grand Avenue the best way to meet the city's employment and spinoff development needs? Additionally, private and public interests have become so blurred by the partnership concept that development projects producing handsome private returns are conceptualized as the epitome of civic achievement.

Urban Economic Development: The Results

Research on urban redevelopment clearly suggests that the entrepreneurial approach has done little to improve living conditions for the majority of urban dwellers and, in fact, has exacerbated inequality. In city after city, redevelopment has been associated with a "tale of two cities": pockets of revitalization surrounded by growing hardship. In New York, for example, more jobs were created in the city in 1983 than in any year since 1950; at the same time, however, the city has seen its poverty rate increase 20 percent since 1979 (*The New York Times* 1985b). Boston has emerged as a "renaissance city" in the 1980s; yet conditions in Roxbury, Dorchester, and other poor areas of the city continue to deteriorate (Ganz 1986). Baltimore's Inner Harbor is a national model of waterfront reclamation; during the 1970s, however, 90 percent of the city's black neighborhoods experienced increases in their poverty rates (Levine 1987).

Redeveloped downtowns, in Brian Berry's phrase, tend to be "islands of renewal in seas of decay" (1985). A Brookings Institution study of urban trends through the late 1970s reports that "by any reasonable measure of the prosperity of places . . . distressed cities were appreciably worse off in the late 1970s than they were ten years earlier. . . . The pattern that emerges . . . is one of isolated improvements in a few pockets of plenty accompanied by continued decline elsewhere" (Fossett and Nathan 1981, 84). In short, while the entrepreneurial city has provided excellent profit opportunities for developers and good jobs for advanced services professionals, it has not improved economic opportunities and living standards for the majority of urban dwellers.

Why has the entrepreneurial approach to urban economic development produced such meager results? The evidence would suggest that both the *content* and the *process* of typical local efforts are deeply flawed.

First, available research suggests that corporate centers—based on advanced services and tourism—are deficient anchors of a local economy. As Thomas Stanback and Thierry Noyelle point out, the income distribution in such economies tends to be "two-tiered," with few occupational ladders and middle-income jobs bridging the tiers. The downtown services sector tends to be isolated from the "local" component of a city economy; with limited linkages to small- and medium-size local firms, there are few ripple effects in neighborhood economic development (1982, 140–42). Finally, the kinds of jobs created in downtown corporate centers are unlikely to provide employment opportunities for urban poor and minorities. Philadelphia, for example, lost 172,000 entry-level jobs between 1970 and 1984; during the same years, the city added 39,000 "knowledge-intensive" jobs (Herbers 1986, 1).

This jobs mismatch helps explain why poverty rates rose and neighborhoods deteriorated throughout urban America, despite the pursuit of economic development. The loss of entry-level employment in basic manufacturing has not been adequately replaced in new, information-based urban economies. Moreover, the entry-level service jobs that *have* been created pay substantially less than the manufacturing employment being replaced. Finally, cities' overall conditions remain distressed because many of the benefits of economic development "leak" to the suburbs. Studies of Boston, Baltimore, New York, and Cleveland all show that over 60 percent of the "good jobs" created by downtown revitalization— those paying over $25,000 a year—have gone to suburban commuters. Such leakage does little to shore up the urban revenue base and support local public services, and it suggests that city residents are not the main beneficiaries of their governments' redevelopment policies (Ganz 1986; Levine 1987; *The New York Times* 1985b, Swanstrom 1985).

The displacement of urban manufacturing and the rise of downtown services are national and international trends virtually impossible for individual cities to alter. But, in embracing a corporate center strategy, urban officials have done little to mitigate the deficiencies noted above, either by channeling downtown growth so that it spurs economic development in distressed neighborhoods or by investing in revitalized public education so that city residents might be better equipped to participate in an information-based economy. In sum, the corporate center approach is flawed because it ignores such issues as the quality of jobs created and linkages between development in one sector and the development needs in another, while relying on "trickle down" benefits rather than public targeting to encourage economic development in the most distressed urban neighborhoods.

The recent focus by cities on tourism and conventions is also deficient. The logic of this approach, according to Dennis R. Judd, is that the industry seems "uniquely beneficial, essentially a 'free' commodity. Presumably, tourists spend money without taking anything out of the local economy" (1984, 388).

However, as Judd, as well as Chester Hartman (1984, 301–309) has detailed, jobs in the tourism/convention trade are mainly low-wage, subsistence jobs, hardly adequate replacements for lost manufacturing employment. Moreover, the industry is highly cyclical and thus an unstable basis on which to build a city economy. Infrastructure costs—added police and fire protection, building convention facilities, increased transportation needs—may significantly reduce the revenues provided by tourists and conventioneers. Finally, virtually all cities are pursuing tourism and conventions (*The New York Times* 1985a, 12), yet there are only so many conventions and vacations to go around, and evidence suggests that the saturation point is now being reached. Several cities are experiencing hotel "busts" after a frenzied boom in construction and may be left with unoccupied publicly subsidized hotels, convention facilities, and tourist attractions, while housing deteriorates for the majority of the cities' populations.

The *process* of entrepreneurial urban economic development—based on public-private partnerships—has helped promote policies that favor developers and the wealthy at the expense of the majority of city residents. Billed as a model for how government and business can cooperate to revitalize a city, these partnerships have been characterized by corporate domination of municipal policy. Having "abdicated" any serious "concept of themselves as stewards of the public interest," to borrow Hartman's phrase, public planning agencies merely identify investment opportunities for private developers or work out the details on projects initiated by developers (1984, 219).

The modus operandi of most partnerships—relegating economic development to quasi-public entities—has also had negative consequences. Purposefully insulated from public influence and dominated by downtown-oriented interests, these institutions have emphasized deal-making and profit opportunities rather than systematic planning to create good jobs and meet pressing neighborhood needs.

Peterson argues that such undemocratic institutions flourish because economic development is a consensual issue: everyone knows that the entire city benefits from policies designed to improve the city's attractiveness to business (1981, 133–34). A more plausible explanation, however, is that quasi-public corporations are insulated from public control in order to keep those groups deriving few benefits from development activity from interfering with the "deal making" process. The *depoliticization* of economic development decision-making effectively stymies groups supporting alternative strategies; it insulates a crucial area of urban policy from democratic impulses.

Under these circumstances, it is not surprising that the chief beneficiaries of urban economic development have been developers and advanced services professionals. These groups, along with pro-business policy entrepreneurs, have dominated typical public-private partnerships. Uneven growth has been the logical outcome of unequal partnerships and closed decision-making processes. As Franklin James points out, "Public-private partnership efforts cannot be expected to have the same commitment to social equity as endeavors can have when the initiative lies in the public sector. . . . Such partnerships are likely to focus on traditional types of activities offering few direct benefits to disadvantaged persons" (1984, 170).

In sum, the economic development strategies of U.S. cities have succeeded in creating a "profit-machine" for developers and investors oriented mainly around a pro-business "growth ideology." Downtowns have been revitalized into corporate services and tourism centers, but the majority of people using these facilities are not city residents. Neighborhood distress and shrinking economic opportunities remain serious problems for large numbers of urban dwellers. The lines between public and private interest have been blurred and urban democracy has been compromised by an approach to economic development that emphasizes state and local governments as "underwriters" of private profits. Recognizing the deficiencies of this entrepreneurial approach, some cities have begun to explore more democratic and progressive alternatives to urban economic development. I shall consider these alternatives in the final section of this chapter as I address the issue of a new economic development role for states and cities.

State Government and Economic Development: from Smokestack Chasing to Strategic Planning

In January 1985 General Motors (GM) announced plans to build a $3.5 billion manufacturing and assembly complex for its new Saturn Corporation line of subcompact automobiles. Envisioned as GM's high-tech, state-of-the-art effort to compete with the Japanese in the small car market, the Saturn facility was projected to employ 6,000 workers directly, with total employment—including suppliers and local services—reaching 20,000 (*Newsweek* 1985a, 56).

GM's announcement set off "the most frantic industrial competition of the 1980s" (Peirce 1985a, 926). Notwithstanding the fact that GM reported record profits in 1984, twenty-four states and one hundred cities offered a dazzling array of giveaways to land Saturn: free land; publicly provided roads, rails, or sewer connections; subsidized worker training; cut-rate financing; and long-term tax abatements. Missouri reportedly offered GM a total package worth about one billion dollars, while Michigan promised to "meet or beat any other state's offer." In an astonishing display of boosterism, seven governors appeared on *The Phil Donahue Show* and ostentatiously peddled their incentives to GM Chairman Roger Smith. In August 1985 GM announced that Spring Hill, a tiny Tennessee town thirty miles south of Nashville, would be the site of the Saturn plant (Peirce 1985a; Glastris 1985; *Newsweek* 1985b).

This "bidding war" over Saturn represented just one—albeit the most highly publicized—skirmish in what has been called the "second war between the states." It revealed the essential irrationality of the entrepreneurial business climate approach to economic development increasingly pursued by states as they battled for corporate investment. In the case of Saturn,

1. GM's intention, even before the bidding began, was to locate the plant in the United States; thus, no new investment was created by the governors' generous incentives packages.

2. The social costs of "smokestack chasing" have already become apparent in Spring Hill, as the huge tax breaks given GM "will force farmers, owners of small businesses and other residents to pick up the balance of the county's tax requirements" (Borden 1986, 852).

3. GM announced in October 1986, presumably as part of its new "cost cutting" competitiveness strategy, that contrary to its earlier forecasts, the Saturn plant would employ only 3,000 workers and produce one-half the volume of cars initially projected (Holusha 1986).

4. At the same time that GM announced its Saturn scale-back, it unveiled a "reorganization and modernization program" entailing eleven plant shutdowns and 29,000 worker layoffs (Prokesh 1986). Thus, the *net impact* of state government economic development efforts involving this corporate giant was substantial diminution in productive capacity and significant job loss.

The Saturn results are not an anomaly; study after study confirms that in the long run smokestack chasing does not pay off, either in net job creation or expanded revenue bases (Peltz 1983, 8–14). Nevertheless, state governments continue to function, in Robert Goodman's felicitous phrase, as America's "last entrepreneurs," bargaining away their taxes, working conditions, environment, and social programs in "entrepreneurial battles" with other states to attract mobile capital (Goodman 1979).

While all states practice entrepreneurial economic development, some, such as Massachusetts, New York, and Michigan, have moved beyond smokestack chasing toward strategic planning designed to encourage indigenous economic development (Epstein 1987; Peirce 1985b; Tese 1985; Schoolman 1986; Task Force for a Long-Term Economic Strategy 1984). States have emphasized new capital instruments—industrial development banks and venture capital funds—designed to help established companies modernize and small entrepreneurs get started. Agencies have been established to help state businesses become successful exporters. Many states have emphasized investments in education and infrastructure as more effective ways of building a thriving economic environment than indiscriminate tax giveaways and business subsidies.

There are crucial differences between these approaches to state economic development. Smokestack chasing puts a state's economic destiny squarely in the hands of giant corporations, with the social costs of giveaways borne by ordinary citizens and with little consideration of whether the sought-after investment meets the state's basic needs: long-term, stable growth and the generation of "good jobs." Strategic planning acknowledges an active rather than responsive role for state government in economic development; it recognizes that effective economic development requires more than tax giveaways and subsidies, and it establishes a process whereby it is at least possible publicly to discuss what kind of economic development strategy would best serve the public interest.

Despite these differences, however, all state economic policies are based on the assumption that "economic development is really a private sector phenomenon"; that a healthy business climate and smooth functioning private markets are the keys to economic well-being (National Association of State Development Agencies 1983, 4). As Vincent Tese, New York State's director of economic development put it in presenting that state's strategic plan, "It is axiomatic that the private sector is the engine that drives New York's economy. Government can clear the roadblocks, it can help steer, and occasionally it can provide an infusion of fuel" (1985, 3). Reliance on the private market and a good business climate, however, are insufficient means of promoting economic development that meets states' basic economic needs: good jobs and increased opportunities for those left out of the economic mainstream. It is precisely this market orientation that limits even the most promising recent state initiatives in economic development.

Conventional State Economic Development: Public Incentives for Business Development

The goal of conventional state economic development policy is simple: to increase business activity in the state by using public policy to lower the costs of doing business, thereby increasing business profits. State governments offer billions of dollars in programs to attract, retain, or expand business activity. While the list of state incentives to business has grown long in the 1980s, the National Association of State Development Agencies outlines the following main "techniques and tools of state economic development":

Financial Incentives
Grants
Loans
Interest subsidies
Equity and near-equity financing

Tax Incentives
Nonfinancial Assistance
Business consulting (i.e. market studies, site selection, etc.)
Research and development
Licensing, regulation, and permitting
Job training
Specialty services
Improvement of the Business Environment
Physical environment (i.e. public infrastructure, land banking).
Business councils and economic development corporations (1983, 9).

States have typically deployed these tools in two main ways. First, as the Saturn case graphically illustrates, states have attempted to attract footloose capital by offering incentives packages: the quintessential smokestack chasing strategy. Desperate for any investment and the promise of jobs, states assemble the most attractive bundle of incentives to lure new plants: Volkswagen, Honda, Toyota, and American Motors have been among the more celebrated corporate beneficiaries of the bidding war approach to economic development.[2] Mobile corporations, explicitly or implicitly, encourage states to bid against one another; therefore, virtually all states have "marketing agencies," whose purpose is to "sell" the state to mobile capital as a place to locate its operations. These state marketing battles are frenzied and generally unconnected to any long-term state development strategy. As Michael Peltz points out, the incentives packaged to attract investment are "offered in a fairly indiscriminate fashion; that is, they are not generally targeted to firms in any particular sector, nor are they generally restricted to firms located or moving into economically distressed areas" (1983, 6).

Second, states have used these tools to nurture an economic environment conducive to entrepreneurial activity and business growth. Low-interest loans to lower the cost of capital are offered to businesses considering expansion; venture-capital loans and subsidies are available for risky, new business operations; job training subsidies are available to industries considering modernization and expansion; export-promotion programs assist in marketing the products of businesses located in the state; and technical assistance, state-supported business "incubators," and capital subsidies are offered to small businesses in the process of starting up or expanding.

Reorienting state public policy in a pro-business direction has also been a central aspect of conventional approaches to economic development. Since the 1970s the politicized business community has repeated its now familiar refrain: state spending on social programs discourages business investment; state taxes are too high for business growth; state wages are too high for business competitiveness; and state regulations too burdensome for business efficiency. States have responded by fundamentally restructuring state budgets in a manner similar to Reaganomics at the national level: slashes in social spending to compensate for deep reductions in taxes for business and the wealthy; greater "flexibility" in state regulation of business; and efforts to restrain wages.

Pro-business budgetary policies are defended in two ways. First, they are viewed as an important symbol to business that the state is sympathetic to business interests and thus a good place to invest. Second, in a quintessential expression of supply-side state economics, such budgetary policies are considered a means of providing more capital for business to invest and reducing "inefficient" government intrusion in the marketplace, allegedly the keys to economic development.

Beyond Incentives: Strategic Planning and the Beginnings of State Industrial Policy

All states, in one form or another, pursue the good business climate approach to economic development. No sane governor is willing to risk capital flight, and virtually all believe it is politically essential to participate in bidding wars for business investment. All states offer at least some business development incentives, and most have restructured their tax and budgetary policies along the lines of the business community's agenda.

Some states, however, have begun approaching economic development from the premise that investment incentives and a good business climate are necessary but *not sufficient* conditions for success. In states such as Massachusetts, Michigan, Rhode Island, New York, and Wisconsin attempts have been made to develop strategic plans that coordinate public and private resources in an effort to maximize a given state's "competitive advantage."

Strategic planning became a vogue in the private sector in the 1970s as a means of helping corporations cope with a turbulent and changing competitive environment (Porter 1980; 1985; Ansoff 1979). The strategic planning process generally involves six elements:

1. Mission statement: identification of the overriding purpose of the organization;

2. Goals identification: specific goals flowing from mission statement;

3. Environmental scan: identification of key external trends—challenges and opportunities—and their implications for the organization and its goals;

4. Resource audit: evaluation of the internal strengths and weaknesses of the organization;

5. Strategy development: formulation of policy, based on the "match" between internal strengths and weaknesses, and environmental challenges and opportunities;

6. Implementation: choice of specific organization and tactics for executing strategy.

Strategic planning offered a method by which to integrate coherently all elements of organizational planning in the organization's ultimate goals, or "mission." In the extraordinarily volatile competitive environment that emerged in the 1970s—new technologies, rapidly changing market conditions, the emergence of global competition—the emphasis in strategic planning on "matching" internal strengths and weaknesses with external threats and opportunities proved attractive to corporations attempting to fulfill their basic "mission": maximizing profits. Strategic planning became enormously popular as a dynamic means of continuously repositioning corporations in a constantly changing competitive environment.

State governments were drawn to strategic planning for the same reasons as corporations: in a rapidly shifting economic environment, strategic planning offered a method through which states could rationally deploy state resources to meet economic threats and exploit economic opportunities (National Council for Urban Economic Development 1984). Underlying state strategic planning was the assumption that the state, like the private corporation, was a "unitary" organization with consensual goals. For the corporation the mission is profit maximization; for the state it is increased investment and jobs. In the manner that, say, GM would use strategic planning to improve its market position vis-à-vis Toyota, Michigan, to take one example, began to think strategically about a) *who* constituted the competition—other Great Lakes states, Massachusetts, Japan, etc.; and b) *how* the state's public and private resources could best be coordinated to maximize its competitive advantage in the investment marketplace.

The strategic plans that have emerged thus far—and the processes that have produced them—have varied from state to state. Nevertheless, there are certain common assumptions in state strategic planning efforts.

1. State policy tools should be coordinated to create a pro-entrepreneurial, pro-investment, pro-business climate. New York's plan discussed "reducing the public burden placed on business" (Tese 1985, 34), while Wisconsin's plan, after delineating business assistance programs the state should pursue, called for state government to "streamline the regulatory process . . . and continue to strive to create a tax and spending climate conducive to economic development" (Wisconsin Strategic Development Commission 1985, 10–11).

2. Although "economic growth is generated from the private sector," to quote New York's planning document, the state can play a vital role in facilitating the rebuilding of salvageable older industries and encouraging the development of new industries (Tese 1985, 33). In particular, most strategic plans propose new financing institutions to help "mature" industries modernize and "emerging" industries flourish. Massachusetts is the leader in this regard, with six state development banks controlling over $3.5 billion for various financing purposes

(Barbe and Sekera 1983, 12–40). New York has proposed an Industrial Development Bank to provide "long-term capital for traditional manufacturing firms in New York that are willing to commit themselves to retooling and the development of new products," as well as a number of less grandiose financing mechanisms (Tese 1985, 36–38).

3. Strategic plans should include a heavy emphasis on investments in human capital and university-based research. Drawing heavily on Robert Reich's argument that flexible workforces and innovative work environments are *the* crucial competitive advantages in the new global economy, states such as New York, North Carolina, and Michigan have all emphasized support for higher education as well as extensive workforce skills development programs as crucial components of their economic development strategies (1983, 229–55; Goldstein and Bergman 1986). The Michigan plan argues that "getting poor"—bringing wages in line with competitor states and nations—is an inadequate strategy, a formula for declining living standards; the plan also rejects "quick fixes," such as elaborate investment incentives, and is critical of strategies relying on high-tech or service jobs. Instead, Michigan's planners propose "getting smart": "replacing the standardized mass production of familiar products, in which we can no longer compete unless we get poor, with competitive new products and processes that require skilled labor." Quoting Reich, the Michigan plan concludes that "getting smart" is a hedge against future deindustrialization: "production processes that rely on human skills must remain where the skilled people are" (Task Force for a Long-Term Economic Strategy 1984, 44–60).

4. Almost all state strategic plans include "targeting" as an explicit component. Conventional economic development uses incentives to leverage private investment, assuming that the precise allocation of that investment is most efficiently determined by the market. In contrast, public sector strategic planning seeks to target development, either by sector or geographic location. All plans seek to direct development resources toward "emerging" or "growth" industries: typically, these include robotics, new materials production, biotechnology, fiber optics, and computers. Many plans focus development tools on creating "good jobs," not simply low-wage jobs that certain businesses may provide (Rhode Island Strategic Development Commission 1983, 12; Mier, Moe, and Sherr 1986). Finally, some states—Massachusetts is again the trend-setter—have used economic development tools to channel investment into distressed areas of the state (Barbe and Sekera 1983, 37–41). The idea here, of course, is that an important role of state government is to compensate for the inadequacies of normal market processes in creating economic opportunities for those in greatest need.

5. Finally, all strategic planning efforts to date have been based on a "corporatist" policy-making model. Rational economic development policy is presumed to flow from a business-government-labor bargaining process, in which key constituencies are represented. Tripartite strategic planning councils or their

equivalents have been established or proposed in a number of states as a means of institutionalizing this "cooperation" process.

Most strategic plans have evolved over time, mainly through public-private commissions appointed by governors seeking to demonstrate their concern about economic development. However, in 1984 the citizens of Rhode Island had the opportunity to vote on a comprehensive strategic development plan. The Rhode Island plan—called the "Greenhouse Compact"—included all the basic elements of state strategic plans: targeted subsidies for industry modernization and development; education and training programs; and new capital instruments to encourage investment. The Compact brought together the state's business, government, and labor leaders in a tripartite consensus approach to economic policy, and the plan was endorsed by virtually every prominent leader in the state (Silver and Burton 1986).

However, groups locked out of this policy-making process, such as welfare recipients, opposed the Compact. In addition, this "neo-liberal" approach to economic policy came under fire from conservative businessmen and economists, who argued that the Compact's architects were undermining the efficiency of the "free market" by imposing "government planning."

In May 1984 the Rhode Island electorate voted down the Compact by a margin of four to one. Subsequent polling revealed that the tripartite planning process that produced the Greenhouse Compact "was viewed as an anti-democratic conspiracy of the state's most powerful interests who were seeking private gain at public expense." Ironically, the same survey indicated that "a substantial majority of those who voted against the Compact believe that government should take a leading role in improving a state's economy. They agreed with the idea that Rhode Island's economy is worse than that of other states, that it can be improved by careful planning, and that state government should take the initiative" (Carroll, Hyde, and Hudson 1985, 110–12).

Opponents of economic planning have touted the Rhode Island case as an example of how and why planning is opposed by most Americans. In fact, what seems clear is that "corporatist" planning elicits strong opposition, but a more democratic approach to planning may generate wide support.

*The Limits of Current State Economic Development
Policy*

The flaws of conventional state economic development policies have been well documented (Peltz 1983; Harrison and Kanter 1978; Goodman 1979). At root, conventional approaches confuse *economic* development—strategies to create good jobs and improve living standards—with *business* development—strategies to increase business activity, mainly by cutting the costs of doing business. Increased investment or business growth may or may not result in quality employment opportunities, and, given the typical criteria for business location decisions, the market is unlikely—without government intervention—to direct such investments to distressed geographic areas most in need of increased business activity. Untargeted business incentives offer few clear public benefits and represent a significant "opportunity cost" of resources that could be directed toward pressing social needs. Moreover, since such incentives are easily duplicated, no lasting competitive advantage accrues to any particular state offering them.

The good business climate underpinnings of conventional economic development are also deeply flawed. Reducing the social wage to encourage business investment is simply a strategy for reducing living standards. State-level versions of supply-side economics are as flawed as the federal model; there simply is no evidence to suggest that spending cuts and tax reductions stimulate economic development. For example, between 1981 and 1985 the ten states with the highest rates of economic growth ranked, on average, *higher* in rates of spending increase than the ten slowest growing states.[3] Finally, to the extent that good business climate budgetary policies stimulate short-term growth, the evidence is overwhelming that the chief beneficiaries have not been those in the greatest economic need. As a recent review of Wisconsin's economic development trends puts it, "State business climate warms as standard of living declines" (Norman 1986).

In contrast to conventional planning, strategic planning represents a promising departure. Virtually all such state plans recognize the limitations of "unfettered markets." As the Greenhouse Compact puts it,

> a. The Commission strongly believes . . . that measures which improve the state's business climate will not by themselves be sufficient to turn around the state's economy. . . . A more activist policy stands a chance of accelerating the process of wealth creation. . . .
>
> b. The public goals of economic development—job creation and increasing real incomes—are . . . not completely coincident with private profit motives. For example, business can increase profitability by either cutting wages or improving productivity. The effect of the latter strategy is far more positive to society than the former, and should be encouraged by economic development programs (Rhode Island Strategic Development Commission 1983, 11).

As noted earlier, Michigan's planners explicitly rejected the "getting poor" strategy of encouraging investment, while New York's plan clearly states: "New York will not follow the lead of some states who [sic] attempt to stimulate their economic development by keeping wage rates low, benefits few, and state social services minimal. The wages and benefits enjoyed by New York's workers were hard won" (Tese 1985, 36).

In short, most strategic plans include a number of positive economic development trends: targeting; attention to issues of equity; concentration on public returns on economic development investments rather than simply underwriting business profits and hoping for the best; and planning to maximize the effectiveness of state economic policy in creating good jobs.

However, even this more sophisticated approach to state economic development is limited. Strategic planning is still overly dependent on the private accumulation process, with all of its distributional inequities and social inefficiencies, as the engine of economic development. One plan explicitly maintains that "states can never conduct a comprehensive industrial policy that makes broad, strategic allocation decisions affecting industrial development" (Task Force for a Long-Term Economic Strategy 1984, 73). Public enterprise is a virtually forbidden option. As long as the state is seen more as a "catalyst" in an essentially sound market system than as a crucial element in surmounting market failure, even the most sophisticated and well intentioned strategic planning ventures will fail to alleviate fundamental economic problems.

Typical state strategic planning, as the voters of Rhode Island correctly perceived, is flawed by an anti-democratic, technocratic policy-making *process*. Planning commissions are often dominated by economic elites. Rarely is there a structured process in which counter-plans, presented by a wide variety of community groups, can make their way on to the strategic planning agenda. Strategic planning is based on the assumptions that a unitary state interest exists, that improving a state's competitive advantage will benefit everyone, and that an explicitly depoliticized planning process that excludes noisy "special interests" is appropriate.

How states improve their competitive position makes a significant difference in *who* benefits from competitiveness strategies. Depoliticized, insulated strategic planning is more likely to be dominated by powerful economic interests than those in the greatest economic need. In short, until the scope of state action and the means for public participation in the process are expanded, the promise of strategic planning as a tool of state economic development will remain unfulfilled.

Rethinking Economic Development: Toward Democratic and Strategic Planning in State and Local Government

Clearly, the time has come for a fundamental reorientation of state and local economic development policy. Since the early 1970s a mobilized business community has succeeded in defining economic development as state support for business activity and the economic development role of state and local government as that of an "ombudsman" for business. The result is that state action has been strictly circumscribed by the notion that the main function of state planning is to aid in the essentially efficient workings of private markets.

Genuine economic development, however, is not simply business growth; it is "the process by which members of a society improve their material and social conditions over time" (Barbe and Sekera 1983, 4). Ultimately, economic development is not about making deals or leveraging investment; it is about creating quality jobs, improving living standards, and increasing the capacity of community residents to be economically self-sufficient. Viewed from this angle, the conventional approach to economic development has been an obvious failure. Only activist state and city governments, reflecting communities' priorities determined in open and democratic policy-making bodies, can engage in the targeted, strategic planning necessary to meet their basic economic development needs.

What would such a restructured state and city government role in economic development look like? While it would be presumptuous to offer a rigid blueprint, applicable to all local settings, we can sketch the broad outlines of a *genuinely strategic*, democratic approach to state and local economic development.

Local governments must take a more active role in economic planning. As Jeff Faux points out, in this country the economy is "the only significant organized human activity where planning ahead is considered irrational" (1983, 447). While local economies will always remain a mix of plan and market, the structural flaws of the private accumulation process—in which the allocation of investment based on private profit calculations ignores the social costs and benefits of alternative investment decisions—necessitate a more directed public planning process.

Public planning, of course, does not automatically result in either rational policies or programs that benefit those in the greatest need. As Richard Fogelsong indicates, the urban planning profession has historically "served to identify, organize, and legitimate the interests of capital in the sphere of urban development" (1986, 6). While some recent state initiatives in strategic planning seem to represent a promise to transcend the limits of corporate-dominated markets, much of what passes for strategic planning is simply the mobilization of public resources to assist capital in one jurisdiction to compete against capital in another.

Nevertheless, when driven by considerations of equity and an understanding of the need for government action to rectify the defects of private markets, local planning can function in the public interest. As Pierre Clavel documents, several cities in the 1970s established progressive planning processes in which local planners, working closely with community groups, delineated *public* economic priorities and then initiated economic development projects targeted to meet the community's basic needs. Using a wide variety of public tools—public investment, development agreements, job training programs—cities such as Hartford, Santa Monica, and Cleveland were able to reorient local planning efforts from "working out the details" over real estate and development deals toward meeting basic economic development needs directly (Clavel 1985; Krumholz 1982).

Effective economic planning by states and cities must build on the promise of current efforts in public-sector strategic planning. According to Robert Mier, Kari Moe, and Irene Sherr, "Planners must identify economic sectors that have promise for providing high-quality, lasting employment locally or in the region. They must determine which opportunities within those sectors can be influenced by local government and direct available resources to them" (1986, 306). If the goal of economic development is to create expanded economic opportunities for local residents, and not merely to nurture a "competitive advantage" over other jurisdictions, then states and cities must use *all* of the tools available to them in pursuit of public goals. Such tools may include public investment, equity holdings in development projects, development agreements assuring public benefits in return for public assistance to private developers, and the selective targeting of public development incentives based on criteria such as equity and whether such activity results in balanced, sustainable economic growth.

The essence of effective strategic planning is the systematic matching of internal strengths and weaknesses with environmental threats and opportunities, with an eye on the basic mission of the institution. Unless states and cities engage in such a systematic matching process, with the mission clearly defined as the creation of high quality, lasting employment, then whatever plans emerge from public-sector strategic planning exercises will not be genuinely strategic and will fall short of meeting the basic economic development needs of communities. Unfortunately, even the most advanced public-sector strategic planning efforts have been constrained by limited notions of the appropriate scope of state action.

There are several examples of such progressive strategic planning in action. The "London Industrial Strategy," developed in 1985 by the Greater London Council, is designed to coordinate strategically public resources to revitalize that deindustrializing city. The plan does not attempt to "repeal laws of value" or use government in a futile effort to resist market-driven economic restructuring. It does substitute social criteria for market criteria in public investment decisions, seeking to use public resources to help restructure the city economy in a way that benefits workers and the community at large. The London strategy targets growth and high "value-added" sectors for public support, is geared toward generating quality employment, and proposes that the city government "take a positive lead in developing industrial investment strategies via an element of municipal ownership and control . . . rather than simply by providing infrastructure and support services or providing assistance to firms in an indiscriminate and 'hands off' manner" (Eisenschitz and North 1986, 422).

Chicago's 1984 development plan, entitled "Chicago Works Together," is one of the clearest examples of an American city trying to harness economic development for its disadvantaged residents. The Chicago strategic plan has five goals.

1   increase job opportunities for Chicagoans;
2   promote balanced growth between downtown and neighborhoods;
3   assist neighborhood development through partnerships and coordinated investment;

4 enhance public participation in development decision-making;

5 pursue a regional, state, and national legislative agenda

The mission of Chicago's plan is clear: strategically to allocate city resources to ensure that the benefits of development accrue to "citizens, businesses, and neighborhoods with demonstrated need." Included in the Chicago plan are such policies as:

a. sectorally and areally *targeted* investment in support of high quality, lasting job creation;

b. local preference in city purchases and hiring;

c. "linkage" policies to promote balanced development between downtown and the neighborhoods;

d. city infrastructure and job training expenditures *coordinated* with the overall strategic development objectives.

As Dennis Judd and Randy Ready point out, Chicago's strategy represents a "frontal assault" on conventional economic development; "it presumes that city government can stimulate an alternative model of economic growth, by sowing seed money for economic development projects in neighborhoods, by involving neighborhoods and small businesses in economic planning, and by using the city government's own purchases to generate business for small and minority-owned firms" (1986, 236–7).

At the state level Massachusetts has moved the furthest from crude smoke-stack chasing toward ongoing, public-sector strategic planning in economic development. Under Governor Michael Dukakis in the 1970s and 1980s Massachusetts has put into place a number of industrial policy tools: capital funds for developing distressed areas; planning councils and public capital to nurture and resuscitate older manufacturing industries; support for community-based economic development; risk capital for new product and technology development; strategic public investments; and human resources policies coordinated with state economic planning (Peirce 1985b). There is a strong neo-liberal, growth ideology flavor to much of Massachusetts' approach, and it is unclear how much public influence exists over investment priorities. Moreover, a number of fortuitous circumstances—the high-tech boom, Massachusetts' unique higher education advantages, a surge of federal defense spending in the region—can arguably be credited with Massachusetts' recent economic success, instead of the efficacy of state industrial policy. Nevertheless, the Massachusetts case does reveal the degree to which state government can actively engage in economic planning, instead of functioning as a passive dispenser of incentives to the private sector. Given the traditional approach to economic development found in most states, the Massachusetts example represents a good intermediate step on the road to genuinely strategic state economic planning.

Establishing active public planning processes will also make it possible to develop genuine public-private partnerships. As I have argued, states and cities today merely provide public benefits for private investors and call such arrangements "partnerships." An activist state, however, can establish public priorities and then, in negotiation with appropriate private-sector interests, work out suitable joint ventures, public-private collaboration, and an equitable sharing of development benefits and burdens—all within the context of the jurisdiction's overall strategic plan (Carnoy, Shearer, Rumberger 1983, 199–214).

The recent adoption of "linkage" policies in several cities is an encouraging example of genuine partnership activity. In return for lucrative development rights, primarily in downtown service centers, some cities require investors to contribute to special funds to meet community needs. In San Francisco, for example, downtown office developers above fifty-thousand square feet of floor space are required to contribute to funds for housing, public transportation, and child-care. Boston similarly requires downtown developers to underwrite low- and moderate-income housing, and Mayor Flynn has suggested using linkage funds for job training. Chicago's plan (still not enacted) encourages downtown developers to increase purchasing from local suppliers, provide technical assistance to neighborhood ventures, directly invest in neighborhoods, or contribute to a trust fund earmarked for neighborhood economic development (Porter 1985; Keating 1986; Chicago 1984).

While linkage policies are not a panacea for the uneven growth typical of urban corporate centers (booming downtowns coupled with deteriorating neighborhoods), they do at least provide a way for the public to benefit from market trends. Perhaps even more importantly, linkage inscribes in government policy the notion that unregulated markets are not necessarily in the public interest, and that there are crucial *public* concerns involved in the allocation of private investment in the community.

The *politics* of state and local economic development planning is as important as the details of strategic plans themselves. As noted earlier, the quasi-public entities that are now so integral to local economic development are purposefully insulated from public access; they exist to consummate deals not to develop strategic plans. In addition, as the case of Rhode Island's ill-fated Greenhouse Compact reveals, corporatist strategic planning lacks the "legitimacy and cooperation it requires to succeed" (Silver and Burton 1986, 287).

New institutional arrangements are required to democratize local economic development planning. Again, the Chicago plan provides a useful, concrete example of what such arrangements might look like. "Enhanced public participation in decision-making" is an explicit goal of Chicago's strategic plan:

> Successful neighborhood planning cannot be a "top-down" process. It must be based on an awareness that neighborhood problems and assets are best known to neighborhood residents and the local organizations devoted to the betterment of their areas. Neighborhood organizations are in the best position to assess

neighborhood needs, establish development priorities, and design workable solutions. (14)

Thus, the Chicago plan includes a number of mechanisms to enhance decentralized planning capacities and encourage wider participation in municipal decision-making. These mechanisms include funding for neighborhood organizations that engage in strategic planning and deliver development services, public workshops on city resource allocation to enhance citizen input into such decisions, and increased public access to information necessary for informed decision-making.

The institutional innovations needed to democratize the political process of economic development will vary from jurisdiction to jurisdiction; Chicago's proposals are just one way of attacking the problem. Community economic development corporations, supported by both state governments and private foundations, may be another useful mechanism for empowering low-income communities to improve their economic opportunities, although their record so far has been rather uneven (Barbe and Sekera 1983; Duncan 1986). Public and private universities can also play important roles by working with community groups, providing "release time" for faculty to contribute their technical expertise to neighborhood planning efforts, and developing broad, interdisciplinary research enterprises directed toward "improving the quality of life" in their communities (Hackney 1986). Unfortunately, the involvement of universities in economic development tends to be exclusively in the areas of technology innovations, product development, and business consulting; opportunities to assist in neighborhood economic development and capacity-building are not a high university priority. They should be.

Democratizing the planning process and developing neighborhood planning capacities are essential for the formulation of economic development strategies that benefit the entire community rather than economic elites. Without the institutionalization of *democratic* planning mechanisms and the revitalization of local politics, state and local planning efforts will continue to be dominated by developers and corporate elites, and economic development policy will continue to serve the private, rather than the public interest.

States and cities are not free to make economic policy exactly as they please. Local economies are shaped by numerous factors not in the control of local governments: national fiscal and monetary policy, the investment decisions of multinational corporations, the position of American industry in a competitive global economy, to name just a few. Moreover, as progressives in Cleveland discovered, local policy-making is constrained by the very real problems of corporate power and mobility—the ability of capital to "go on strike" against jurisdictions perceived as anti-business—as well as the need for local governments to maintain access to conservative, pro-corporate credit markets (Swanstrom 1985). All of these factors suggest that progressive economic development at the state and local level requires the support of *national* level planning (of the sort suggested by Jeff Faux in Chapter 6) that helps manage the velocity of capital movements, provides adjustment and retooling assistance to jurisdictions with declining industries, and facilitates regional economic cooperation rather than "beggar thy neighbor" rivalries along the lines of the Saturn war.

Even within this constraint, there are clearly options that promise significantly greater public benefits than the conventional approach to state and local economic development. Instead of passively responding to the investment agenda of private elites, states and cities can strategically plan for quality jobs and lasting growth. Instead of bottling up economic decision-making in quasi-public bodies, new institutions can be established that facilitate bottom-up economic planning. The disastrous consequences of the Reagan-era incantation that "government is the source of all problems" are clear. The time for blind faith in market-based solutions is over.

In the early part of the twentieth century progressive states and cities showed that government could play a positive role in such areas as social welfare and labor policy, and the stage was set for the national reforms of the New Deal. Today, the opportunities are there for states and local governments again to show the way by developing the progressive, democratic, and strategic economic plans necessary to meet vital public needs and provide improved standards of living in communities across this country. Reinvigorating state enterprise at the local level may be the first step toward revitalizing the capacity of the federal government—so tattered by the policies of Ronald Reagan—to meet the basic social and economic problems facing this country in the years ahead.

NOTES

1.   I have borrowed extensively in this section from my analysis in Levine (1987).

2.   Big auto plants promising large numbers of jobs have obviously been the most alluring objects of state bidding wars, but thousands of smaller enterprises, ranging from sports franchises to meat packers have benefited from state government largesse. As this list suggests, hard-headed, strategic economic analysis is apparently absent from state participation in bidding wars. Wisconsin, for example, has bid as energetically for the quintessential loser, American Motors, as it did for the plant Toyota was peddling in 1985.

3.   Growth data—defined, in the absence of a state-level equivalent to GNP, as income from wages and proprietorships—were compiled by the Congressional Joint Economic Committee in its study (1986). State expenditure data were drawn, for 1980–83—the most recent available— from the U.S. Bureau of the Census (1986).

References

AFL-CIO. 1986. *Crossroads for America*. Washington, D.C.: AFL-CIO.
Ansoff, G. I. 1979. *Strategic management*. London: Macmillan.

Barbe, N., and J. Sekera. 1983. *States and communities: The challenge for economic action.* Washington, D.C.: National Congress for Community Economic Development.

Berry, B. 1985. Islands of renewal in seas of decay. Ed. P. E. Peterson. *The new urban reality.* Washington, D.C.: Brookings Institution.

Bluestone, B., and B. Harrison. 1982. *The deindustrialization of America: Plant closings, community abandonment, and the dismantling of basic industry.* New York: Basic Books.

———. 1986. *The great job machine: The proliferation of low-wage employment in the U.S. economy.* Washington, D.C.: Joint Economic Committee.

Blumenthal, S. 1986. *The rise of the counterestablishment: From conservative ideology to political power.* New York: Basic Books.

Borden, A. 1986. G.M. comes to Spring Hill: Hidden costs. *The Nation* 21 June.

Business Week. 1986. The hollow corporation. 3 March.

Carnoy, M., D. Shearer, and R. Rumberger. 1983. *A new social contract: The economy and government after Reagan.* New York: Harper and Row.

Carroll, J., M. Hyde, and W. Hudson. 1985. Economic development policy: Why Rhode Islanders rejected the greenhouse compact. *State Government* 58:110–12.

Chicago, City of. 1984. *Chicago works together.* Chicago: City of Chicago.

Clavel, P. 1985. *The progressive city: Planning and participation, 1969–1984.* New Brunswick: Rutgers University Press.

Committee for Economic Development. 1982. *Public-private partnership: An opportunity for urban communities.* N.Y.: CED.

Congress of the United States, Office of Technology Assessment. 1986. *Technology and structural unemployment: Reemploying displaced adults.* Washington, D.C.: Government Printing Office.

Data Resources, Inc. 1983. *Report on U.S. manufacturing industries.* Washington, D.C.: DRI, Inc.

Duncan, W. 1986. An economic development strategy. *Social Policy* (Spring):17–24.

Edsall, T. B. 1984. *The new politics of inequality.* New York: W. W. Norton and Company.

Eisenschitz, A., and D. North. 1986. The London industrial strategy: Socialist transformation or modernising capitalism. *International Journal of Urban and Regional Research* 10(3):423–48.

Epstein, N. 1987. It works, but don't call it industrial policy. *Washington Post National Weekly Edition* 12 January.

Fainstein, S. S. et al. 1983. *Restructuring the city: The political economy of urban redevelopment.* New York: Longman.

Faux, J. 1983. Who plans. Ed. M. Green. *The big business reader.* New York: Pilgrim Press.

Fogelsong, R. 1986. *Planning the capitalist city: The colonial era to the 1920s.* Princeton: Princeton University Press.

Fossett, J. W., and R. P. Nathan. 1981. The prospects for urban revival. Ed. R. Bahl. *Urban government finance: Emerging trends.* Beverly Hills, CA: Sage Publications.

Frieden, B., and L. Sagalyn. 1986. Downtown shopping malls and the new public-private strategy. Eds. M. Kaplan and P. Cuciti. *The great society and its legacy: Twenty years of U.S. social policy.* Durham: Duke University Press.

Ganz, A. 1986. Where has the urban crisis gone? How Boston and other large cities stemmed economic decline. Ed. M. Gottdiener. *Cities in stress.* Beverly Hills, CA: Sage Publications.

Glaab, C. N., and A. T. Brown. 1983. *A history of urban America.* New York: Macmillan.

Glastris, P. 1985. The governors' bidding war: What goods for G. M. *The New Republic* 1 April.

Goldstein, H. A. 1986. The state and local industrial policy question. *Journal of the American Planning Association* 52(3):262–64.

———, and E. M. Bergman. 1986. Institutional arrangements for state and local industrial policy. *The Journal of the American Planning Association* 52(3):265–76.

Goodman, R. 1979. *The last entrepreneurs.* Boston: South End Press.

Gunts, E. 1985a. Rouse projects stand out as symbol of rejuvenation of U.S. downtowns. *The Baltimore Sun* 26 May.

————. 1985b. Rouse works with cities as partners—or not at all. *The Baltimore Sun* 27 May.

Hackney, S. 1986. The university and its community: Past and present. *The Annals of the American Academy of Political and Social Science* 488(November):183–201.

Harrison, B., and S. Kanter. 1978. The political economy of states' job creation incentives. *The Journal of the American Institute of Planners* 44(4):424–35.

Hartman, C. 1984. *The transformation of San Francisco.* Totowa, N.J.: Rowman and Allanheld.

Hartz, L. 1948. *Economic policy and democratic thought: Pennsylvania, 1776–1860.* Cambridge: Harvard University Press.

Herbers, J. 1986. New jobs in cities little aid to poor. *The New York Times* 22 October.

Hill, R. C. 1983. Crisis in the motor city: The politics of economic development in Detroit. Eds. S. Fainstein et. al. *Restructuring the city: The political economy of urban redevelopment.* New York: Longman.

Holusha, J. 1986. G.M. cuts estimates for saturn. *The New York Times* 3 October.

James, F. 1984. Urban economic development: A zero-sum game? Eds. R. Bingham and J. Blair. *Urban economic development.* Beverly Hills, CA: Sage Publications.

Joint Economic Committee, U.S. Congress. 1986. *The bicoastal economy.* Washington, D.C.: Joint Economic Committee.

Judd, D. R. 1984. *The politics of American cities: Private power and public policy.* Boston: Little, Brown, and Company.

————, and R. Ready. 1986. Entrepreneurial cities and the new politics of economic development. Eds. G. Peterson and C. Lewis. *Reagan and the cities.* Washington, D.C.: Urban Institute Press.

Kasarda, J. D. 1982. Symposium: The state of the nation's cities. *Urban Affairs Quarterly* 18(2):163–86.

————. 1985. Urban change and minority opportunities. Ed. P. E. Peterson. *The new urban reality.* Washington, D.C.: Brookings Institution.

Keating, W. D. 1986. Linking downtown development to broader community goals: An analysis of linkage policy in three cities. *Journal of the American Planning Association* (Spring):133–41.

Krumholz, N. 1982. A retrospective view of equity planning: Cleveland, 1969–1979. *Journal of the American Planning Association* (Spring):163–83.

Levine, M. V. 1986a. Downtown redevelopment and uneven growth: The political economy of the Baltimore renaissance. Paper presented at Annual Meeting of the Urban Affairs Association.

————. 1986b. Public-private partnerships and uneven development: Baltimore, 1950–1985. Paper presented at Annual Meeting of the American Political Science Association.

————. 1987. Downtown redevelopment as an urban growth strategy: A critical appraisal of the Baltimore renaissance. *Journal of Urban Affairs* In press.

Louv, R. 1983. *America II.* Los Angeles: J. P. Tarcher.

Lyall, K. 1982. A bicycle built for two: Public-private partnership in Baltimore. Eds. R. S. Fosler and R. Berger. *Public-private partnership in American cities.* Lexington, MA: D. C. Heath.

Mier, R., K. J. Moe, and I. Sherr. 1986. Strategic planning and the pursuit of reform, economic development, and equity. *Journal of the American Planning Association* 52(3):299–309.

Mollenkopf, J. 1983. *The contested city.* Princeton: Princeton University Press.

Molotch, H. 1976. The city as a growth machine: Towards a political economy of place. *American Journal of Sociology* 82 (2):309–30.

National Association of State Development Agencies. 1983. *Directory of incentives for business investment and development in the United States.* Washington, D.C.: The Urban Institute Press.

National Council on Urban Economic Development. 1978a. *Coordinated urban economic development: Development finance.* Washington, D.C.: National Council on Urban Economic Development.

————. 1978b. *Coordinated urban economic development: Public/private development institutions.* Washington, D.C.: National Council on Urban Economic Development.

———. 1984. *Competitive advantage: Framing a strategy to support high growth firms.* Washington, D.C.: National Council on Urban Economic Development.

Newsweek. 1985a. The ardent suitors for saturn 11 February.

———. 1985b. Saturn gets a launching pad 5 August.

New York Times. 1985a. States turn to tourism for new funds and jobs 16 August.

———. 1985b. A symposium: A city divided 20 January.

Norman, J. 1986. Progress at a price. *The Milwaukee Journal* 16 February.

Peirce, N., R. Guskind, and J. Gardner. 1983. Politics is not the only thing that is changing America's big cities. *National Journal* 26 November.

Peirce, N. 1985a. Smokestack chasing and lady luck economics. *National Journal* 27 April.

———. 1985b. Massachusetts, after going from rags to riches, looks to spread the wealth. *National Journal* 25 May.

Peltz, M. 1983. *State legislation for community economic development.* Berkeley: National Economic Development and Law Center.

Peterson, P. E. 1981. *City limits.* Chicago: University of Chicago Press.

Porter, D. 1985. *Downtown linkages.* Washington, D.C.: Urban Land Institute.

Porter, M. E. 1980. *Competitive strategy: Techniques for analyzing industries and competition.* New York: Free Press.

———. 1985. *Competitive advantage: Creating and sustaining superior performance.* New York: Macmillan.

Prokesh, S. 1986. General motors to shut 11 plants; 29,000 workers will be affected. *The New York Times* 7 November.

Reich, R. B. 1983. *The next American frontier.* New York: Times Books.

Rhode Island Strategic Development Commission. 1983. *The greenhouse compact.* Providence: R.I. Strategic Development Commission.

Schoolman, M. 1986. Solving the dilemma of statesmanship: Reindustrialization through an evolving democratic plan. Eds. Schoolman and A. Magid. *Reindustrializing New York state: Strategies, implications, challenges.* Albany: State University of New York Press.

Shaiken, H. 1985. *Work transformed: Automation and labor in the computer age.* New York: Holt, Rinehart, and Winston.

Shefter, M. 1985. *Political crisis/fiscal crisis: The collapse and revival of New York City.* New York: Basic Books.

Silver, H., and D. Burton. 1986. The politics of state-level industrial policy. *Journal of the American Planning Association* 52(3):276–89.

Smith, C. F. 1980a. Two trustees and a $100 million 'bank' skirt restrictions of city government. *The Baltimore Sun* 13 April.

———. 1980b. Baltimore's trustees playing high finance on a tightrope. *The Baltimore Sun* 14 April.

———. 1985. City's 2 trustees made secret pact. *The Baltimore Sun* 22 December.

———. 1986. Trustee process was controversial within small circle. *The Baltimore Sun* 16 March.

Stanback, T., and T. Noyelle. 1982. *Cities in transition.* Totowa, N.J.: Allanheld-Osmun.

Stevens, W. K. 1985. Philadelphia takes on a new identity. *The New York Times* 24 November.

Stewman, S., and J. A. Tarr. 1982. Four decades of public-private partnerships in Pittsburgh. Eds. R. S. Fosler and R. A. Berger. *Public-private partnership in American cities.* Lexington, MA: D. C. Heath.

Swanstrom, T. 1985. *The crisis of growth politics: Cleveland, Kucinich, and the challenge of urban populism.* Philadelphia: Temple University Press.

———. 1986. Strategic planning for cities: Problems and possibilities. Paper presented at the Annual Meeting of the Urban Affairs Association.

Tabb, W. 1982. *The long default: New York City and the urban fiscal crisis.* New York: Monthly Review Press.

Task Force for a Long-Term Economic Strategy for Michigan. 1984. *The path to prosperity.*

Tese, V. 1985. *Rebuilding New York: The next phase. From recovery to resurgence: A strategic plan for expanding economic and job development in New York state.* State of New York, Department of Economic Development.

U.S. Bureau of the Census. 1986. *State and metropolitan area data book 1986.* Washington, D.C.: Government Printing Office.

———. 1972. *County and City Data Book.* Washington, D.C.: Government Printing Office.

U.S. Conference of Mayors. 1984. *The Baltimore city loan and guarantee program: A trustee system.* Washington, D.C.: U.S. Conference of Mayors.

U.S. House of Representatives, Committee on Energy and Commerce. 1983. *The United States in a changing world economy: The case for an integrated domestic and international commercial policy.* Washington, D.C.: Government Printing Office.

Wisconsin Strategic Development Commission. 1985. *The final report.* Madison, WI: Strategic Development Commission.

Zevin, R. 1977. New York City crisis: First act in a new age of reaction. Eds. R. E. Alcaly and D. Mermelstein. *The fiscal crisis of American cities.* New York: Random House.

6   New Institutions for the Post-Reagan Economy

Jeff Faux

The United States has entered a new economic era marked by the rapid erosion of U.S. industrial dominance and greatly heightened international competition. While the world has changed dramatically, the ideological and institutional framework of U.S. economic policy has not. This discontinuity between the new realities and the old institutions has resulted, externally, in a deterioration of U.S. economic power and, internally, in a decline of U.S. living standards. This gap may also present an opportunity to gain political support for a credible progressive alternative that both addresses central economic issues and the political realities of late twentieth-century America.

Any such alternative must make expanding high-wage employment its central goal. In turn, expanding high-wage employment will require some new and more explicit forms of economic planning. The forms will have to be *new* because the existing structures of institutional governance are no longer adequate. They must be *explicit* because we can no longer afford the inefficiency of a system based on haphazard, ad hoc government intervention hidden from democratic scrutiny by laissez-faire ideology.

The Old Era

The old era began with World War II, which lifted the United States out of the Great Depression by generating a massive demand for industrial production and destroying the productive capacity of most of our foreign commercial rivals. The United States emerged from the war with most of the gold, the world's strongest currency, and most of the world's effective manufacturing capacity.

The question facing the architects of the post-war era was how to create enough purchasing power and investment to put Europe and Japan back on their feet and provide markets for U.S. goods. The answer was a set of Keynesian institutions and policies that nurtured expansion both at home and abroad. At the national level the progressive income tax, unemployment compensation, and other automatic stabilizers were built into economic policy to modulate the business cycle by using changes in government spending to offset changes in private demand. Targeting government spending built up public infrastructure and pulled a reluctant market into areas of national priority. The GI Bill and the National Defense Education Act, housing programs, expansion of Social Security benefits, Medicare, and a variety of anti-poverty programs reflected an understanding that the government was responsible for maintaining economic growth and increased opportunity, as well as providing a compassionate safety net. The National Aeronautic and Space Administration, the highway system, and a permanent high level of military spending further expanded the post-war boom.

The New International Economic Order

Internationally, the United States, which had retreated from world leadership after World War I, embraced its superpower status after World War II. The Bretton Woods agreement, the Marshall Plan, the General Agreement on Tariffs and Trade, the World Bank, and similar institutions all reflected the shift toward using U.S. post-war financial power to undergird a new international economic order. In order to solidify the global anti-communist alliance, the United States agreed to become the lender and the market of last resort for most of the non-communist world (Kindleberger 1985, 18, 19). American Keynesianism was a necessary condition of Pax Americana.

John Maynard Keynes's preferred a more social-minded context, including generous expansion of urban planning, rural development, and international economic coordination aimed at stabilizing trade and currency flows and balancing global growth. He would certainly not have chosen to concentrate such a large share of scientific and technical resources in the military sector. Still, by most historic standards, the new order was a success. The standard of living of the U.S. middle class rose dramatically, Europe and Japan were quickly rebuilt, and the development of the Third World was begun.

This very success transformed the global economy beyond the managerial capacity of post-war institutions. As the industries of Japan and Western Europe recovered, they began to nibble away at U.S. market supremacy. By 1960 Western Europe and Japan were capable of supplying most of their internal needs for manufacturing products. By 1970 they began to undercut the United States in world markets. By 1980 they were taking huge bites out of the U.S. domestic market.

The internationalization of capital was also transforming the global marketplace. Multinational corporations found that locating facilities around the world was as easy as moving them within a country. Goods, services, managers, and even workers moved across national boundaries with increasing frequency. U.S. corporations increasingly became, in a phrase used by *Business Week*, "hollow corporations." Design was farmed out to the Europeans, and production moved to the Far East. The job of the U.S. subsidiary was to slap a label on the product and sell it at home (Jonas et. al. 1986, 56).

By the mid-1980s the global economy had been transformed from a relatively stable, steadily expanding system dominated by the United States to an unstable, increasingly competitive system with no economy strong enough to provide either discipline or a safety net. In particular, the global extension of the multinational corporation has expanded productive capacity to the point where it is outrunning the system's ability to generate sufficient income and credit to clear the market. Excess capacity has been growing in industrial goods, commodities, and agricultural products. Markets are glutted not only in mature industries, such as autos, steel, and consumer electronics, but in many high-tech areas as well. As in the 1930s, this excess capacity has resulted in price-slashing, dumping, out-sourcing, and protectionism.

The expansion of supply occurred at the time that economic growth as a whole, and the consequent demand for goods, slowed down (see Table 6.1).

In the United States low growth has meant a lower demand for labor, the weakening of the union movement, and attacks on the welfare state. It has resulted in a lower standard of living for wage earners and their families. Real weekly wages in 1985 were 14 percent below the 1973 level. Over the same period real median family income dropped from $29,169 to $27,735 in 1985 dollars (U.S. Bureau of the Census 1984, 9, 33; 1985, 5; Bureau of Labor Statistics 1986, 79–81).

Low growth has also meant that income is distributed less equally. The share of income received by the lowest 40 percent of the income distribution curve dropped from 20 percent in 1967 to 15.7 percent in 1984. On the average, families in this category earned $470 less in real income in 1984 than they did in 1980. The share of income going to families in the middle 20 percent dropped from 17.9 in 1967 to 17 percent in 1984. On the other hand, the top 40 percent of families received 67.3 percent of all income in 1984, their highest share since 1947 (Joint Economic Committee 1986, 81).

Table 6.1. Average Annual Rates of Economic Growth, 1961–1985

	1961–1965	1966–1970	1971–1975	1976–1980	1981–1985
Developed Countries	5.2	4.8	3.7	3.2	2.4
United States	4.6	3.0	2.2	3.4	2.3
Canada	5.7	4.7	5.0	3.3	2.4
Japan	10.0	11.3	4.6	5.1	4.3
European Community	4.7	4.4	2.7	3.0	1.2
Developing Countries	6.3	6.7	7.0	5.6	1.8
Communist Countries	4.4	5.0	4.2	2.8	3.0

Source: Council of Economic Advisors 1987, 368

In order to maintain their living standards, consumers have had to squeeze savings—now near record-low percentages of income—and borrow heavily. The consumer debt-income ratio climbed to record levels in 1986, delinquent payments rose, and mortgage delinquencies increased. In the fall of 1986 the General Accounting Office reported that 43 percent of the country's savings and loan institutions were either insolvent or dangerously overextended (Berg 1986).

In the short run the expanding U.S. national debt has helped maintain domestic demand. The ballooning fiscal deficit was the major cause of recovery from the 1982 recession. The ensuing high U.S. dollar also opened up the U.S. market to outsiders, allowing foreign countries to sell off their mounting surplus production.

The United States has now reached the limit of its ability and willingness to absorb the world's exports. Despite its previous hostility to government interference in currency markets, the Reagan administration, in the winter of 1985–1986, permitted a swift drop in the dollar-yen ratio. The United States then attempted to convince Germany and Japan to grow faster in order to increase their imports of world goods. Neither country, however, is willing to assume the burden of responsibility for the world's growth.

The global market conflict is therefore likely to worsen. Debt among Third World countries already threatens to swamp the international banking system. In the less developed countries (LDCs) debt was 22 percent of total Gross Domestic Product in 1973. In 1983 it was 35 percent and rising. Debt in the developing world is growing much faster than either income or exports. In fact, many countries are servicing their debts by taking on more debts.

Efforts by the International Monetary Fund (IMF) to solve the debt problem through imposing austerity and forcing Third World countries to export more are in the long long run self-defeating, since they reduce demand even further and constrain the growth in global income. The result has been a drastic reduction in imports by Third World countries, while exports have continued to grow. This has added to the deterioration of the U.S. trade balance. Between 1981 and 1984 the U.S. trade balance with six Latin American countries alone worsened by $20 billion (Feketekuty 1985).

IMF "adjustment" policies have led to a 20 percent decline in per capita income in the Latin American debtor countries since 1980 (Epstein 1985, 641). In addition to austerity, the IMF has pressured Third World countries to dismantle much of their public sectors. Abuses and inefficiencies in these public sectors are of course not hard to find, but there is little evidence that "privatization" is the path to successful development. Indeed, the problem may be *too much* privatization. Latin American citizens are estimated to hold between $60 and $85 billion of liquid assets in U.S. banks (Koretz 1986). Part of the U.S. fiscal deficit is therefore being financed by investor classes in underdeveloped countries with funds skimmed from loans intended for their own countries' development.

The U.S. fiscal deficit would be small cause for concern if the United States were making investments in human and physical capital that would eventually increase productivity, incomes, and future tax revenues. But the fiscal deficit does not represent an investment in the future. We are not borrowing to improve public education, to raise the skill level of our workforce, to support researchers in making technological breakthroughs, or to encourage entrepreneurs to translate such breakthroughs to the market. We have been borrowing to pay for a military buildup and to support the shortfall in revenues resulting from inadequate rates of growth.

With its own markets under serious competitive pressure, the United States has for the last fifteen years been losing the ability to control its own internal economy with traditional Keynesian macroeconomic techniques. Thus, a sudden rise in the prices of oil and food, originating outside U.S. borders, sparked a second inflationary spiral in the late 1970s. By appointing and reappointing Paul Volcker to the chairmanship of the Federal Reserve, Presidents Carter and Reagan applied conventional responses to inflation—high interest rates and tight money. The result was a surprisingly severe recession, reflecting an unexpectedly weakened economy. Reagan then applied the conventional fiscal stimulus of deficit spending, which sparked a moderate recovery. Only a decade before a comparable deficit stimulus would have sparked a boom, creating full employment and generating sufficient revenues to reduce the deficit to a minor problem. By the early 1980s the United States' competitive position had deteriorated to such an extent that much of the new deficit-induced spending leaked out of the country. This has aggravated the trade deficit to a gigantic $170 billion in 1986.

Ironically, the Reagan program somewhat paralleled the French effort to reflate their economy in 1981. The difference between Reagan's apparent success and Mitterand's failure is found in the greater creditworthiness of the United States. So long as foreigners are willing to lend, the United States can cover its deficit without reigniting inflation.

Since we are not borrowing to invest in income-producing assets, there is obviously a limit to how far such a strategy can take us. In a few short years the United States has become the largest debtor nation in the world. Like anyone borrowing to cover operating expenses, the United States will eventually be unable to cover its mounting interest charges. At some point, our credit rating will drop and the bank lending windows will close. Then, finally, we will have to confront the reality of our own sluggish productivity.

For years the conventional wisdom held that slower U.S. productivity growth was not important because our rivals were simply "catching up." Analysis by Data Resources, Inc. shows that Japan and most of our Western European competitors are at or just below our overall level of productivity and that two of them—France and Germany—have passed us (Thurow 1985a, 22). Continuing along our current path will only guarantee more of the same.

A Full Employment Economy

Breaking out of our current stagnation will require making economic growth *and* full employment national goals. It is no accident that stagnant growth and a widening gap between rich and poor have appeared together. Economic growth is not a sufficient condition for fairness and equality, but in a modern, work-oriented society it is a necessary one. Full employment—the condition of there being a job available for everyone willing and able to work—is how most benefits of a high-growth society get distributed downward.

In theory it is possible to have full employment with a large number of low-paying jobs. But in practice high demand for labor raises all wage earners' income in advanced industrial countries—which is the reason corporate interests are ideologically opposed to full employment. Historically, times of full employment have been associated with improving income distribution.

In turn, full employment contributes to the productivity of the national economy in the following ways:

1. Full employment reduces the portion of the population that must be supported by those who are working. It increases public revenues and decreases public expenditures. This leaves more funds available for maintaining the incomes of those who are unable to work and for investment in human and physical capital, which further enhances national productivity.

2. Full employment and the associated high rates of capacity utilization and wages are constant incentives to private-sector expansion and the introduction of more efficient, labor-saving machinery.

3. Full employment reduces worker resistance to automation and changing technologies. The spectacular success of the Japanese economy is in large measure a result of the willingness of workers to accept and even encourage automation because they have a high degree of job security and receive the benefits of higher productivity.

4. Full employment maximizes opportunities for risk-taking and creative entrepreneurship.

5. By helping to equalize the distribution of income and wealth, full employment helps maintain the steady expansion of the domestic mass market for goods and services needed to keep factories running at high levels.

6. By creating more opportunities for victims of discrimination, full employment increases the pool of talent and creative skills available to the national economy.

Full employment is not simply a question of income; it has a *political* strategic importance as well. All of our experience shows that the overwhelming majority of Americans, on moral grounds as well as on the grounds of what makes sense for society, prefer a paycheck to a welfare check. Less consciously understood perhaps is the link between a high demand for labor and the personal experience of democracy. In a market economy, where money is power, personal dignity and freedom is at least partially a function of the value of one's labor. Where labor is scarce, employees retain a greater ability to tell their bosses to "take this job and shove it," thus restricting the arbitrary authority of management.

The democratic implications of high demand for labor extend to the community as well. Cities and rural areas of high unemployment are forced to make tax, environmental, and other concessions to attract business investment. Political leaders in prosperous areas are much freer to pursue public purposes beyond the mercantile agenda.

For several decades the Democratic Party's identification with full employment was the backbone of its strength at the polls. Full employment, however, was abandoned after 1976 by the increasingly conservative politics that gave us the Carter presidency. There remains a popular assumption that Jimmy Carter lost the presidency because of liberal policies that no longer appealed to the U.S. public. Yet the evidence indicates that the problem was not his liberal sentiments, but his conservative policies. Polls taken as people left the voting booths in November 1980 showed that the issues uppermost in their minds were inflation, unemployment, and foreign policy—in that order. (Foreign policy ranked third even as hostages were being held in Iran.)

Carter's inflation problem was a direct result of the huge jump in oil prices between early 1979 and Election Day. The energy price increase, along with a sudden jump in the world price of grain, rapidly ran through the economy and drove the Consumer Price Index up 11.5 percent in 1979 and 13.5 percent in 1980. Carter was helpless to stop it because three years earlier he had refused the offer of the Democratic leadership in Congress to renew presidential authority for standby wage-price controls. Continuing his anti-government campaign rhetoric, Carter announced that he had confidence in the free market's ability to handle inflation. Even Richard Nixon knew better than that.

Having denied himself the tools to stem inflation directly, Carter reached for the traditional conservative medicine. He cut back domestic spending drastically and increased military spending. Then he appointed Paul Volcker as chairman of the Federal Reserve Board. Volcker tightened up money and credit, sending interest rates sky high and rapidly adding a million and a half Americans to the unemployment rolls. Traditionally, Democratic blue- and pink-collar workers did not vote against Carter on ideological grounds; they were either out of work or afraid they soon would be.

To be sure, Democratic administrations had not previously lived up to the promise of full employment. Carter's de facto abandonment of full employment as an explicit goal, however, gave the issue to the Republican Party for the first time since before the Great Depression. In the elections of 1980 and 1984, while the Democratic candidates stressed austerity and budget-balancing, Reagan's campaign stressed economic growth and jobs. Indeed, while mainstream Democrats avoided the very term "full employment," Reagan has used it quite often.

Carter's type of conservatism that still dominates much of the Democratic Party virtually ceded the employment issue to Reagan. In early 1987 midterm Democratic victories and the Iran-Contra scandal had shaken the administration's confidence, but the political landscape was still barren of Democrats willing to attack Reagan on the jobs issue. Reporters and editorial writers who insisted on Reagan's success in creating jobs went unchallenged even when the facts showed that his record was worse than Carter's had been. Civilian unemployment under Carter averaged 6.5 percent, versus 8.1 percent for Reagan's first six years. Over 10.5 million new jobs were created during the four years of the Carter administration, versus less than 10 million during Reagan's first six years in office (Council of Economic Advisors 1987, 288, 290).

The unwillingness of conservative Democrats to address the question of jobs creates an opportunity for progressives to capture an issue that has broad appeal and is in the mainstream of the Democratic Party's own tradition. Under current conditions, however, the issue is no longer simply one of creating jobs. It is an issue of creating *good jobs*—jobs that will allow workers to support themselves and their families at a middle-class standard of living.

Clearly, such a goal is not possible within the current policy regime, which accepts and promotes wage competition between the U.S. labor force and the rest of the world. U.S. living standards simply cannot survive competition with workers who make $1.30 an hour in Brazil, $1.60 an hour in Mexico, $.30 an hour in China. Yet the increasing mobility of capital and technology daily widens the number of markets in which such competition occurs. The impoverishment of the U.S. middle class is the inevitable consequence of the laissez-faire policies being followed by the Reagan administration.

It is possible to imagine a "Fortress America" alternative, in which we barricade the United States against the global economy with tariffs, quotas, and other protectionist devices to encourage substitute production for imports and generally isolate ourselves from the rest of the world. The United States' internal market is certainly large enough to maintain a respectable, if not dynamic, level of living for its population. This option, however, is academic. The pull of the global economy is too powerful at this point to be reversed by anything but the most draconian of domestic social and economic controls, which are incompatible with fundamental freedoms and democratic institutions.

The other option is to recognize that the only realistic alternative to a low-wage strategy is to make products that are desirable enough to be sold at prices that can support high wages. This will require a set of policies and planning institutions that permit the United States to compete in the world on the basis of quality and innovation.

A Plan for Full Employment

An effective strategy for revitalizing the U.S. economy in the current global context involves three major elements: 1) microeconomic planning policies to improve U.S. productivity; 2) macroeconomic policies to raise the rate of domestic economic growth; and 3) international arrangements to raise the rate of global economic growth.

Microeconomic Planning

After a decade of research and debate we know there is no single cause of our productivity problem (Thurow 1985a, 69–71). Rather, the evidence suggests a problem of "death by a thousand cuts." An inadequate educational system, an anemic level of civilian research and development, no real system of worker retraining and adjustment from declining to emerging industries, poor labor-management relations, a low savings rate, a declining level of public investment in economic infrastructure, a lack of "patient" long-term capital, and a management culture obsessed with short-term profits have all been convincingly identified as major sources of our wounded productivity. There are a host of concrete ideas for cures already in the public debate. They include:

● improving education by increasing salaries for teachers, strengthening curriculum requirements, lengthening the school year;

● increasing training for workers, portable pensions, and tax changes to discourage labor turnover;

● raising the savings rate through a variety of tax changes;

● discouraging wasteful diversion of investment into megamergers, speculation, and other kinds of "paper entrepreneurship" through tax changes, rules against unfriendly takeovers, and representation of communities and workers on corporate boards;

● assisting civilian research and development through a national development bank, as well as new measures to finance public investments by state and local government;

● encouraging better labor-management cooperation through industrial extension service (Reich 1983; Thurow 1985b).

Detailed examination of the items on this list can be found in a number of books, congressional hearings, and foundation reports. Obviously, some have more merit than others. Some reflect more of a political consensus that others. But they are all reasonable suggestions that should be considered.

They do not, however, add up to a strategy. They offer a list of management tools without a manager. Building a productivity policy from this collection of reasonable "new ideas" is like building an automobile without a driver's seat or steering wheel. The parts may fit together, but they are not credible unless there is someone to run the machine and steer it in some direction.

The Japanese have not flourished just because of their educational system or just because of their greater investment in civilian research and development or just because the first $15,000 of a family's savings is exempt from taxes. They have flourished because they have been able to manage their economy, choose the appropriate strategy for particular economic purposes, and create their own comparative advantage.

The Japanese systems of economic planning—or the Swedish or Austrian or French or German systems—are not by any means clear-cut, smoothly working mechanisms for rational decision-making. Disagreement, jockeying for position, incompetence, and individualism are all present. Active planning abolishes neither the drive for power nor the drive for profits. What it does do is channel them in a way that serves a more or less explicitly identified national interest. And it locates responsibility for that national interest in the national government.

To raise the question of who should be responsible for the performance of the U.S. economy is to take the issue out of the mainstream of political debate. The ideological proscription against Big Government has so permeated our political consciousness (ironically, on the left as well as the right) that serious discussion of how to organize the economy distintegrates into vague and often fatuous nonsense or is cut off by its proponents' fear of being labelled soft on Big Government.

"We are not talking about centralized planning" is a standard opening line for practically every speech or book on the subject of industrial policy, equating the common sense notion of government goals with Stalinism. This not only abuses the language and distorts thought, it undercuts the advocates' own position. Of course we are talking about planning, and of course it has to be centralized to some degree. Exactly how much and in what form is a critical part of the discussion.

The political attractiveness of scapegoating the public sector has allowed a myth to develop over the last eight years—during the latter Carter as well as the Reagan years—that national wealth is exclusively the function of individuals and corporations investing in the private marketplace. The private sector is society's "producer." The public sector—however desirable some of its activities may be—is a "consumer" of what business produces. Therefore, economic growth can only be stimulated through tax incentives, deregulation, and other direct assistance to the private sector.

This proposition, even in a market-worshipping culture such as ours, is absurd. When reminded, most people understand that prosperity is generated by a web of activities in both the public and private sectors. Virtually every business benefits from investments in highways, health, clean air and water, law enforcement, transportation, sanitation, and other public responsibilities. Many industries have been nurtured to profitability by public spending. The greatest single contribution to business productivity comes from our public schools—an educated workforce.

Our one-dimensional notion of economic growth has led to serious economic policy mistakes. For example, the proportion of our gross national product devoted to public investments has declined considerably over the last ten years. The Joint Economic Committee of the U.S. Congress estimates that current levels of funding are roughly $450 billion short of what is needed to maintain roads, bridges, parks, and other public facilities through the end of the century. Furthermore, reduced investments in training for teenagers and nutrition for children will soon show up in a less skilled and less healthy workforce—and therefore lower national productivity. In the public sector, as in the private, there is no free lunch.

The Reagan administration promised that the massive 1981 tax cuts for business would stimulate an explosion of business investment, which in turn would create such rapid growth that the federal budget would be balanced in no time. The opposite happened. Business investment tumbled for two years and was revived during the next two only by the stimulus of a sustained budget deficit. Real business purchases of new plants and equipment in 1986 dropped 2.6 percent from 1985 (Department of Commerce 1986, 18).

As a study by Citizens for Tax Justice has shown, companies such as General Electric, Weyerhaeuser, and DuPont paid no taxes at all during the period 1981–1984, and companies that had the highest tax rates since 1981 actually invested more than companies with the lowest tax rates (1986, 5, 17). By 1984 U.S. corporations were contributing only 6 percent of federal revenues, down from 23 percent in 1960. In contrast, corporate taxes in Japan in 1984 provided 30 percent of national revenues.

Our international capitalist rivals have understood the importance of the public sector for some time now. The Japanese have flourished because that country's government has self-consciously taken responsibility for managing the economy, for choosing the appropriate strategy for particular economic goals, and for creating their own comparative advantage. In effect, they have a national plan for development. Thus, while our competitors are treating their countries as economic units, fitting individual industries and sectors together in cooperative planning from the shop floor to the international negotiating table, the consensus of U.S. governance remains stuck in an ideological time warp. The idea that laissez-faire and individual entrepreneurship are the sole sources of wealth and progress was always a myth. But now that the fruits of our victory in World War II have been consumed, we no longer have the luxury of indulging ourselves in them.

The secret of economic management is not some centralized government Gosplan, but a culture of planning and cooperation in which private and public institutions work together to achieve both private and societal goals. Former

Labor Secretary Ray Marshall once asked the chairman of the board of a major U.S. steel company why his firm took profits made in the steel industry and invested them in acquiring oil companies, real estate, and so forth. The chairman replied that the company was not in the steel business but the money business and that his responsibility as a businessman was to get the highest possible return for his shareholders. Shortly afterwards, Marshall asked the head of Nippon Steel why he was taking profits from the steel business and reinvesting them in steel when he might make more money elsewhere. His answer was that Japan needed a steel industry.

Whether the United States needs a steel industry or an auto industry or *any* industry is not a recognized policy question for the government, although it is of course a *political* question in Pittsburgh or Detroit. There is literally no person or institution in the United States responsible for increasing U.S. productivity. On the other hand, this does not mean that there is no industrial policy. We have one, and it is run by the Pentagon. It is the de facto policy of the United States today to concentrate its technological future in weaponry. In 1987 two-thirds of all federal research and development was spent by the Pentagon. The next phase of that industrial policy—the "Star Wars" Strategic Defense Initiative—will absorb massive numbers of our most talented scientists and engineers when they are desperately needed to shore up our declining competitive position. The absence of any explicit responsibility for industrial policy has shielded this critical aspect of the militarization of our economy from scrutiny. Because our public dialogue does not admit the function of public planning, there is literally no acceptable word for the economic function the Pentagon is performing.

The taboo against planning makes it impossible to discuss publicly and seriously the institutional framework for sectoral planning. Our collective wisdom in this area is therefore very underdeveloped. The following outline attempts to specify the major organizational functions involved.

First, we need a national economic agency responsible for developing long- and short-range economic strategies. Whether this is a completely new agency or an amalgam of existing agencies is a secondary question. What is important is its function as a center of expertise and public discussion about U.S. strategic economic interests.

This planning agency should consciously develop a permanent, high-level bureaucracy to provide depth, expertise, and continuity to the ongoing planning process. The agency should incorporate mechanisms for advisory councils, public hearings (in conjunction with the Joint Economic Committee of the U.S. Congress), and other means of public dialogue and discussion. These activities should culminate in specific goals identified by the president and the Congress for employment, trade, inflation, and productivity.

Second, we must strengthen the capacity of state and local governments to formulate their own long-term plans and integrate their goals into the national economic planning system. In the last few years, state governments have developed industrial policy strategies, consolidating their planning expertise and authority. To date, most have been hampered by the grinding pressure to compete with other states for mobile capital on the basis of various subsidies. A national full employment program would go a long way toward lessening that pressure. In the last few years, for example, full employment in Massachusetts has enabled that state to develop innovative job training and welfare programs.

One way to encourage democratization in the planning process is through a community investment agenda, a prioritized listing of local public and private investment needs. Such an agenda would be central in the national planning process, which would consciously target new industries in areas now occupied by declining ones.

Industrial mobility can often be separated from geographic mobility. It is sound economic policy to encourage capital to move from obsolete technologies and declining industries to more efficient and expanding ones. It does not follow, however, that capital mobility should be promoted among regions and communities. Unregulated flight of private capital leads to waste: to reproducing in San Diego and Houston the housing, shops, and public works abandoned in Detroit and Youngstown. Some industries clearly have special geographic requirements. They must be physically near sources of supply and markets. But many do not. What we know about industrial location suggests that the decision about where to put a plant typically has more to do with wage levels, local attitudes toward unionization, and the idiosyncratic preferences of management— factors that might be altered or overcome by appropriate public policies—than with strictly geographic factors.

Third, we need a new set of national and state institutions to finance, guide, and disseminate civilian research and development. A high-wage, high value added strategy is not possible unless we steadily invest in civilian research and development at least at the level of our major competitors. For a long time we have lagged behind most Western European countries in the proportion of our economy devoted to civilian research and development. And now the Japanese, whose growth was spurred by commercializing our own research, have surpassed us.

The market alone has simply been unable to call forth the research and development investment that is necessary for long-term growth in productivity and the development of new products. Indeed, the obsession with laissez-faire solutions has in some cases made things worse; the breakup of AT&T, for example, hurt Bell Labs—the most important single source of industrial innovation in the United States today.

There is, of course, the National Science Foundation, which supports technical research, primarily at universities. But NSF is a "reactive" institution, responding to ideas and proposals that are sent to it. Japan's MITI, in contrast, is much more aggressive, setting priorities and taking responsibility for identifying the most promising state-of-the-art technologies. A new U.S. Civilian Technology

Foundation could operate in much the same way, financing projects in partnership with private firms that agree to use the results to create products manufactured in the United States. The process should certainly involve labor unions and employees in selecting and implementing new technologies.

The nature of the U.S. economy requires that new technologies be disseminated in a much more decentralized way than in Japan and Western Europe, where business is more concentrated and closely connected to government. One model is a state-operated, joint federal- and state-financed industrial extension service, patterned after the Agricultural Extension Service of the U.S. Department of Agriculture. A number of states, most notably Michigan, have already developed such programs that could be adapted to a national system.

Fourth, the federal government must take responsibility for directing the allocation of U.S. capital to more productive investments. Capital investment is the key to shaping a modern economy. The federal government already directly supplies and/or guarantees a large part of the capital invested in the United States (Magaziner and Reich 1982, 235–47). Moreover, its tax, spending, regulation, and monetary policies make the federal government the most important single determinant of where today's capital will be invested to create tomorrow's world.

To plan competently, two new functions are needed. First, the government must make long-term investments in strategic industries that the private sector is unwilling to make. Such investments essentially amount to underwriting a strategic market. For example, in order to get a global jump in robotics, Japanese government agencies created a corporation to guarantee purchase of enough robots to justify their production by private companies. It then leased them out to industry in order to build the market in the private sector. As a result, Japanese industry was using approximately two-thirds of the world's robots by 1982 (President's Commission on Industrial Competitiveness 1985, 23). The U.S. response should be a national development corporation willing to organize such investments. Ideally, such long-term risks should be shared with private investors, but where necessary, the public agency should be willing to act independently.

Second, the Federal Reserve Board's power over reserve requirements, rediscount rates, and other tools of financial regulation should be used to discourage speculation and excessive merger and acquisition activity. By making loans for such speculative activities more expensive than loans for more productive purposes the Fed could dramatically influence the pattern of investment.

Macroeconomic Institutions

The popular assumption that the fiscal deficit per se is the cause of sluggish economic growth distorts a more complex reality. There is some connection between higher interest rates and the fiscal deficit, but the connection is not rooted in immutable laws of economics. Rather, it emerges from the institutional arrangement in which the Federal Reserve Board, independent from the administration, is solely responsible for fighting inflation. High interest rates are a result of the Fed's perception that they are necessary to prevent both inflation and, just as important, the expectation of future inflation.

The major structural issue is the Federal Reserve Board's resistance to reducing interest rates more than what is necessary to compensate for the deflation effect of a lower budget deficit. The Federal Reserve's domination by private bankers and its independence from the executive branch have historically made it reluctant to risk igniting a rise in the price level.

The solution is to liberate the central bank from its inflation responsibility. In its place we need a specific set of anti-inflation, "incomes," and other policies aimed at stemming inflation. Such policies, described in a growing body of economic policy literature, include:

- sectoral policies which would limit price shocks in volatile commodity markets, particularly food and fuel (Alperovitz and Faux 1984, part 3);

- incomes policies to restrain wages, profits, and other incomes from accelerating far beyond increases in productivity (Thurow 1985b, 320–31);

- targeted employment and training programs to avoid skill shortages and geographical imbalances in labor supply and demand (Reich 1983, 239–41);

- stand-by authority for temporary price and wage controls to prevent inflationary pressures from escalating in the short run (Alperovitz and Faux 1984, 227–28).

Finally, the Federal Reserve Board should become a part of the executive branch. Any effective strategy for short-term full employment and long-term wage-price stability requires a centralization of economic policy authority. The separation of responsibilities that distributes monetary policy to the Federal Reserve Board and fiscal policy to the administration and the Congress makes little sense. The inherent propensity for fiscal and monetary policy to work against each other has reached irrational heights in the last several years, but the problem is endemic. The system is fundamentally undemocratic; it puts enormous public power in the hands of unelected people whose loyalties lie with the financial sector of the economy. It also allows elected officials to escape responsibility for the workings of the economy by pointing their fingers at the Federal Reserve. The Fed should be put squarely under the authority of the president. At the same time, the Fed's authority to regulate the proliferation of bank-like financial institutions should be extended to ensure that it can influence financial markets effectively.

Global Planning

The problem of inadequate institutions is of course even more pronounced in the area of global economic stability. World government is an idea whose time has obviously not yet come. But it had not come in 1945 either, and the United States managed to create the institutions needed to generate unprecedented global prosperity. Now, as then, it will be up to the United States to take the lead—not as an all-powerful conqueror but as a leader in the community of nations. We all have a stake in avoiding catastrophe.

If world markets do not grow, the U.S. standard of living will not rise, even if we become more competitive. Without an expansion of world markets, more competition simply means wages and living standards will be driven to unacceptably low levels. Neither an expanding piece of a shrinking pie nor a shrinking piece of an expanding pie will do the trick.

As in the case of industrial policy, the main elements—or at least categories—of a global planning solution have appeared in recent literature and policy discussions. They include:

1. *Exchange Rates*. The market system of floating exchange rates has failed. Exchange rates no longer reflect trade relationships but rather volatile short-term capital flows. This is destructive to trade and makes it difficult for all countries to stabilize their economies. In the short-term the major currency nations (the United States, Japan, West Germany, United Kingdom, and France) should commit themselves to maintain exchange values within a target range that reflects realistic trade relationships. A U.S. tax on large movements of capital would also retard short-term speculation with or against the dollar. Over the long-term a new form of international reserve—baskets of strong currencies or commodities—will have to replace the dollar to assure sufficient liquidity and free the dollar from the increasing burden of being the world's unit of exchange (Cooper 1984, 180–83; Epstein 1985, 646–49; Makhijani and Browne 1985–1986, 70–71).

2. *Coordinated Growth*. Since the United States can no longer spur economic growth by itself, Japan and Germany (followed by the rest of Western Europe) must agree to stimulate their own economies in tandem through fiscal and monetary expansion. Growth policies must be continually coordinated. Expanding the current system of ad hoc summitry to one where explicit targets for growth, inflation, and employment are agreed upon annually will go a long way toward stabilizing the global system.

3. *Third World Debt*. Some combinations of lengthening maturities, forgiveness of the debts of the most destitute nations, limits on interest payments, and massive new credits is needed. Large banks will have to take some losses, but to preserve financial stability, governments should shore them up and guarantee some of the new debt. In return for its participation the U.S. government could take an equity position in the banks themselves. Future lending should be conditional on limitations on military spending and luxury consumption and the prevention of capital flight.

4. *Labor Conditions*. As part of a global plan Third World nations should be required to adhere to international labor standards for health, safety, workers'

rights to organize, and other conditions. Steps should be taken toward an international "sliding scale" minimum wage tied to productivity to prevent permanent pockets of low-wage labor from dragging down wages in developed countries.

5. *Managed Trade.* For the foreseeable future, unlimited free trade is not a useful guide to policy. All countries practice some sort of protectionism, the United States no less than others. The tendency of the international system toward excess capacity will keep the pressure on. The issue is whether the strong tendency toward protectionism can be managed and limited. Precedents for some accommodation—such as the Multifiber Arrangement, which limited less developed country textile imports into the United States and Western Europe—have some promise but there are no entirely satisfactory models. Reality suggests a series of long, difficult multilateral and bilateral negotiations, out of which, if the world is lucky, we shall see a new arrangement appropriate to the world's uneven development.

The process of global restructuring involving these issues will be drawn-out, frustrating, delicate, and complex. For the United States it will be particularly difficult both to lead and defend its own interests. To say that we are not prepared for this task is an understatement. At present we participate in such negotiations at the nation's peril. Our negotiating team is an assistant secretary backed up by a few nervous, temporarily recruited bureaucrats and political appointees who will tomorrow be back at work in a Wall Street investment house. The mindset is short-run "deal-making," not positioning for strategic advantage. With all the patriotic intentions in the world the U.S. team is no match for well trained planners from Japan's MITI and other agencies who have spent years thinking through ways of advancing the long-term economic interests of their countries. The very idea of identifying overarching national economic interests is beyond the capacity of our bureaucracy.

Despite the public relations flourishes of summitry, the rest of the world is desperately girding for economic warfare while we blindly trust our fate to a Maginot line labelled "free trade" supported only by multinational corporations that no longer consider themselves American.

The internationalization of capital has not been without benefits. The flow of trade has aided in developing many areas of the world and has encouraged an interdependence of East and West that makes increased political tensions economically inconvenient. But it has also freed much of U.S. banking and corporate capital from the constraints implied citizenship once imposed, and this, as we have seen, has drastically reduced the power of the U.S. government to maintain steady economic growth.

The emergence of the truly multinational corporation makes development of an international economic management system even more urgent. The unregulated international marketplace has become dangerously volatile; dramatic shifts in exchange rates, prices of oil, food, and other commodities, and sudden political disruptions threaten to snap the interdependent economic fabric thinly stretched around the globe.

Excess industrial capacity is an inevitable consequence of the inability of present world economic institutions to accommodate the internationalization of capital. The multinational corporation is a supply-side engine of expanded production. On the demand side no equivalent public mechanism is responsible for maintaining purchasing power. Nor is there an equivalent institution for maintaining the bargaining power of labor.

There can be a tendency to think of the multinational corporation as simply a loose grouping of what are essentially national companies. Is Ford in Great Britain or Shell in the United States much different from any other company, after all? So long as prospects remain good, branches of multinationals have historically reinvested in expanding operations in the host country. But the evolution of the multinational is far from complete. Peter Drucker, for example, points out that the newer Japanese corporations are more "transnational" than "multinational"—far more centralized and less connected to the local national economies where they invest (1986).

Drucker suggests this is the wave of the future. If so, we can expect the international economy to become even more unstable. Tomorrow's countries, like today's communities, will be subject to the booms and busts associated with absentee owners constantly on the prowl to maximize short-term profits. As part of any restructuring plan, we must therefore consider strategies for reconnecting the unaccountable free-wheeling multinational corporation to the national soil that gives it its economic strength. Since experience suggests that such corporations have the capacity to frustrate any serious effort at regulation, one promising path is to consider expanding the ownership of U.S. corporations by institutions rooted in the United States.

One possibility is that the U.S. government itself demand an equity share in corporations that get special tax and regulatory treatment as part of a quid pro quo. Another is to broaden the participation of U.S. workers in their firms through redesigning pension fund laws and reinstituting tax advantages to foster and aid employee-owned firms. One model worth considering is the Meidner Plan in Sweden. Established in 1983, it mandates that a portion of major corporations' profits be put into special funds to enable workers gradually to buy shares in the companies. By the year 2000 a growing portion of Sweden's largest companies will be owned by Swedish workers. As Robert Kuttner observes, the plan somewhat mitigates labor's demand for higher wages. But unlike typical profit-sharing, the shares will be administered collectively, giving workers' representatives potentially more influence in industrial strategies across corporate boundaries (1984, 155).

The United States does not of course have the cultural homogeneity of Japan (or Sweden or Austria or Germany or even France), which is on its way to a more developed system of economic management. In particular, the United States does not have a close-knit ruling class. The U.S. economy is sprawling, diverse, pluralistic, and basically unorganized. The business communities of all our commercial rivals are much more cohesive; members are tied together by class, school, culture, and formal association. Among the largest U.S. corporations such connections are much looser. There are 14 million businesses in the United States, and the vast majority are unrepresented by anyone. Organized labor represents only 19 percent of the U.S. workforce, as opposed to 29 percent in Japan, 43 percent in West Germany, 94 percent in Sweden, and 38 percent in Canada (Bureau of Labor Statistics, unpublished). Moreover, U.S. labor has little of the socialist tradition that gives European labor some sense that it is responsible for helping to run the country.

To state these obstacles is to define the task. It is precisely because the United States lacks those informal planning mechanisms that it is in such desperate need of formal, politically explicit ones. Managers want more flexibility, workers want more security, and the country needs more investment. But there is neither an institutional framework nor a space in national political dialogue where the bargaining over a new social contract can begin.

Ironically, the absence of formal and informal planning institutions makes the government more dangerous to the economic freedom and security of U.S. citizens. Macroeconomic policies lurch from expansion to contraction, crushing workers, farmers, small businesses, and others in their wake. Trade policies become primarily a function of the political cycle. Government regulations and contract awards—because they are subject to no overarching plan—become prizes won in a lobbying contest. Government by crisis in the end becomes government by political whim.

The situation is both a cause and effect of the unevenness of power between large corporations and other social institutions. Free market ideology and support for institutional pluralism obscure from public discussion the enormous power of business over U.S. public affairs. This private power has always been a fact of life in the United States, but in recent years it has grown to immense proportions. It has been aided by a number of factors: the increasing importance of media in elections and the disastrous post-Watergate campaign financing reforms that opened the door for corporate political action committees (Edsall 1984, 76–78); the high rate of unemployment, which holds federal, state, and local governments hostage to decisions about the location of business investment; and the deterioration of the power and militancy of organized labor.

The result is a deepened sense of unfairness that accurately reflects reality. The United States has the most unequal distribution of income of any modern industrial state, with the possible exception of France. The message from U.S. leaders to U.S. citizens is: "You are all on your own. If you are inclined to small acts of individual charity or altruism you may or may not be appreciated. But it is of no importance. Above all, do not put your faith in the system or its major institutions because these do not care about you."

Under these circumstances is it any wonder that U.S. workers who are likely to be unemployed by automation resist technological change, while Japanese workers assured of job security welcome it? Is it any wonder that businessmen scramble to maximize immediate profits and say to hell with the longer-term interests of the firm or the country? Is it any wonder that bureaucrats use their government jobs as a training ground for higher-paying jobs in the private sector? Is it any wonder that public streets are strewn with the homeless and terrorized by the alienated?

This leads to the final question: how realistic is it to expect U.S. politics and culture to accommodate a serious commitment to national economic planning?

For those who care about the future of the planet, there is of course no choice but to attempt to build a political constituency for policies and institutions to manage a global economy that is now out of control. Nevertheless, there are some reasons to be optimistic. At the very least, the current political environment is more amenable to change than it was during the late 1920s and early 1930s, when the conditions leading to World War II solidified.

First, the level of education and awareness of global issues among the U.S. electorate—as abysmal as it seems—is far greater than it was half a century ago, when people were more isolated and suspicious of one another and had less contact with other cultures.

Second, despite the fact that advocates of laissez-faire solutions to our problems were given an extraordinary opportunity to prevail—a popular, lucky, conservative Republican president succeeding a failed Democrat—they still have been unable to dismantle the basic structures of our mixed economy. Indeed, by 1987 the Reagan administration was giving unintended legitimacy to such "liberal" ideas as tax reform, international cooperation to stabilize exchange rates, and expanded national health insurance for catastrophic illness.

Finally, the last few years have seen a wide variety of efforts at grassroots economic planning—halting, uneasy, yet continuing efforts at labor-management cooperation at the level of the shop floor and state and local government experiments at channeling market forces into activities with more social benefits. A committed, progressive political movement could make these efforts the building blocks for a set of competent national and international planning institutions.

The fact that political conditions may be somewhat better today than they were prior to the Great Depression does not guarantee that we will avoid World War III. But it does mean we have a better chance. And, given the stakes, we have little choice but to take it.

References

Alperovitz, G., and J. Faux. 1984. *Rebuilding America*. New York: Pantheon.
Berg, E. N. 1986. Thrift ills disguised, study says. *The New York Times* August 18.

Bureau of Labor Statistics. unpublished data. International Comparisons Division.

————. 1986. *Employment and earnings* 33 (3).

Citizens for Tax Justice. 1986. *Money for nothing: The failure of corporate tax incentives, 1981–1984*. Washington, D.C.

Cooper, R. 1984. A monetary system for the future. *Foreign Affairs* 63 (1):180–183.

Council of Economic Advisors. 1987. *Economic Report of the President*. Washington, D.C.: U.S. Government Printing Office. January.

Department of Commerce. 1986. *Survey of current business*. Washington D.C. December.

Drucker, P. 1986. The changing multinational. *The Wall Street Journal* January 15.

Edsall, T. B. 1984. *The new politics of inequality*. New York: W. W. Norton and Company.

Epstein, G. 1985. The triple debt crisis. *World Policy Journal*. Fall.

Feketekuty, G. 1985. Statement of Assistant U.S. Trade Representative before the House Subcommittee on Economic Stabilization. April 16.

Jonas, N., et al. 1986. The hollow corporation. *Business Week* March 3.

Joint Economic Committee. 1986. Report on the February 1986 Economic Report of the President. Washington, D.C.: U.S. Government Printing Office.

Kindleberger, C. 1985. International public goods without international government. Presidential address delivered at the 98th meeting of the American Economic Association. December 29.

Koretz, G. 1986. Has capital flight made the U.S. a debtor of Latin America? *Business Week* April 21.

Kuttner, R. 1984. *The economic illusion*. Boston: Houghton Mifflin.

Magaziner, I., and R. Reich. 1982. *Minding America's business*. New York: Harcourt, Brace, Jovanovich.

Makhijani, A., and R. S. Browne. 1985–1986. Restructuring the international monetary system. *World Policy Journal* Winter: 70–71.

President's Commission on Industrial Competitiveness. 1985. *Global competition*. Vol. 2. Washington, D.C.: U.S. Government Printing Office.

Reich, R. B. 1983. *The next American frontier*. New York: Times Books.

Senate Democratic Group on Trade Policy. 1985. The new global economy: First steps in a United States trade strategy. April.

Thurow, L. 1985a. A time to dismantle the world economy. *The Economist* November 9.

————. 1985b. *The zero sum solution*. New York: Simon and Schuster.

U.S. Bureau of the Census. 1984. *Money income of households, families and persons in the United States: 1984*. Washington, D.C.: U.S. Government Printing Office.

————. 1985. *Money income and poverty status of families and persons in the United States: 1985*. Washington, D.C.: U.S. Government Printing Office.

7   Democracy versus the National Security State

Marcus G. Raskin

From our beginnings as a nation Americans have been engaged in a profound struggle about the character and form of their government. Although the Constitution guarantees the nation and each state within it a republican form of government, who is entitled to be represented and who will participate in governing are questions that have been a continual source of conflict.[1] Those men who wrote the Constitution favored a concept of citizenship that entrusted control of the state to those with property and wealth sufficient to provide them with the time and dispassion to govern for their class and for others not in their class. These founders believed people without property, wealth, and education were prone to mob rule and concluded that because this group had little if any stake in the nation, it should not have the power to make decisions for the common good. These were not full citizens but *associates*; associates needed rights because they had no power. Indeed, associates have favored those parts of the Constitution that have the least to do with the actual, day-to-day operations of government, namely the preamble and the Bill of Rights. Citizens, on the other hand, concerned themselves with the practice of governance and therefore those parts of the Constitution that spell out the authority and powers of the government.

The early American republic was exclusionary. It did not take into account countless people who worked, who had inventive ideas, and who thought of themselves as part of "We, the people." In other words, the republic did not take workers, blacks, and women into account, groups that, while politically unnoticed, were central to the economic success of the United States. Almost from its beginning, therefore, a struggle occurred over who was a citizen. The original republic proved too static, reflecting an eighteenth-century ideological straitjacket against which the "left-outs" had to struggle to realize the promise that democracy held out to them. Indeed, the struggle to democratize the American republic by removing property and subsequently racial and gender restrictions on the right to take part in government has been a focal point of battles fought

This chapter is a condensed and revised version of an article published with the same title in *Law and Contemporary Problems* 40:3 (Summer 1976). John Kushma provided able editing assistance in preparing the present chapter.

by disadvantaged groups to become full members of American society. These battles have been fought in our legislatures, courts, workshops, and factories, and from time to time they have spilled into the streets, turning our land in a battlefield.

In the eighteenth century, as today, democracy meant participation in politics and property. And for just those reasons it was disdained by "the better classes." In the United States democracy has been identified with increasing participation of the associates in the political process, a legal and cultural condition of equality, and a measure of economic justice. The disadvantaged, the associates, refused to accept the notion that the republic created by the Constitution was a finished product, a fetishized eighteenth-century commodity. They struggled to wrest control of the state from the oligarchy of wealth and property that dominated it. For them democracy meant the extension of the republic through constitutional means to spread access, participation, deliberation, and justice for all—a process to make all associates into full, active citizens.

As titanic as this continuing struggle has been, a new form of governance, the national security state, came into being to further bedevil those who sought to realize democracy.[2] The national security state is the form that U.S. leaders framed after World War II to deal with the problems of the new role the United States took on itself internationally. The national security state was also designed to serve as a gyroscope, a balancer, for the crisis-prone U.S. economy. The logic of these requirements necessitated the formulation of a forced internal social consensus among disparate classes and groups, as if the United States were still at war. This consensus was fashioned around anti-communism, a loyalty system, continuous military conflict, and an open-ended technological arms race premised on nuclear weapons, missiles, and military engagement in other lands through an alliance system that allowed the United States direct and indirect political and military intervention. More important, those in control of the national security state demanded the cloak of secrecy for their actions and denied the need for independent or autonomous judgment on the part of the citizenry.

From the inception of the Cold War an iron curtain came down between the people and the state, between citizens and the actual way government operated in foreign and domestic affairs. The citizenry, except those who were part of the secrecy network that represented a new oligarchy, was excluded from knowledge of the covert activities undertaken in its name by its now nominally democratic government. By 1949 continuously increasing defense expenditures ordained by the national security state became the central economic planning mechanism to assure a stable and relatively prosperous economy. Post-war economic growth served as a mask to hide the character of U.S. involvement abroad, while the belief that individualism, in the sense of consumer choice, was "real" democracy disguised continuing inequality at home.

The 1987 hearings held by Congress on the Iran-Contra affair have starkly demonstrated anew the threat that the national security state poses not only to democracy but even to the republican form of government guaranteed by the

Constitution. It now appears that the national security state cannot be contained by public law or the Constitution and that Congress cannot assure the nation of either a republican or a democratic form of government.[3] As democracy has advanced through the civil rights and women's movements, the growth of the national security state has simultaneously restricted the scope of political choices available to the American people. This fact leads directly to the recognition that there is a virtual impossibility of revitalizing U.S. politics and rebuilding U.S. society without transforming and dismantling the national security state, a state apparatus that has few roots in our Constitution and in civil society.

The Historical Origins of the National Security State

In 1945 the United States appeared invulnerable. It held, or so it seemed, all the economic, social, scientific, and power cards. Its allies depended on it for the kind of economic aid that was needed to restore their pre-war social and economic structures, and the vanquished were, of course, totally dependent on its largesse (Kolko 1968, 618–26). Colonial areas of the world looked to it for aid in their national independence struggles against France, Great Britain, and the Netherlands (Fleming 1961, 661–706; Kahin 1952, 334–35, 417–23). U.S. scientists, with help from their European friends, scaled the heights to become "the destroyer of worlds" with the atomic bomb, as J. Robert Oppenheimer put it (Stern 1969, 81). Roosevelt and Churchill had decided in 1944 that the weapon was to be kept secret from the Soviet Union to assure immediate and complete supremacy at the close of the war (Sherwin 1975, 209).

It was no wonder then that U.S. leaders felt a certain omnipotence and arrogance during the immediate post-war period. The U.S. leadership had gained enormously in prestige and power during World War II (Janeway 1968, 28), and Americans were honored by communists and colonized people alike. Indeed, during the war, the American Communist Party dissolved itself to become an "association" because, according to Earl Browder, American capitalists were different from the European brand (Howe and Coser 1962, 426). Revolutionaries like Ho Chi Minh modeled their declarations of independence after the American document (Fall 1956, 5).

Yet there remained profound doubts about the viability of U.S. capitalism at the close of the war, doubts that had their roots in the Depression and that the accomplishments of the New Deal had not eradicated.

Many "citizens" and "associates" alike had viewed the Depression as a period in which our constitutional republic might be more fully democratized. Embedded in this view was the need to break the hold that an oligarchic few retained on wealth and income. The leading instruments for this change were to be a labor movement organized along class lines and a presidency committed to a progressive democratic agenda. During and immediately after the war the movement of women into the workforce and millions of blacks out of the rural plantation ghettoes of the South into northern factories once again inspired the hope of domestic democratic social reconstruction. Needless to say, democratic social reconstruction did not occur after World War II. The implementation of an economic bill of rights, promised by Franklin Roosevelt in his last budget message, did not happen.

The domestic economic agenda that had been set aside during World War II in order to fight Germany and Japan again played second fiddle during another war. The Cold War—often not quite as cold as Americans were led to believe—became the new mobilizing and unifying mechanism that made the social democratic agenda the tail to the national security dog of continuous conflict. The immediate slide into the Cold War reinforced martial values, not democratic ones, just as it "softened up" the population for a continuous hatred of an "enemy." The 80th Congress embraced Truman's alternative to social reconstruction, namely the national security state. It reasserted the associate and hostage condition of virtually all U.S. citizens.

On the eve of World War II the United States had not recovered from the effects of the Depression. The various measures that had been tried by Franklin Roosevelt and his advisors, such as creating public works programs, curbing the excesses of the stock market, and guaranteeing loans to farmers proved insufficient. In 1938 and 1939 the unemployment rate was 8 percent, and there did not seem to be a means of rationalizing the needs of the people with the short- and long-term interests of capitalists. Between 1931 and 1940 the jobless rate never fell below 14 percent—and for four of those years it averaged more than 20 percent. In 1941, the last year before mobilization during the wartime economy, unemployment hovered at 10 percent. It was generally assumed by government economists that after pent-up demand had been met, the post-war United States would again be faced with serious unemployment (Ginsberg 1975, 3, 6).

There had been, of course, an active anti-business ideology during the Depression years. Broken-spirited people had been demoralized by the economic failure, and they reclaimed the Populist hostility to corporate capital. Although this anti-business hostility did not lead to widespread demands for systemic change, it remained sufficiently strong at the end of the war to spur business and political leaders to find ways to stabilize capitalism. They, as well as the people who stood in them, remembered the bread lines of the Depression. During the war most unions had accepted no-strike pledges in exchange for minor management prerogatives in the plants. These arrangements were dissolved at the war's end as management sought to take back all control over life in the factory. Strike turbulence was consequently profound in major industries in the immediate post-war years. Harry Truman threatened to take over the coal mines and railroads, while draftees in the armed forces rioted to return to civilian life (Goldberg 1956, 44; Taft 1964, 546).

Despite post-war optimism life in the United States seemed to be returning to the economic and social chaos of the Depression. After World War II the British informed the United States that Greece and Turkey were now U.S. imperial responsibilities. In March 1947 the United States intervened in both nations and established its new sphere of influence (Dulles 1953, 231–32). The convergence of domestic problems and international "opportunities" gave rise to a new kind of governing structure designed to enable the United States to exercise world hegemony while ensuring internal social and economic stability. In response to this new situation the U.S. leadership attempted to reorganize the government so that it would appear at once to be democratic and to steer an economic and political course between socialism and fascism. This new governing structure was the national security state. The leaders who first constructed and later guided the national security state were a small group of men who, through ties of social class and interest, reacted to the post-war world in essentially the same way.

The National Security Act of 1947 and the National Security Council (NSC), which it created, formalized the structure of the national security state. Three major structural purposes were intended to be served by this legislation. One was the development and creation of an intelligence capability known as the Central Intelligence Agency (CIA). It legitimated secrecy as necessary to peacetime government. Another was the reorganization of the independent armed services under the Secretary of Defense, with a Joint Chiefs of Staff system. The system grew out of the need to "rationalize" global responsibilities in a common planning system. The third was to ensure that the domestic economy would make available resources and material for defense and national security purposes. It should be noted that while a "National Security Council" was created, no definition of national security was formulated in the act or in ensuing acts that ostensibly dealt with national security. The concept remained one that was defined through positive action and, tautologically, by those who exercised the powers of the state. The National Security Act allowed various agencies to broaden and interpret their own mandates. The consequence of vesting the national security apparatus with such unchecked discretion soon became apparent. According to Arthur Macy Cox, a former member of the CIA, the agency entered into covert data collection operations from its inception, hiring former Nazi general Gerhard Gehlen[4] to develop an intelligence network on the Soviets (1975, 93).

Initial steps toward creating the national security state had immediate domestic consequences as political leaders began to forge the links between it and U.S. labor. Reinhold Niebuhr, an intellectually influential exponent of the national security state and the Cold War, argued that a partnership between capital and labor had been achieved and that this partnership could be maintained if organized labor were given a role in the national security system (Niebuhr 1953).[5]

Such was the impetus behind the passage of the Employment Act of 1946 (15 U.S.C. § 1021 [1970]), a piece of legislation that was viewed by its supporters as an instrument for taming capitalism and giving workers a stake in its maintenance. The incongruities of the act are apparent. Aimed at creating conditions "under which there will be afforded useful employment opportunities, including self-employment, for those able, willing and seeking to work, and to promote maximum employment, production, and purchasing power," the act reflected the commitment on the part of the federal government to "maximum employment" and to fit this need into the overall economic picture. But this picture also included policies directed toward protecting the high profits of the largest corporations, fostering a climate for the enterprising, and building a hedge against inflation. In a word, the act was to be consistent with the needs of an economic system that required unemployment. (A Senate version that committed the nation to full employment and guaranteed a right to employment was defeated in the House and deleted in conference committee.)

While the Employment Act of 1946 at least gave the illusion of worker participation in the economic well-being of the United States, the Taft-Hartley Act (Labor Management Relations Act 29 U.S.C. § 141–97, 1947, 1970) placed explicit limits on the power of organized labor. In response to a wave of strikes between 1945 and 1947 the Taft-Hartley Act implemented a right to refrain from organization and concerted activities, allowed management to lobby against unionization of the workplace, outlawed the closed shop and subjected the union shop to certain limitations, and proscribed a number of union unfair labor practices, including secondary boycotts and jurisdictional strikes. In short, the Taft-Hartley Act served, as an AFL-CIO resolution concluded, as the instrument "to block union organization, to weaken unions and to interfere with free collective bargaining" (Goldberg 1956, 205). The law also kept Communists from holding leadership positions in unions.

Nevertheless, the position of U.S. workers improved substantially during the Cold War period from their position during the Depression (Taft 1964, 587–88). The defense contract system guaranteed workers a role of sorts in the national security system. In the fifteen-year period from 1959 to 1974, 75 percent of federal government purchases of goods and services was for military purposes (Ginsberg 1975, 9–16). The overall size of the economic pie was increasing, but the selling of the American dream, made tangible by this economic growth, masked the question of who would share the slices. An important, indeed crucial, actor in selling the American dream was the president.

The power of the presidency increased dramatically under the new institutional structure and ideology of the national security state. Since the New Deal economic and political decisions had been shifting to the executive. At first it was thought by hopeful liberals and fearful conservatives that the presidency was the instrument for bringing about social reform in the face of a Congress that did not care to disturb the constitutional *stare decisis* and favored the power of local oligarchic groups. But the presidency became instead the rationalizing instrument for the most powerful groupings in society. By the beginning of Roosevelt's third term it was clear to the great corporations, and then the military, that they needed the presidency as a fundamental instrument to extend their power or to assure that they would continue to reap benefits.

If given certain legislative tools, a president apparently can act unchecked by the theoretical restraints that are written into our Constitution and our political system. The president can act out of whim or in furtherance of carefully laid out plans. Congress has in fact given the president those legislative tools and the task of being point man to save the "system" and to rationalize the various conflicting interests of ruling groups (Raskin 1974, 28).[6]

The power of a modern president rests on several elements. One is his willingness to rationalize class relations in the society. This must not be done by tampering with those who hold great agglomerations of property. If he is liberal-minded, he will put forward schemes of economic growth that supposedly render unnecessary any redistributive plans. Additionally, until 1975 he was not to undermine the military and national security apparatus. Finally, he is to pay obeisance to constitutional forms such as Congress and not threaten their existence (Raskin 1974, 18–25, 53). He is to recognize Congress' legitimizing function and find a means of coopting it into the national security apparatus or the lockstep of the great corporations. A president who acts according to these rules can be assured of the support of established power.

Effects of the National Security State in Undermining the Rule of Law

During the Cold War period the president and his entourage became brokers for the illegitimate power wielded by the CIA, the FBI, and the various gangs within them. They also sought to use these groups for their own purposes. The powerful sought maximum flexibility for their objectives. Ad hoc committees treaded the lines between legitimacy, illegality, and crime ("Hearings on S Res. 21, Before the Senate Select Committee to Study Governmental Operations with Respect to Intelligence Activities, Volume 7, Covert Action," 94th Cong., 1st Sess. [1975], 1–136, 148–210). Much of the president's and his advisors' time was spent curbing or ratifying the excesses of lower-level bureaucrats emboldened by the imperial stance and the shroud of secrecy. Thus, for example, after the CIA's failure at the Bay of Pigs the President, the Attorney General, and Special Assistant for National Security Affairs McGeorge Bundy undertook to control the national security bureaucracy through President Kennedy's Special Military Advisor (and later Chairman of the Joint Chiefs of Staff) Maxwell Taylor and presidentially-appointed committees. This "reform" more deeply implicated the presidency in paramilitary and criminal affairs.

It should be noted that the framework of "maximum flexibility" for leadership and the national security bureaucracy is intended to encompass both domestic and foreign activity. The control techniques that wartime and Cold War presidents sanctioned against the poor and the "subversives" at home and that had been transported abroad during the Cold War, were used as well against the middle class, the bureaucrats, and finally the leaders of the major political parties.

The FBI, as well as other police agencies of the federal government, proceeded to enforce the Procrustean bed of anti-left conformist ideology inside and outside the government. President Truman's Executive Order 9835, issued in March 1947, required loyalty oaths of government officials. Many who held positions in institutions such as labor unions, universities, and the media were purged. By 1949 they found themselves eliminated from policy debates on the character of U.S. society, treated as objects of contempt or benign tolerance. The effect of the Truman loyalty probes and those later undertaken by Senator Joseph McCarthy and J. Edgar Hoover was to enforce a view of the world based on hatred of "Communism" and to prepare an automatic defense of corporate capitalism as the reason for U.S. prosperity and the justification of U.S. military adventures and alliances, both covert and overt. To this end the national security state was dedicated.

In *The Powers of Government* Bernard Schwartz outlines three fundamental elements of the rule of law: "1) The absence of arbitrary power; 2) the subjugation of the State and its officers to the ordinary law; and 3) the recognition of basic principles superior to the State itself" (1963, 26). Schwartz and others, in assuming that the rule of law is crucial to the existence of representative democracy, echo the words of the radical revolutionary Thomas Paine: "Let a crown be placed thereon, by which the world may know that, so far as we approve monarchy, that in America *the law is king*" (1953, 332).

Arbitrary Power

The national security state and the rule of law are mortal enemies. The national security state apparatus needs arbitrary power by nature and mission. Such power has its own code, which is meant to govern or to justify the behavior of the initiated—after the fact. It operates to protect the state apparatus from the citizenry. In its defensive form it is hidden under instant and specious doctrines such as executive privilege. This apparatus seeks to cede to the discretion of officials the power of the nation's citizens to manage their future or participate with others in that management. Government officials attempt to control the kinds of politics and citizen activities they do not favor. They see no distinctions between geographic boundaries and are apt to operate in essentially the same way against Americans and non-Americans. Thus, the attempt of the CIA to assassinate Patrice Lumumba in the Congo is directly analogous to the FBI's attempt politically to destroy Martin Luther King, Jr., in the United States. President Nixon's sanctioning of the decision of the 40 Committee (made up of CIA, National Security Council and State and Defense Department staff, which passed on covert operations) to intervene and attempt to prevent the election of Salvador Allende in Chile through bribe offers and other means is strikingly similar to the methods the Committee for the Re-election of the President (CREEP) used in Nixon's re-election campaign or the methods used against the Socialist Workers Party in the United States.

The police agencies have served as a brake on the political process. The Counter Intelligence Programs (COINTELPRO) of the FBI have employed an astonishing variety of means to disrupt the activities of groups that sought to exercise their participatory rights. Programs like Operation Hoodwink, for example, were meant to incite organized crimes against the Communist Party, to entrap war objectors into undertaking bombings, as in the case of the Camden, New Jersey, draft board affair, and to break up human and social relations by sending forged documents and threatening letters to victims of federal and police enterprises. Break-ins, burglaries, wire-taps and bugging of the citizenry have been a central aspect of the FBI's work as it has undertaken to humiliate, ridicule, and harass civil rights workers, anti-war groups, radicals, conservatives, and any grouping that did not share the assumptions or the influence of those "in charge." The CIA has taken pride in training local police in bugging, photo surveillance, and surreptitious entry (Perkus 1975; "Hearings on FBI Counter-intelligence Programs before the Civil Rights and Constitutional Rights Sub-committee of the House Committee on the Judiciary," 93rd Cong., 2nd Sess., pp. 10–47; Borosage and Marks 1976).

The line between criminal gangs and the police is crossed often in the national security state. Why government uses criminal gangs may appear obscure to the average law-abiding citizen, but the process of tyranny uses all manner of power and threat to sustain domination. Too often it calls the process national security. The attempt by holders of arbitrary power to inhibit people from exercising their participatory rights is invariably accompanied by forms of personal harassment against people who have no interest in the exercise of their rights, but simply in carrying on the ordinary functions of life. Here the arbitrary power of the national security apparatus operates less obviously, in a more automatic and, to the victim, less obtrusive way. Files on individuals are built up and used for a variety of purposes, such as blackmail or to control possibilities of future employment for the object-victim. This type of bureaucratic behavior became especially popular as bureaucracies grew larger, computers more sophisticated, and leaders more insecure. It is punctuated with the predictable danger of vying leadership elites using police and other records as weapons to destroy opponents or settle old scores. Such activities are common practice in the bureaucracy of the national and "internal" security apparatus. There is nothing in public law that limits the FBI or, indeed, suggests that legal authority exists for its comprehensive surveillance activities in the area of "subversive activities."

Officers Above the Law

The national security state is the U.S. version of the dual state. In the dual state, specifically rejected by U.S. law, "legal concepts are not applicable to the political sphere, which is regulated by arbitrary measures, in which the dominant officials exercise unfettered discretionary prerogatives" (Schwartz 1963, 12). Within the national security agencies, several levels of para-legal and illegal activities may be discerned.

At one level the national security apparatus operates according to a para-legal structure. It is "private," with its own standards. Thus, the 40 Committee is an example of an attempt to draw the various police, military, and criminal forces at the command of the leadership into a private and self-justifying administrative system. "Beginning in 1955, the responsibility for authorizing CIA covert action operations lay with the Special Group, a subcommittee of the NSC composed of the President's Assistant for National Security Affairs, the Director of the CIA, the Deputy Secretary of Defense and the Undersecretary of State for Political Affairs" (Senate Select Committee to Study Governmental Operations with Respect to Intelligence Activities, Alleged Assassination Plots Involving Foreign Leaders, S. Rep. No. 465, 94th Cong., 1st Sess., p. 10). Today this group has expanded to include the chairman of the Joint Chiefs of Staff. This part of the national security apparatus operates according to its own rules and regulations, taking little or no account of public law and asserting its own definition of national security and national interest—a definition that is invariably ruling-class-oriented. We may refer to it as "lightly-covered" because it may or may not surface from time to time, as in the case of the 40 Committee. When it does surface, it seeks to justify its actions by embracing principles of positive law and of the dual state.

On another level the national security state carries on activities that are flatly illegal. At this level criminal behavior becomes an important operational instrument. National Security Defense Memorandum 40 of 1970 points out that the intelligence apparatus must be ready for all contingencies and must have responses basically researched and ready to go. In other words, preparing for criminality and involving or nurturing criminal behavior are part of the national security state, since it is never clear when their results will prove useful. This illegal activity includes forgery and counterfeiting, assassination, the employment of known criminals, and so on.

One NSC Directive frighteningly states:

CIA must necessarily be responsible for planning. Occasionally suggestions for action will come from outside sources but, to depend entirely on such requirements would be an evasion of the Agency's responsibilities. Also, the average person, both in government and outside, is *thinking along normal lines* and to develop clandestine cold war activities properly, persons knowing both the capabilities and limitations of clandestine action must be studying and devising how such actions can be undertaken effectively. (Directive of the National Security Council, NSC 5412/2, cited in Alleged Assassination Plots, 9, n.4 [emphasis added])

This kind of thinking goes beyond the para-legal procedure. It gives rise to plans and actions of a frightful nature. An unlimited choice of means has been extended to agents or hired contract officers. Thus, the sober William Colby planned and carried out the Phoenix program, which resulted in the killing of some 20,000 Vietnamese. They were killed because they were ostensibly part of the "Viet Cong's infrastructure" (Borosage and Marks 1976, 190).

Another example of the policy criminal is the imaginative General Edward Lansdale. He was put in charge of the MONGOOSE program to overthrow Cuban Premier Fidel Castro through covert means. He recommended exploiting the potential of the underworld in Cuban cities to harass and "bleed the community control apparatus." Added to this plan was another suggestion (among thirty one other planning tasks) to utilize biological and chemical warfare against the Cuban sugar crop workers (Alleged Assassination Plots 1974, 139–69).

The Special Group minutes of June 19, 1963 suggest the manner in which the executive undertook war and warlike activities on its own initiative, pulling itself and the government into unaccountable policy crimes. At a meeting in which Defense Secretary Robert McNamara, CIA official General William Kee, Assistant Secretary of State Averill Harriman, Director of Central Intelligence John McCone, Desmond Fitzgerald of the CIA, and McGeorge Bundy were present, a sabotage program was described by the CIA to the members of the Special Group. It was to be directed at "four major segments of the Cuban economy": a) electric power; b) petroleum refineries and storage facilities; c) railroad and highway transportation; and d) production and manufacturing. Raids were to be conducted from outside Cuba, using Cuban agents under CIA control. Missions would be staged from a U.S. base (173).

Here were officers of the government, with statutorily defined responsibilities in the constitutional order, acting in their hidden role as officers of the dual state. They could not be reached or controlled through constitutional or legal means. At the first meeting of the NSC, in December 1947, "covert operations" were authorized, giving the go-ahead to criminal action. It would take us too far afield to analyze the class bias of this and other "executive committees" that assumes a consensus by the members of the government for actions against the under-privileged and powerless persons of the earth. What are we to make of our ambassador to Chile, Edward Korry, who said that once Allende the Marxist was elected president, the United States would do "all within our power to condemn Chile and the Chileans to utmost deprivation and poverty" (231 n.2)? What about President Nixon and Secretary of State Kissinger who, having been emboldened by various multinational corporations such as IT&T and PEPSICO, pursued another attempt to bring down Allende, operated through the White House and kept secret even from the 40 Committee? According to Kissinger, this plan involved a group unknown to others for "reasons of security" and charged with the responsibility of working with the Chilean military in bringing about a coup against Allende (246–55). They succeeded.

The role of the courts is exceedingly limited with regard to the national security apparatus, thus permitting the expansion of its para-legal and illegal activities. The judiciary has handled precious few cases involving the CIA or the National Security Agency (NSA). Furthermore, when such cases have been presented to the courts, judges have been reluctant or unable to rule against the secret agencies or inquire as to their activities.

Why does the doctrine of *Marbury v. Madison* stop at the gates of Langley, Virginia? One reason is that secret agencies specialize in lying. It is hard to know when CIA officials are telling the truth. They have been given the devilish power to lie. Thus a stock in trade of the CIA has been "plausible deniability." This "doctrine" is meant to protect operatives "from the consequences of disclosures" and "to mask decisions of the president and his senior staff members." The masking process is "designed to allow the president and other senior officials to deny knowledge of an operation should it be disclosed" (Alleged Assassination Plots, 1974, 11–12). In other words, plausible deniability is a doctrine that encourages the invention of false information or lies that will be acceptable to other government agencies, the courts, and the public as well as to competing or uninformed groups within the secret agencies themselves. Related to the doctrine of plausible deniability is the "need to know" principle. The operational effect of "need to know" is, as Richard Barnet has said, need not to know (Stavins, Raskin, and Barnet 1971, 246). Thus, the FBI and the CIA operate on the basis that various groups within their own agencies, including higher officials, have little idea of what others in the same chain of command are doing.

But democracy and its operative principle, the rule of law, require a ground on which to stand, and that ground is, as former President Ford said when he was installed as president, truth. In this regard the government has a higher duty than the citizen to tell the truth because it is the government that embodies the traditions and values of the body politic as a whole. Where the government lies or is so structured as to permit only lies and self-deception, it is clear that the governing process and the organization of power have become some other form than that originally intended or generally understood by the citizenry as constitutional. The doctrines of "plausible deniability" and "need to know" present problems of particular significance for the judiciary as enforcer of the rule of law because with the development of the national security state the duty of truth-telling has been substantially waived. Indeed, it is taken for granted that lies and masks are officials' tools for self and group protection.

One example of the kind of falsification that is routine within the national security apparatus is the *Gatto* incident. In 1970 the *U.S.S. Gatto*, against orders, drifted within one mile of the Soviet coast. A Soviet sub rammed the *Gatto* somewhere near the White Sea. The *Gatto* was ready to fire a nuclear missile at the Russian sub but escaped without needing to do so. The ship's officers were requested to file two sets of reports. One was to consist of six copies describing the incident as it actually occurred; the other was to be twenty-five copies falsifying the incident. The Pentagon admitted filing the falsified reports but said that it filed the true report with the 40 Committee. However, when interviewed, officials could not locate or remember any reports about the *Gatto*. There have been at least four mid-ocean collisions between U.S. Navy and Soviet nuclear-powered and nuclear weapons-carrying submarines since the mid 1960s. These were ostensibly intelligence operations that could easily have resulted in nuclear disaster (Command Study Group 1974, 1–7).

Since "unacceptable" acts—that is, actions that are constitutionally, legally, or morally questionable—are denied as a matter of course, there has been no way for courts to test the veracity of statements of the secret agencies. For example, how are we to know when the FBI engaged in wiretapping, burglary, or entrapment? Under Hoover the FBI kept at least two separate sets of books. The set that is available to the courts reflects the FBI's "acceptable" or "legitimate" purposes. The other set appears to have been less pretty and was unknown except to the initiated (Inquiry into the Destruction of Former FBI Director J. Edgar Hoover's Files & FBI Recordkeeping, Hearing before a Subcommittee of the House Committee on Government Operations, 94th Cong., 1st Sess. [1975], 36–48). This set apparently shows the actual operations of the FBI and special groups, their special missions, and special purposes undertaken for themselves and for special friends. But this is not the record the courts receive. *Marbury* is defeated by national security practice.

Basic Principles Superior to the State

According to Schwartz, the third element of the rule of law is a recognition that there are principles superior to the state itself. This is an important safeguard against legislatures that pass laws that may be criminal. It is also a justification for the citizenry to act in a civilly disobedient manner against laws or governmental acts that shock the conscience of the society. The history of the twentieth century is replete with para-legal orders for bombings, concentration camps, assassinations, and break-ins. A citizen does not affirm or assent to every proclamation, every law, every secret rule of a secret policy agency, whether it operates within the United States or abroad, nor does the citizen affirm every executive order that appears to operate under the color of the law. What we may discern instead is limited assent, which must be continuously won from its citizenry by a government. It does so by doing justice and by recognizing human and natural rights as qualities that indeed define personhood.

Notions of human rights seem to be engaged in a race against the inclinations of a national security state swollen with nuclear weapons. There exists a seeming willingness on the part of the bureaucracy, the military, and science to build and use weapons of mass destruction on hundreds of millions of people because they, as a group, or their leaders, do not see the world in similar ways as a rival set of leaders does. This situation poses a question that cannot be dodged: What rights does a state have to commit suicide for the people? This issue, in its baldest form, has yet to be considered by the people, the Congress, or the courts.

Can the rule of law begin to deal with any of these issues? What help can citizens expect to have if they raise questions about whether the state can commit suicide for the body politic through a policy of mindless armament or use of nuclear weapons to destroy whole classes of people?

The courts have attempted to recognize constitutional rights as they relate to equality of opportunity. They have also attempted to give proper credence to the civil rights of the people, thereby recognizing "personhood" and those rights that attach to a person qua person as well as those that attach to a person qua citizen. This objective has not been shared by the police apparatus. Thus, throughout the civil rights struggles of the 1960s the FBI had the unfortunate habit of allowing the local police to beat and jail civil rights demonstrators. It, as well as the CIA, infiltrated black nationalist groups in the ghetto for the specific purpose of ridiculing and discrediting their organizing attempts (Perkus 1975, 9–17, 110–18). There was no recognition by police agencies that the struggles of the civil rights movement were for natural and human rights. This is not surprising. To guarantee such rights would mean that their own activities would have to come under strict scrutiny and finally be dismantled in favor of local neighborhood and community police. It should be noted that according to a study of the Media Papers, stolen from the FBI files in Media, Pennsylvania, 40 percent of the FBI's time is spent in harassing and keeping tabs on political groups that seek some measure of recognition of their personhood (*Ibid*). It is hardly surprising that the national security apparatus, built as it is on principles of unaccountability, secrecy, ultra-allegiance to the state, and willingness to lie to the courts and legislatures, is unconcerned with human or natural rights. Yet within the U.S. Constitution there is the seed of a radical understanding of the rights of the people. Under the Ninth Amendment the rights of the people cannot be disparaged, i.e., they cannot be disparaged by the government, the secret apparatus of the government, the gangs that operate within the secret apparatus, or the president. How can these rights be upheld? Only in a continuous dialogue from the "grassroots."

The National Security State and Democracy:
Recent Developments

In the previous two sections of this essay, updated from an article I wrote in the wake of the Watergate scandal and end of the Vietnam War (see acknowledgements), I explored the development of the national security state, a system of government outside of traditional legal and public controls. At that time millions of people protested the U.S. military intervention in Indochina, a war where no clear purpose could be manufactured by the U.S. leadership. These protests illustrated that a significant part of the populace was unwilling to accept the idea that leaders knew best. Established authority was threatened by a populace that seemed to have found its voice and was determined to make the point that the war was unconstitutional and immoral. At the same time congressional and establishment opinion was that the national security state should be curbed. The FBI, the CIA, and the military had spied on the establishment as well as on the left, and they had sought to corrupt and make paranoid the entire political process through such activities as COINTELPRO and OPERATION CHAOS. These activities were necessary to the national security state, as escalation of the war yielded no positive results and as many citizens rejected so-called strategic considerations for moral and legal arguments.

Palladins of the national security state like Samuel Huntington called this public response too much democracy and complained that it would destroy orderly elites and their capacity to speak for the body politic. Yet calls for increased democratic participation had little effect on the structure and operation of the national security state. In this section I will briefly address the reasons why the national security state was able to maintain its role in the face of public opposition during this period and touch on its recent history, particularly during the Reagan administration.

In the mid-1970s the national security state was faced with how to escape taint and blame for a flawed war and a flawed presidency. It had been central to the war in Vietnam, just as it had been involved in illegal activities for President Nixon. The question was how to explain its role to an increasingly uncontrollable press and to a populace that was reeling from the loss in Indochina.

The activities uncovered in congressional investigations in the 1970s were not considered impeachable offenses by Congress, which itself had been coopted into the national security system, the arms race, and the war itself. There were honorable exceptions, such as Congressman Robert Kastenmeier of Wisconsin, but most politicians did not grasp the reality of the contradiction between the national security state and authentic democracy.

It is in this contradiction that we can see that the definition of democracy that guides the national security state is tied to authoritarian forms throughout the world. The national security apparatus encourages authoritarian regimes if it appears that a national movement is underway that would thumb its nose at U.S. dominance. Programs to aid such regimes, often through the Department of Defense, have the color of law and regulation to them even though by their very nature they have undercut representative democracy in the Third World and in the United States itself. Without Congress' realizing it, such programs have trivialized Congress and justified national security escapades. (The Iran-Contra affair was no different in style or direction from any other situation in which congressional representatives were told about specific covert or military actions only after they had occurred, if at all. And when they are told, the actions are justified in terms of markets, anti-Communism, and giving aid to "moderates.")

A valiant effort to provide a veneer of legality for the national security state was subsequently made by President Ford's Attorney General, Edward Levi. He framed regulations designed to make CIA and FBI operations more congruent with the public and statutory aspects of federal law, if not with constitutional democracy. The regulations limited CIA and FBI intrusion into political groups that dissented from the government's policies. In this manner he hoped to erect a fence around the national security state so that it would not corrode civil society. The paradox of the Levi guidelines, however, is that they were not meant to interfere with or curtail the CIA. They were meant as a paper administrative trail for monitoring national security operations so that the more egregious crimes detailed by the Senate in 1974 would not be repeated. Covert actions were thus rationalized, even though Congress, through its intelligence oversight committees, would only be informed, not consulted, about actions deemed covert.

The national security state was also protected politically because it provided jobs either directly or indirectly to over eleven million people. It acted as the paymaster for U.S. science, guiding it toward more and more sophisticated technologies. It likewise played a major economic role in addressing an unfavorable balance of payments caused in part by the U.S.-sponsored military alliance system. The Defense Department under Nixon conducted an arms sales and military assistance program far greater than those under previous presidents.

Finally, the public outcry against the national security state did not directly challenge the U.S. triumphal ethos. Americans are comfortable with a division of the world into categories of good and evil that demand continuous struggle (managed by the national security state) to assure victory of the good. Of course, there has been enough evil in the twentieth century to reinforce this sentiment. Triumphalism holds sway for the populace, with three caveats. It should not lead to a long, drawn-out war with U.S. troops. It should not contradict the positive image Americans have of themselves. And it should not lead to a war fought on U.S. soil. In the aftermath of Vietnam these conditions seem clearly met.

Ultimately, the national security state's tentacles had completely entwined the presidency, making it all but impossible for any president or Congress to sever the institutional links between the national security state and the executive. The national security state has always predicated its covert activities on plausible deniability for the president, thus implicating the president as the legitimator of activities that have no legal defense except that of *raison d'état*. For example, in the egregious case of a first or second nuclear strike, the president, as the legally constituted authority, may be bureaucratically pressured into destroying millions of people for cause or whim. Each president thus finds himself trapped into immoral nuclear imperatives. Carter, for example, came into office hoping to cut strategic delivery missiles to two hundred as a deterrent and ended his term in office by authorizing a decapitation strategy—that is, destroying the Soviet government in the hopes that the Soviet Union could be broken apart in the course of a nuclear war or otherwise—made possible with a buildup of Trident 2, MX, Pershing 2, and Minuteman 3 missiles and a five percent per year real increase in the defense budget. Good intentions are not enough to tame, transform, or dismantle the national security state.

Under President Carter some restraint was exercised over NSC staff operations. Carter appointed his old classmate Admiral Stansfield Turner to head the CIA.[7] Turner fired or retired a number of covert operators who believed in the kind of direct espionage and "sublimited" war that the national security state had favored throughout the Cold War. This style of operation had become a bone of contention within the intelligence community by 1977. One reason was that the CIA's analysts had been against the Vietnam War, stating as early as 1964 that the U.S. could not win. (This belief did not, however, prevent its operatives from killing tens of thousands of people in Vietnam in order to "pacify" the Vietnamese peasantry.) Furthermore, the technocrats in the intelligence community believed in a more antiseptic way of managing an empire—using intelligence gathered by satellite and other technical means. Carter, who was himself technologically-oriented, favored this approach. Yet, according to Admiral Turner, Carter did not stint on covert actions.

The structure of the national security state continued to suggest that "surgical" force could be used to attain U.S. objectives, such as the return of the hostages in Iran. Under President Carter, however, some restraint was exercised over NSC staff operations until Zbigniew Brzezinski won the battle against Secretary of State Cyrus Vance, who then resigned in disgust at the imprudent course on which Brzezinski had taken the President. Brzezinski pressed the President to increase substantially the defense budget, intervene militarily in Iran to obtain the return of the hostages, and put SALT II on the back burner after Soviet intervention in Afghanistan.

With the Reagan administration came the return of "old hands" who were committed to covert activities for espionage and the overthrow of other nations. Activities such as the backing of guerrilla war in Angola through covert aid, indirect aid to Pol Pot's Khmer Rouge, an extensive undeclared war against Nicaragua, as well as extensive operations in Afghanistan, Yemen, Asia, and Central America were quickly taken up by the national security state. Covert and "sublimited" actions were greatly increased. National security state staff reverted to the principle that they would have to transcend the bureaucratic and stodgy character of the government.

The one part of the national security apparatus that operated under statutory provisions with some public scrutiny and legislative control, the Department of Defense, was anything but stodgy during the Reagan administration. From January 1981 forward Carter's fiscal constraints were effectively removed from the Department of Defense and the CIA. Caspar Weinberger's defense budget was meant to make clear that the United States intended to have a first strike capacity and that it would increase the numbers of weapons and troops at each level of the violence scale. In reality, however, the costs of defense had become so high and technology so sophisticated that the defense procurement process continued at a pace little different from that laid out by the Carter administration.

The other parts of the national security state—the CIA and the NSA—from 1981–1986 were given free rein to operate at whim, accountable only to the samurai-like rules of the old-boy network both inside and outside of government, and not to Congress or the public. Although President Reagan maintained the presidentially appointed intelligence oversight board that Carter had established to exercise some control over covert actions, it was a sham. When its counsel, for example, asked Oliver North whether he might be doing anything illegal, North said no. That ended the matter. National security state bureaucrats were told by Reagan advisors that the Vietnam syndrome was over and that the ethos of the Green Berets and sublimited war, now called "low-intensity warfare," would be enshrined and strengthened. During the Reagan administration, the nation had to rely on the Joint Chiefs of Staff's understanding of military limits so that no totally crazy activities would be undertaken by the right-wing bureaucrats of the national security state.

Under Director William Casey, the CIA quickly reclaimed its former grandeur as an intervenor in all manner of activities. Reagan, who had served on the Rockefeller Commission to review the CIA during the Ford administration, knew exactly the kind of man he wanted for the job. The CIA had come to describe itself as nothing more than a liberal-minded university whose scholars just happen to work on intelligence matters. A number of Harvard professors, especially William Langer and Robert Bowie, helped to set up and, in the latter's case, run the CIA. While both of these men specialized in analysis, Casey represented the "other side of the shop." His biography was a story of how covert operations could be used in domestic elections and in the corporate world. In 1980 he was Reagan's campaign manager, and under President Nixon he was chairman of the Securities and Exchange Commission. Like the buccaneer businessman he was, Casey had increased the use of the agency's intelligence "product" while geometrically increasing the number of covert and black operations. On the National Security Council, men like Oliver North played out their roles as operators and analysts, taking the lead from the Kissinger-Haig NSC period when few distinctions were made between operators and analysts.

Reagan's CIA operatives courted extreme rightist and neo-fascist groups in much the same way their predecessors had done in the 1950s when fascist and Nazi exiles were brought into the battle against Communism through the work of Frank Wisner, a former CIA deputy director. At the behest of the Reagan administration and with the encouragement of the NSC the CIA supported fascist groups outside of the United States. It played ball with all contending groups, finding ways to work with South African intelligence as well as members of opposition groups. A new wrinkle has been added by the Reagan administration whereby large-scale operations were contracted to former agents and free-booting capitalists who saw personal gain as a higher ethic. That any of these arrangements could serve U.S. interests as a constitutional democracy has yet to be demonstrated.

Most important, the Reagan administration brought new groups into the operation and support of the national security state. Since World War II the national security state has operated with the blessings and support of the Eastern establishment, a condition that began to change under Nixon. President Reagan was beholden to a constituency that had played no significant part in the national security state, namely the radical right. Of course, it had long supplied the music for a virulent anti-Communism during the Cold War through such groups as the John Birch Society and the Anti-Communist Christian Crusade. In the 1950s its most powerful representative was Senator Joseph McCarthy, who for a time challenged the national security state as not being sufficiently anti-Communist. He was finally brought down by the army and the CIA, when he went after those institutions of the national security state.

The radical rightist movement of the 1950s failed, but its ideas resurfaced again in the late 1970s. Rightist emigré groups had long favored a strategy of dismantling the Soviet Union, since they believed it to be nothing more than an agglomeration of individual nations and peoples. The idea of dismantling the Soviet Union spread in rightist circles since they considered the aging Soviet leadership to be suffering from hardening of the political arteries and having no way to deal with the disenchantment of the intellectual classes and the revival of religion. Such ideas had long played a small part in U.S. strategic thinking about the national security state; they were always marginal to the main thrust of seeing the Soviet Union as an implacable adversary that would neither change nor collapse under the weight of its own problems.

It was not until PD 59, an NSC action memorandum on basic national security policy issued late in the Carter administration, that U.S. policy was fashioned according to the specific strategy of decapitation. By 1981 a variety of emigré groups, mercenaries, and rightist capitalists who were part of the CIA's stable changed from work horses to race horses as they moved from the fringes to the executive offices of the National Security Council. This band of believers intended to move the national security state into arenas of conflict around the world to do battle with the evil Communist Grendel at every turn. The Reagan administration sought to generate an anti-Communist league of guerrillas, "freedom fighters," extreme rightist U.S. businessmen, and retired generals to secure the blessings of their illusions to other nations.

Since this program was not one that the U.S. people either knew about or cared to "pay any price" to support, its budget had to include secret funds beyond the $350 billion a year already spent by the United States on national security and defense. Some of these funds came from the hundreds of corporations the CIA operates throughout the world that officials believe to be necessary for U.S. security. (It should not be surprising to anyone that many personal fortunes have been made by those who operate them.) Other funds were secured from joint ventures with operators such as retired General Richard Secord who was confused about whether he was working for the purposes of U.S. security or for a profitable bottom line. These revenues were mixed together with public funds. Nevertheless, the bulk of funds was reflected in the national security state budget, which the movement sought to guide.

It is important to emphasize that while the budgets of the CIA and other sectors of the national security apparatus are considerable, the bulk of national security funds in the national budget are spent on retaining conventional forces in Europe and Asia and on research and development for new weapons systems. The Reagan defense budgets have been a bonanza for the largest defense contractors. While President Reagan has leveled much criticism at central economic planning and public expenditures, the defense budget has been used as a financial subsidy to stabilize and provide a floor under U.S. industry in its precipitous decline and as an ineffective means to balance our trade deficit.

Perhaps the zaniest of the Reagan initiatives in the field of military technology is the Strategic Defense Initiative (SDI). This idea was first proposed during the Dwight D. Eisenhower administration; it retained currency among important but marginal groups of the national security state who were emboldened under Reagan to seek new initiatives. It is universally agreed that the system is infeasible. So why did the Reagan administration press for a strategy that so obviously is without merit? There are several reasons. First is the ideology that governs the national security state, a mixture of science, strategy, fantasy, and greed packaged as tough-minded rationality. Second, military planners cannot find any more targets to be destroyed in the Soviet Union, and there are no more types of nuclear weapons that can be made that fit a strategic purpose. What better way to maintain a nuclear weapons industry of some two hundred thousand people and an annual budget of $35 billion than by chasing the holy grail of "total defense" (while still allowing for a first strike on the Soviet Union)? Finally, SDI was a way to tighten the link between scientific and technical exploration and the military enterprise. The Reagan administration has attempted to buy up the technical knowledge class of workers and the institutions employing them. Even so, some eight thousand physicists have refused to work on SDI projects.

The continued militarization of society and the vast funds required to support it demand a complaisant public. President Reagan has continued and amplified methods of manipulation that have been used by different administrations throughout the Cold War. The first involves symbols of consent: patriotic trappings, the use of sports to encourage young people to join the armed forces, and identification with absurd film characters, whether James Bond or Rambo. In addition, President Reagan has shaped military maneuvers and incursions to divert the public attention from disasters as, for example, in the case of the invasion of Grenada, which was timed to distract attention from the deaths of some 250 marines in Lebanon (an unnecessary loss caused by sloppiness, hubris, and the callous American bombing and shelling of Lebanese villages). One does not have to rehearse the agitprop character of the Reagan presidency, with its Hollywood popular front-type presentation of Americanism, to comprehend the fusing of hope, pretension, illusion, and hype that comprises Reagan's American dream.

The use of hard cash has been the second method of securing allegiance to the national security state, a method that the Reagan administration does not favor for the poor. There is no citizen wage (or guaranteed income) for the majority of the U.S. population. Caught among unemployment, inflation, and spiralling personal and public debt, income guarantees become very important to working-class and middle-class families. The benefit that comes closest to the citizen wage and that was once critical in creating a skilled work force is veterans' benefits. The Veterans Administration has calculated that some fifteen million Americans per year are direct recipients of veterans' pensions and other benefits. Thus, war and preparation for it have provided an economic floor for many citizens who might otherwise be impoverished. Veterans groups, with some exceptions, offer a ready mass support system for the national security state.

We need not be economic determinists to recognize the importance of such underpinnings to the national security state, especially when one seeks to formulate a strategy for dismantling it. For example, it will require the most subtle statesmanship to bring about a situation in which veterans' benefits are seen as part of a general guaranteed citizen's wage tied to peaceful pursuits and not the fighting of wars. Veterans organizations are averse to seeing benefits as a welfare arrangement. They view their benefits as an entitlement distinct from social security.

The character of the armed forces themselves suggests that the working class and the poor, especially the black poor, need the armed forces training and security fallback. Fully 36 percent of the army is black and 20 percent of the armed forces is black. The fact is that the armed forces are an important outlet for young men and women who have no place to turn in the market economy, no funds or opportunities. There is evidence to reinforce the argument that the armed forces have helped black youth in their search for skills and status. Clearly, in a full employment economy there could be other chances for the poor.

Finally, the national security state has been based on public insecurity, that is, fear of war. The paradox of U.S. use of violence, or its threatened use, is that it has become less and less successful in international affairs while it has become more and more frightening to the American people in an age of nuclear weapons. It is not easily demonstrated that the trillions of dollars spent for military preparations since World War II have provided psychic security. The national security state operates most successfully when its antagonists automatically back down because of fear that U.S. leaders will employ force, including nuclear weapons. The problem, of course, is that this textbook view of how others will "cave" at U.S. threats is not our experience. The result is that the U.S. populace has to be psychologically mobilized for war on a perpetual basis as crises to which national security operators and managers have committed U.S. resources multiply around the world. Anti-communism had been the chief means used to raise the spectre of war. The Reagan administration offered a new justification for insecurity and fear: terrorism. It was in the name of anti-terrorism that the national security entrepreneurs were able to use the U.S. military to initiate raids against Libya and obtain both CIA and Pentagon resources in mining the harbors of Nicaragua.

The most serious difficulty with a national security and foreign policy that rests on the principle of threat and fear is that there is little to tell us whether what we do causes us to engender threats to ourselves or the appearance of them. Perhaps even more serious is that the national security state apparatus insulates itself from any criticism that could foster such self-awareness. Throughout the Cold War period the national security state was managed in such a way as to assure that dissenting views be kept outside of the government. If the views were from the left, they were labeled unpatriotic, and those who held them were branded disloyal.

Public fear breeds on the secrecy that the national security state demands as a matter of course in virtually all its activities. State secrecy is designed to assure loyalty. It is meant as a bonding principle to create solidarity among the "witting," who then are privileged to make judgments for the uninitiated populace. Of course, secrecy also invariably masks activities undertaken by the national security state that are either illegal or unconscionable. That the purpose of these activities is to protect the national security can only be proclaimed, almost never proved. In 1972, there were over 130 million pieces of classified information (Miller, 1973). This number has greatly increased. As William G. Florence, a specialist in security classification, said at that time:

> Secrecy in the executive branch of the federal government continues to be one
> of the most serious problems of our times. There is abundant proof that the
> false philosophy of classifying information in the name of national security is
> the source of most of the secrecy evils in the Executive branch. The insistence
> of people in that branch operating under security classification of secrecy has
> created a state of antagonism between them and the American people. (76)

Secrecy reduces the public side of government to a subsidiary condition. As the national security state's hold on the federal budget expands, the element of the budget that reflects the general welfare shrinks. This is not only because of the costs of security and defense, but because we are caught in a dynamic of undemocratic governing that is technologically, economically, and bureaucratically driven by the national security state. Government officials use the pretext of security and their own misperceptions as justifications for decisions and operations made for other reasons. For example, the commitment to the arms race is related to the need of a scientific and technological elite to keep their laboratories and consultancies going. The armed services, which last defined their mission and purpose in 1946, operate according to a principle of continuous budget expansion. Congress has long since given up the task of providing a fundamental critique of the military purpose. A significant segment of U.S. business expects and needs contracts from the Department of Defense as its guarantee either of profit margin or continuation in business. It is taken for granted that we must have a national security agency that has the capacity to listen to all communications traffic throughout the world. Public welfare is argued in terms of national security. Domestic programs, when they are granted, become nothing more than a means of buying off domestic populations that may be too difficult or expensive to police.

That the major structural and policy questions of life have been diverted or kept entirely off the political agenda by the national security state is a disaster similar in scope to the one that Americans faced in 1860, when slavery could not be expunged without a civil war. It is not likely that we will be able to muddle through an arms race nurtured by the national security state, entrapped as its members are in a myth and paranoia system of threat and counterthreat prepared for them over forty years ago, without a series of very intentional actions taken by political actors and social movements that see the contradiction between the national security state and the promise of democracy.

President Reagan, on different occasions, sought to end the Cold War and begin a new relationship of *entente* with the Soviet Union. The possibility of this policy succeeding under future administrations is intertwined with fundamental changes in our definitions of common defense and national security which would then lead to the transformation of the national security state. The following is designed to encourage those who are committed to democracy to decide what actions should be for such a transformation.

Toward a Common Defense for the United States

The historical and political conditions that gave rise to the national security state have changed. At the end of World War II the United States appeared to have inherited an empire consonant with its newly found affluence. For forty years the United States has bled itself as it has prepared for and participated in inconclusive wars, military engagements, and "national security" escapades (often for the personal profit of those involved). The United States has propped up tin-horn dictators in every area of the globe to suppress revolutions that threaten our economic and social control over vast geographic regions. Whether it was the regime of Somoza in Nicaragua, Rhee in Korea, Mbuto in Zaire, the Shah in Iran, or Marcos in the Philippines (a brief sample of a very long list), the weight of U.S. authority and wealth has welded authoritarian governments to our own national security establishment. It will be difficult indeed for any historian—whether conservative, liberal, or radical—to justify such policies on any grounds, including national security. The current tragedy in Central America, resulting from the failure of U.S. leaders to come to terms with the poverty of the region and the right of those nations to choose their own governments, abundantly testifies to the absence of political insight and the narrow class basis that characterize our national security policy.

The continuation of this type of foreign and national security policy is not without its economic and political costs. The belief that the best one could hope for is guns with some butter is no longer tenable. Even those constituencies formerly prepared to live with the national security state as long as they gained some measure of economic and social decency are beginning to recognize that inherent contradiction. There are few ways for the United States to revitalize its society and politics without radically changing its military posture, its attitude toward disarmament, and its "lone ranger" role in the world. The end of the Cold War and the dismantling of the national security state would release for the purposes of democratic development enormous resources and creative energies that are now frozen by institutions and habits of mind.

Those concerned with domestic reconstruction have the responsibility to give practical and modern meaning to the constitutional phrase that the people will provide for the common defense of the United States. If the national security state has any legitimacy at all, it stems from this constitutional principle. Although some have recently fought for the principles of the national security state by insisting that only people—not procedures—were at fault in the Iran-Contra affair, the facts indicate otherwise. Cover actions are illegal, either in terms of U.S. law or some other nation's law, yet the CIA has consistently used "cutouts," "assets," "plausible deniability," assassination, bribery, and other devious means since its inception. Their purpose is to fool rather inform the people and the Congress, and sometimes these deceptions have even extended to the president. The ability to commit suicide for civilization through the use of nuclear weapons consigns the constitutional right of Congress to declare war and manage the armed forces to the dustbin of history unless it can be retrieved through a new legal and ethical concept of national security. The national security state threatens both democracy and our constitutional republic.

A common defense system consistent with the modern constitutional democracy requires that its managers be concerned with the permanent interests of humankind. No democratic government will find such interests in a dual state system in which the constitutional form is manipulated by a national security grouping that operates in secrecy and outside the rule of law. National security policy must be openly debated, and actions in accord with that policy must be performed in the full light of public scrutiny. Without escaping the institutions and habits of mind of the national security state, the chance for internal democratic reconstruction is virtually nil.

Our international impasse will be overcome only if we recognize that the connection among power, violence, and threat is the problem, not the solution. Politicians who play a role in this system are unlikely to recognize an alternative to the institutions and procedures of the national security state. The Tower Commission report is an example of what we can expect from politicians and national security managers under the existing system. Major political parties will not challenge the national security state except in the most ornamental and casuistic way. The Republican Party, if it controls the executive branch, will continue President Reagan's course, asserting that military engagement is the central and virtually only task of the federal government. The Democratic Party, fearful of being labeled "soft" on Communism and revolution and concerned about not being properly reverential to military Keynesian programs, is not likely to attack the root assumptions of the national security state and the Cold War unless pressed by outside movements, much in the manner that the party was pressed during the 1960s by the civil rights and anti-war movements.

The path back to democracy bounded by law does not have to be invented out of whole cloth or out of a utopian grab bag of ideas. The basis is already present in the ideas of the founders of our republic, in many resolutions of the United National General Assembly, in decisions of the International Court of Justice, in UN convenants on economic, social, and political rights, and in judgments made against aggressive war and war crimes after World War II. Both movements and political parties need a different mentality than that which now governs the national security state and international politics. The following propositions are dedicated to this goal.

1. The United States should end its role as guarantor, policeman, or guardian at the gate in favor of an international organizational structure, namely the United Nations, that would secure the peace through mediation, arbitration, economic boycott, and an international security agreement. The United States would abide by the UN Charter by refraining from making threats to the peace and would instead work with other nations to build international institutions, including economic, security, and peacekeeping agencies within the UN family.

2. Any administration committed to ending the dual system of government that characterizes the national security state will be required to redraft the National Security Act of 1947. A new national security act should eliminate the institutional structure that has operated beyond the scope of public, judicial, and congressional control; an undefined concept of "national security"; the notion that the executive is excused from public accountability for "national security" actions. This administration should outlaw all covert activities and infringements on other nations and end all secret national security budgets, such as the CIA and NSA budgets, assuring that they are debated publicly and made publicly available. Finally, this administration should draft a public charter for the NSA that would relate that agency's work to the public and to joint multilateral and UN activities.

3. In order to transcend arms control and incrementalist steps that merely rationalize the arms race and the national security state, the United States, through its government and citizenry, should develop and present proposals for general and complete disarmament. Continuous dialogue on new commitments to assure that general disarmament will occur should be carried out through public groups such as unions, corporations, voluntary associations, churches, universities, and political groups.

4. The United States, through its government and citizenry, should formulate development plans for an international order and join other nations in an international economic development program funded through cuts in national defense budgets.

5. The United States should recognize the integrity of other states and should not act unilaterally, either with covert or overt means, to overthrow any foreign government. Where a government has been declared an aggressor against peace by the UN General Assembly and the Security Council, the United States should, with the permission of Congress, allow some of its forces to be used by the United Nations.

6. Governors and mayors should participate in the formulation of a national defense plan for the United States. Such a defense plan should have two aspects: 1) it should conform to the defense interests of the American people, its institutions, and its land; 2) it should conform to world law and the judgments at Nuremberg and the Asian War Crimes Tribunal. The United States should also integrate into law principles of personal accountability of government officials for activities outlawed at Nuremberg.

7. Any national defense plan—if there is no multilateral disarmament agreement—should concern itself with the defense of the United States, not an alliance system. The United States should not enter into military alliances with other nations outside the UN that are meant to establish rival blocs. All alliances of mutual defense to which the United States is presently obligated should be transformed into mutual disarmament and security agreements.

8. The military strategy of the United States—even if there is no multilateral disarmament agreement—should not rely on nuclear weapons as a passive deterrent or active threat. Because of their clearly criminal nature, stemming from

horrendous consequences, the United States must not use nuclear or other weapons of mass destruction as first strike weapons or in retaliation.

9. U.S. forces should be used in defense of land, institutions, and people only in the United States and its possessions, legally recognized as such in the international realm. Thus, the United States should reject covert operations because of their criminal character, their tendency to distort U.S. diplomatic relations, and their reenforcement of lawlessness unsupported in the Constitution.

Under no circumstances, however, should a U.S. government surrender to attack on its soil. Where collaboration with an enemy occurs or is attempted, that group or government should be held treasonous. Having established this basic principle, the United States, state and local governments, and voluntary organizations should work with foreign nations and groups in the development of world security arrangements that will parallel a disarmament program.

10. All space and undersea explorations should be peaceful and conducted jointly with other nations under the aegis of a UN authority. The common defense of the United States does not require a militarization of science.

11. The United States should participate fully in establishing a regulation, monitoring, and compliance system to assure that environmental hazards caused by military, industrial, and technological invention and application are minimized.

12. The United States should abandon the military assistance program as a means to assure the stability of its alliance systems and as a means of addressing its international trade deficits. The U.S. government and citizenry should develop a comprehensive plan for economic reconversion of the defense industry to rebuild its productive capacity for civilian purposes.

13. The United States should not use its national security budget as a substitute for domestic economic and social development. Instead, communities should conduct continuous audits to assure that the security of the people is being met through public and private means. This means that communities must ensure that trade is not independent of community needs. In particular, U.S. corporations that hold no loyalty to the United States should not be permitted to "double dip" by setting up industrial enterprises abroad to escape wage requirements of domestic workers while seeking no tariffs on imports of their goods into the United States.

14. The use of U.S. foreign and military policy to assure markets for U.S. products abroad and to protect U.S. investment in foreign nations is now outmoded and distinctly secondary to internal economic reconstruction. Thus, our first line of common defense should be to rebuild our industries, towns, and cities. Accordingly, the federal government should ensure that investments by U.S. corporations are allocated primarily in the United States by curtailing and then ending subsidies for corporate investing abroad. Ownership of U.S. resources should remain in U.S. hands. Just as there is no good reason U.S. investors should control other nations' wealth and minerals, there is no justification for

U.S. firms, banks, and lands to be controlled by foreign investors. That system of international investment leads to a foreign policy characterized by misunderstanding, xenophobia, and resentment.

Those concerned with a common defense for a constitutional democracy will recognize that the values reflected in this essay and in the propositions I have suggested are significantly different from those generated by the national security state. In a constitutional democracy leaders, citizens, and managers of foreign policy must realize that power is not a threat to humanity only when it is derived from principles of legitimacy and justice. If such principles were to be our guide, the American people would have a chance at democratic reconstruction, undisturbed by military threats. The propositions I have advanced are meant to suggest how to integrate social and political reconstruction with national security policy. Democracy is the only proper approach to domestic and national security policy, for it holds to certain founding precepts of our nation: the quest for happiness, the fulfillment of promises for social and economic justice, and the generation of a vibrant local, national, and international culture that helps to lift the sword of war from humanity's neck. The propositions outlined above are intended to make democratic forces within the United States the shapers and judges of any set of national security policies.

It is not too late to stop the dance of death, but good intentions are not enough to tame, transform, or dismantle the national security state as both Carter and Reagan found out. Only a movement with a genuine commitment to constitutional democracy can speak directly to the needs of our society. Such a movement has already begun. The social movements of the last generation confronted directly and successfully the national security state apparatus during the Indochina War and sought to democratize U.S. society. Today, this movement will start from a premise other than guns and butter. It will have a clearly defined understanding of democracy as a process and an end, and it will be prepared to suggest a more optimistic social covenant than the mutually assured destruction of the planet promised by the arms race. The Reagan period has made this movement more important than ever. And the changes in the Soviet Union have removed the Soviet Union as an implacable enemy.

NOTES

1.   Article 4 of the Constitution guarantees a republican form of government to the states while asserting protection against the lower classes. "The United States shall guarantee to every state in the Union a Republican Form of Government and shall protect each of them against invasion; and on the application of the Legislature or the Executive (when the Legislature cannot be convened) against domestic Violence."

2.   I first began using the term "national security state" in 1966 as a way to distinguish the more restrictive term used by Harold Lasswell in the late 1940s, "the garrison state," which asserted that those who were specialists in violence would no longer be on tap, but on top. The course of the war in Indo-China made clear that an entire governing structure could be taken over by an imperial criminal enterprise. Its managers had no interest in constitutional niceties, for they believed that the rules of governance had changed at the end of the World War II.

3.   From 1982 to 1984, Oliver North was given the responsibility as a National Security Council staff officer of preparing a martial law plan with the Federal Emergency Management Agency (FEMA). It "called for suspension of the Constitution, turning control of the United States over to FEMA, appointment of military commanders to run state and local governments, and declaration of martial law during a national crisis. The plan did not define national crisis, but it was understood to be nuclear war, violent and widespread internal dissent, or national opposition against a military invasion abroad" (Charady 1987, 15).

4.   Gehlen had been a senior planner for "Operation Barbarossa," the German invasion of the Soviet Union. The decision to employ Gehlen had immediate international significance. As Spiro concludes, "there can be little doubt that the Soviets, fearing the Germans more than any other people, were greatly influenced in their assessment of U.S. intentions by the fact that the United States selected Gehlen for this role" (1972, 42).

5.   Niebuhr was the senior advisor to the Policy Planning Staff of the Department of State during the crucial early stages of the Cold War. For a sympathetic account of his pre-World War II views, see Nichols (1967).

6.   It should be noted that first for economic reasons and then for imperial ones the United States has organized itself according to national emergency rules since 1933. There are some 470 provisions of the federal law that delegate to the president, and therefore his agents, extraordinary powers during states of emergency. This congressional delegation, coupled with the so-called inherent power of the president, gives him carte blanche to act as he sees fit. "Under the powers delegated by these statutes, the President may seize properties, mobilize production, seize commodities, institute martial law, seize control of all transportation and communications, regulate private capital, restrict travel, and—in a host of particular and peculiar ways—control the activities of all American citizens." (Senate Special Committee on the Termination of the National Emergency, Emergency Power Statutes, S. Pre. No. 93–549, 93d Cong., 1st Sess., [1973]; 17. See also Raskin 1974, 29.)

7.   President Carter's first choice for CIA Director, Theodore Sorensen, was forced to withdraw because he had once been a conscientious objector. There was fear that he would have caused a review of the CIA's curious operations at the time of the Kennedy assassination. Sorensen was also distinctly not a favorite of those who argued that the United States was behind in the arms race with the Soviet Union. Sorensen remembered the bill of goods President Kennedy had been sold on the "missile gap" in 1960, a canard put out by the ubiquitous Paul Nitze. In 1977 Nitze was performing the same public service, grossly inflating the Soviet Union's military capacity. Nitze's citizen committee, the Committee on the Present Danger, stood as the public guard dog for the assumptions of the national security state, some of which would have been questioned by Sorensen, a man who remembered the failure of Richard Bissell and Allen Dulles, the chief promoters of the Bay of Pigs fiasco.

References

Charady, A. 1987. Reagan aides and the "secret" government. *Miami Herald* July 5.
Chomsky, N. 1975. Introduction. Ed. C. Perkus. *COINTELPRO: The FBI's secret war on political freedom*. New York: Monad Press.

Command Study Group. 1974. Ralph Stavins, Chairman. *Study on U.S.S. Gatto, Problems of nuclear accidents*. February. Unpublished report, available at the Institute for Policy Studies, 1601 Connecticut Ave. NW, Washington, D.C.

Cox, A. 1975. *The myths of the national security state*. Boston: Beacon Press.

Dulles, F. R. 1953. *America's rise to world power, 1898–1954*. New York: Harper & Row.

Fall, B. 1956. *The Viet Minh regime: Government and administration in the democratic regime of Viet Nam*. Rev. ed. Ithaca, N.Y.: Cornell University Department of Far Eastern Studies.

Fleming, D. F. 1961. *The Cold War and its origins, 1917–1960*. Garden City, NY: Doubleday.

Ginsberg, H. 1975. *Unemployment, subemployment and public policy*. New York: New York University School of Social Work.

Goldberg, A. 1956. *AFL-CIO: Labor united*. New York: McGraw-Hill.

Hearings on FBI counterintelligence programs before the Civil Rights and Constitutional Rights Subcommittee of the House Committee on the Judiciary. 1976. 93rd Congress, 2nd session.

Hearings on S Res 21, before the Senate Select Committee to Study Governmental Operations with Respect to Intelligence Activities, volume 7, Covert action. 1975. 94th Congress, 1st session.

Howe, I., and L. Coser. 1962. *The American Communist Party*. 2nd ed. New York: Praeger.

Inquiry into the destruction of former FBI Director J. Edgar Hoover's files and FBI recordkeeping. 1975. Hearing before a Subcommittee of the House Committee on Government Operations. 94th Congress, 1st session.

Janeway, E. 1968. *The economics of crisis: War, politics and the dollar*. New York: Weybright and Talley.

Kahin, G. 1952. *Nationalism and revolution in Indonesia*. Ithaca, NY: Cornell University Press.

Kolko, G. 1968. *The politics of war and U.S. foreign policy, 1943–45*. New York: Random House.

Media papers. 1972. *WIN* VIII, 4-5 (March).

Miller, A. S. 1973. Watergate and beyond: The issue is secrecy. *The Progressive* 37 no:12 (December):15.

Nichols, J. H. 1967. Reinhold Niebuhr—prophet in politics. Eds. L. Krieger and F. Stern. *Responsibility of power*. London: Macmillan.

Niebuhr, R. 1953. *Christian realism and political problems*. New York: Charles Scribner's Sons.

Paine, T. 1953. *Common Sense, the American Crisis, and the Age of Reason*. Philadelphia: Franklin Library.

Perkus, C. ed. 1975. *COINTELPRO: The FBIs secret war on political freedom*. New York: Monad Press.

Raskin, M. 1974. *Notes on the old system*. New York: David McKay.

Ross, T. 1976. Surreptitious entry. Eds. R. Borosage and J. Marks. *The CIA file*. New York: Grossman Publishers.

Schwartz, R. 1963. *The powers of government*. New York: Macmillan.

Senate Select Committee to Study Governmental Operations with Respect to Intelligence Activities, Alleged Assassination Plots Involving Foreign Leaders. 1977. S. Rep. No. 465. 94th Congress, 1st session.

Senate Special Subcommittee on the Termination of the National Emergency Power Statutes. 1973. S. Pre. Nos. 93–549. 93rd Congress, 1st session.

Sherwin, M. 1975. *A world destroyed: The atomic bomb and the grand alliance*. New York: Knopf.

Spiro, E. 1972. *Gehlen: Spy of the century*. New York: Random House.

Stavins, R., M. Raskin, and R. Barnet. 1971. *Washington plans an aggressive war*. New York: Random House.

Stern, P. 1969. *The Oppenheimer case: Security on trial*. New York: Random House.

Taft, P. 1964. *Organized labor in American history*. New York: Harper & Row.

Yost, C. 1981. *History and memory*. New York: W. W. Norton and Company.

8   Realizing the Promise of Democracy in America's Third Century

John J. Kushma

One central theme pervades the essays in this book—that the cure for the present ills of government in the United States is more democracy. The expansion of political participation is the first step toward revitalizing both American democracy and the American state. Each chapter explores this theme in a different political context. This concluding chapter examines our common philosophy and summarizes our programmatic recommendations.

Identifying democracy simply as a form of government strips it of its radical *élan* and transforming potential. Democratic governance is not something that one group of people "does" to another, and it is more than the right to complain when "the shoe pinches." Democracy should be a collective endeavor of all citizens, not the privilege of a select few. Participation in governing is intrinsically ennobling, recognizing the inherent dignity and political equality of all citizens. It is also developmental, encouraging citizens to explore their public responsibilities and enlarge their moral vision.

The historic traditions of liberal democracy in the United States have bequeathed us an array of vital individual rights. The extreme emphasis on the individual that now permeates liberal thought—coupled with the classic liberal fear of collective action—has resulted in an "interest-group" politics that has actually lost sight of real individuals and communities by parcelling out political authority and defining the public good according to imputed "interests" of citizens. In contrast, we believe that human and social needs are ultimately discovered and forged through collective processes of discussion, deliberation, and decision-making. Citizens are not merely consumers of goods and services produced by the state. Political values cannot be reduced to simple economic ones. Authentic democratic values cannot be replaced by the standards of the marketplace.

Conservatives in the last decade have successfully exposed the weakness of liberalism as a public philosophy. The ability of the Republican Party under Ronald Reagan to stigmatize Walter Mondale's supporters in 1984 as a collection of "special interests" abundantly testifies to this success. Yet conservatives have been unable to put forward any alternative public philosophy beyond a sentimental nostalgia for a mythic past or an equally unsatisfying glorification of self-interest.

The failure of the right to capture the public mind is manifest in increasing public disaffection and predictable cynicism about celebrated episodes of greed, irresponsibility, and outright criminality. Conservative anti-statist diatribes have lost their power to command public attention and the Iran-Contra scandal demonstrated how the abdication of public responsibility by governmental officials serves only to court national and international crises. Finally, conservative claims to more effective management of the economy have proved false. The standard of living of millions of U.S. citizens has deteriorated while the national debt has exploded.

The "post-Reagan revolution" Thermidor has, we believe, encouraged too many progressives to adopt too narrow a vision of an alternative public philosophy. Promising to "do better" than conservatives in managing the economy and the state represents a tacit accommodation to contemporary right wing visions. Traditional liberal pieties fail to address the structural and ideological weaknesses that led to the "Reagan revolution" in the first place. Although beating the right at its own game may result in short-term success, we have argued throughout this book that this strategy does not go far enough in addressing our national political crisis.

Our argument is that an alternative to conservatism must be based in a genuinely democratic public philosophy. We reject the definition of democracy as merely a political system in which citizens can choose who will govern them from among competing candidates or rival elites. That definition impoverishes not only contemporary politics but also our national heritage. It constricts our vision of what can be done to transform the political life of our country.

Genuine democracy, as we conceive it, involves the active participation of all citizens in decisions that affect their lives. Yet, while it obviously involves more than this, we have been content in these essays simply to demonstrate how contemporary U.S. political institutions systematically frustrate widespread public participation in the process of governing and how those institutions are biased against those individuals most economically disadvantaged in our society.

Although our theoretical focus is primarily on political institutions, we share a common normative concern for political culture and public values, because we recognize how powerful institutions are in shaping debate and the public agenda. Accordingly, in our advocacy of procedural and institutional reforms, we do not outline strategies or techniques to win specific political battles within the existing set of political institutions. Rather, we examine institutions and structures to assess how they restrict our choices, limit our visions of the possible, and ultimately rob us of our democratic heritage. The essays that comprise this book are exercises in what Max Weber called "substantive rationality" or what Jürgen Habermas termed "practical reason." We examine the rationality of political institutions and decisions not just from the perspective of the internal logic of the existing political system but also from ideal democratic values and norms.

This book assesses both the means and ends of our politics, a critical framework that stands at the center of a genuinely democratic political culture.

It is to the development of such a culture that our agenda for reform is directed. The procedural and structural reforms we propose are designed to realize two complementary goals: to bring about more vigorous, effective, and equitable public participation in political life; and to establish a "public space" where debate and discussion can occur without the biasing effects of undemocratic constraints.

Our vision of a positive, effective, social democratic state incorporates all of the hard-won social welfare guarantees that have to date been enacted into law. But we go further. We view the state as the embodiment of democratic authority in the United States. As such, it must assume responsibility for actively promoting more genuine democracy in all its institutions and for establishing agencies and procedures to encourage widespread, informed, and effective citizen participation. The state must not only ensure an acceptable level of economic existence for all citizens but also provide citizens with the means to become involved in the governing process and to acquire the efficacy and knowledge to make their participation meaningful.

Before reviewing our major recommendations, we can anticipate the critical question that will undoubtedly be asked. Given the low level of political awareness in the United States and the frequent manifestations of anti-communitarian values, how can people be entrusted with an active role in governing? This is, of course, the perennial argument of opponents of real democracy.

Our response is twofold. First, we reject the right of any group to establish limits on public participation in the process of governing. We need no self-appointed censors who would exclude citizens from participation in order to maintain their own privileged access. Second, we do recognize the political "disengagement" of the U.S. public, a reality that, in fact, prompted this collection of essays. But we submit that this low level of political awareness stems not from individual limitations but rather is structurally and institutionally induced. Some of the reasons stem from the social, economic, and educational inequities that directly affect individuals' political skills, knowledge, and values. There are important structural aspects of our political institutions that also contribute to the low level of political knowledge and interest of U.S. citizens.

Lamentably few substantive incentives encourage citizens to become actively engaged in politics and to acquire the facilitating skills and knowledge. Because so few of the major political decisions in the United States today are subject to public intervention, citizens have little reason to invest time and energy in becoming politically informed. Additionally, the extraordinary fragmentation of political authority means that even those citizens who are knowledgeable and interested are faced with too many agencies and procedures to enable them to participate meaningfully and effectively. Finally, given the significant inequality in access to resources that are currently effective in influencing political decisions, most citizens feel understandably powerless. These and other constraints discourage citizens from acquiring the knowledge, skills, and values necessary in a genuine democracy. And our point is precisely that our current political system is far from a genuine democracy.

Throughout this book we have argued that as citizens are afforded more meaningful participation in public decision making and as more effective avenues of public intervention are created, citizens will be encouraged to invest time and energy in acquiring political information and skills. Similarly, effective and meaningful participation in public decisions will, we believe, inculcate and nurture authentic democratic values and a sense of civic and social responsibility. We view the current response of the U.S. people to politics—inattention, indifference, lack of interest and knowledge, and disaffection—as entirely reasonable given the political options open to them. We maintain that a new structure of political institutions and procedures will result in an equally reasonable public response—activism, interest, knowledge, and civic responsibility.

Our analysis of these themes, and our specific recommendations for revitalizing U.S. democracy and the U.S. state, can be conveyed most effectively by answering four major, interrelated questions.

1. *Why is there today a lack of open, democratic discussion of significant public policy alternatives?* The simple answer is that the most effective means of limiting public deliberation and citizen participation is to provide no arena where they can occur. As Jeff Faux demonstrates, the absence of democratic national economic alternatives is directly attributable to the lack of "an institutional framework [or] a space in national political dialogue where the bargaining over a new social contract can begin" (page 165).

Similarly, democratic control of public policy is frustrated when public authority is fragmented and uncoordinated. Charles Noble shows how the unreasonable fragmentation of regulatory agencies has persistently frustrated effective regulation of toxic and hazardous substances. Citizens wishing to influence regulatory policy are confronted with a political labyrinth that demands an unreasonable and unfair expenditure of their political resources.

Our set of recommendations includes proposals for changes in the structure and procedures of existing political and governmental institutions and the creation of new ones to promote more effective and open policy-making. These institutions should be structured so as to enhance public awareness and should be legislatively controlled so as to maximize public oversight and control.

For example, as Carol MacLennan suggests, the Office of Management and Budget (OMB) is one vital target for reform. Administrative centralization has lodged too much power in the OMB, an agency removed from legislative and public scrutiny. At the direction of the President, the OMB can now make decisions about what information will be collected and disseminated by the state, decisions that directly affect the public's knowledge and thereby its opportunities for effective political participation. We therefore recommend that Congress review OMB operations, strictly define its appropriate management and budget functions, and provide for more extensive legislative and public oversight of the agency.

Another reform in the area of institutional design is Charles Noble's proposal for the creation of a Department of Worker and Environmental Protection. It would, as he concludes, result in more effective public control of regulatory policy by providing coordination among separate agencies. The existence of this department would also require Congress, at least when considering the new department's budget, openly to debate important regulatory issues that are now frequently decided in venues removed from public intervention.

2. *Why has public participation become primarily ritualistic and ineffective in influencing public policy?* The answer seems clear. In a wide variety of political arenas genuine alternatives are foreclosed or suppressed. John Kushma suggests that many electoral and political party reforms have in fact operated historically to restrict the influence of public participation and substitute instead the power of money and technological expertise. We advocate reforms to redress this inequity, among them public funding for all elections and governmental responsibility for registering voters and providing information about candidates and referenda. In order to provide citizens with the opportunity to do more than simply select candidates in primary elections, we recommend changes in party rules to provide the local party with greater autonomy, increase the scope of its activities, and enhance its role in the policy process.

Carol MacLennan also demonstrates how recent administrative reforms, particularly the centralization of bureaucratic oversight in highly politicized executive agencies, have limited public intervention and promoted more closed, elitist, and technocratic tendencies in administrative agencies. To counter this tendency, we propose a number of reforms, including requirements for agency response to citizen recommendations and inquiries and appropriate funding for citizen advisory boards. Reforms such as these would enhance public intervention in the administrative process and encourage public workers to respond creatively to authentic democratic demands and not the demands of the state itself.

More far-reaching reasons for the weakness of local participatory mechanisms are the economic constraints within which these mechanisms operate. Kushma, Noble, Levine, and Faux all point out that the absence of effective national policy reduces the number and scope of meaningful policy alternatives available to citizens in states and local communities. For example, without a national economic policy guaranteeing full employment at a realistic social wage, citizens are compelled to yield to market considerations and the power of capital. Most have no real choices at all. Workers cannot be expected to make "free" choices about local economic development or health and safety policy when those choices are tied to palpable threats of capital flight and the loss of jobs. Citizens cannot be expected to evince much concern for local economic development policy when the choice being offered is public investment under terms demanded by private investors or no investment at all.

In related fashion Marcus Raskin discusses how the dimensions of the national security debate are constrained by economic considerations. When the military serves as the employer of last resort for disadvantaged youth and when a significant part of the social welfare apparatus is directly tied to the military, many citizens' options are practically foreclosed. Likewise, when so much of U.S. public economic investment is tied directly to defense contracts, public consideration of national security policy, as well as economic policy, is artificially constrained.

We have advocated some specific economic policies to ensure a wider set of political choices for the American people, full employment in particular. Guaranteed employment would provide people with the realistic option of exercising their political, as opposed to economic, judgment in a variety of important policy areas. Until this option is given practical meaning, our democracy will remain underdeveloped, and the quality of our public policies will suffer. In line with Faux's analysis, we also recommend an institutional restructuring or the creation of new institutions to provide greater coherence in economic policymaking and planning. This would highlight the linkages among regulatory, national security, and economic policies and thereby encourage more realistic public deliberation. It would reduce the military role in determining national economic policy and augment the public role. It would also, as Faux suggests, provide the public with greater power to demand accountability from governmental officials by centralizing monetary and fiscal policy.

Finally, the existence of national economic planning capacity would help to realize the full democratic potential of federalism and decentralization strategies. No longer would local and state governments be compelled to compete with their neighbors for jobs and economic development funds. No longer would local and state governments be forced to respond to policies set elsewhere. Rather, citizens in states and local communities would have the opportunity to make meaningful and effective choices, the very essence of democracy.

3. *How can the public participate effectively when so many aspects of public policy-making involve highly technical and complex issues?* Elitists have defined public policy issues in highly technical or specialized terms to their advantage. "Secrecy" is also promoted as an essential element of policy effectiveness. When citizens accept this "technocratic" notion of the policy process—yielding to the claims of "experts" and the need for "secrecy"—they voluntarily limit their active participation.

Some policy matters do require expert knowledge, and some may even require secrecy. In these cases mechanisms to ensure public accountability must be in place. In too many areas, however, from the national security state (see Raskin) to administrative agencies (see MacLennan), local economic development agencies (see Levine), and regulatory bodies (see Noble), the insistence on expertise and secrecy is but a gambit to limit public participation and minimize governmental accountability.

We do not disparage the role of technological or scientific expertise (many experts are in fact good democrats), but we propose reforms that uphold the public's right to determine, as Noble puts it, the "fundamental choices about our priorities" (p. 108). Accordingly, we advocate the extension of right-to-know legislation to all state agencies and expanded public access to information. We also call on Congress to reduce the number of secret committee hearings. Finally, we ask Congress to fulfill its constitutionally-defined roles of managing the armed forces and declaring war, thereby giving the public a more effective voice in decisions about national security.

4. *How can citizens participate effectively when there are so many decisions to be made and so many decision-making arenas?* There are obvious limitations on the ability of the public to participate realistically in all or even most government decisions. Our concept of participatory democracy is not a fatuous vision of a town meeting attended by quarter of a billion citizens. It is, however, a vision of openly debated policy alternatives and public participation in *key* decisions that establish national priorities and that in turn effectively regulate the state's activity. We have suggested that a party-driven Congress is the most appropriate institution in the U.S. political system through which to realize the goals of widespread public participation, public accountability, and effective decision-making. Hence, many of our recommendations would increase the scope and agenda of legislative activity and strengthen political parties as mediating institutions.

The Congress, in both constitutional design and practice, has been the component of the state closest to and most subject to control by the people. Our suggested reforms, such as the changes in the electoral system discussed above, are intended to minimize the distance between them. Likewise, political parties have historically been the chief agencies of democratic politics, and our proposals for reinvigorating them are designed to facilitate and maintain this role. Most important among these proposals are changes in campaign and party financing that would institutionalize greater collective responsibility for governing by shifting the focus of elections from candidates and interest groups to the political parties themselves.

We have argued throughout this book that proposals for revitalizing the state must begin with a consideration of our nation's democratic roots. The democratic state we envision is unlike our contemporary American state. We have *not* advocated, in any of our reforms, a powerful yet "autonomous" state, entrusted with the responsibility of governing "wisely." Rather, we hope to foster the development of a state that is an extension of an inclusive public process of self-government, a collective agency for carrying out the public's decisions and transacting the public's business.

Conservatives advocate a less autonomous state, but their vision is predicated on a defense of existing inequality and privilege in our economy and society as well as on a preference for market values over democratic ones. We find this vision morally unacceptable and antithetical to our democratic traditions. In contrast, we have suggested that reforms that give practical meaning to "the consent of the governed" can create a less autonomous but more powerful state, one able to realize the collective goals of the American people.

Our vision of the positive state rests on the fundamental premise of democracy—the political equality of all citizens. In this fashion, positive government and democratic renewal are inextricably linked. It is through this reform agenda that progressive efforts can be united. For too long we have neglected to ask how the state can promote democracy. It is time once again to address that question. The spirit of egalitarianism has always been the revolutionary legacy of democratic ideals in the United States. We cannot reclaim this legacy by embracing a nostalgia for past democratic aspirations or by invoking the authority of historical figures. To do so would be to ignore how many times democratic goals have been thwarted and how well intentioned reforms often have repressed rather than furthered a more democratic polity. To possess our democratic heritage, we must grasp it anew. This book is a collective effort to extend our reach.

Index

Administration: separation from politics, 52, 54

Administrative failures, 51, 52

Administrative orthodoxy, 53–4, 74–5, 75–6n; countering anti-democratic aspects of, 59–60. *See also* Business principles; Managerial control; Political neutrality

Administrative Procedures Act (APA), 50, 67, 68, 69–70, 92.

Administrative reform: and assumptions about public work, 61–2; during Carter and Reagan administrations, 60–8; history of, 51–3

Advisory Committee Act, 69, 74

Agricultural Extension Service, 74, 160

Alliance systems, proposal to alter, 193

Arbitrary power, in national security state, 175–6

A–76 Circular, 65–6

Attack on the state: class basis of, 1–2, 6–7; by conservatives, 5–6; populist dimension of, 1; and public administration, 49

Automation; and full employment, 152

Business climate: *see* Investment climate

Business principles: of administrative orthodoxy, 57–8

Campaign finance, 40, 165. *See also* Political action committees.

Capital: mobility of, 113, 159

Capitalism: and environmental hazards, 83–4; and regulatory policy, 85–6, 93–4, 97. *See also* Investment climate; Market

Central Intelligence Agency (CIA), and national security state, 172, 174, 175, 176, 177, 179, 181, 182, 183, 184, 185–6, 187, 191

Citizen Research Centers, proposal for, 74

Citizenship: historical struggle to define, 168–9; moral qualities of in republican ideology, 22

Civil Service Commission, 56, 57, 61. *See also* Office of Personnel Management; Merit Systems Protection Board

Civil Service Reform Act (CSRA), 50, 60–1; and federal workers, 62–4; reversing effects of on public administration, 72–3

Civilian Technology Foundation, proposal for, 159–60

Cold war, 171

Common defense, proposals for, 192–5

Community investment agenda, proposal for, 159

Congress: proposed role in administrative reform, 73, 74; proposed role in regulatory policy, 106; reduction of scope of activity and role in governing, 32, 50; and revitalization of democracy, 204; role in national security state, 174, 182–3

Constitution: and design of the U.S. state, 23, 86–7; and republican form of government, 168, 170, 196n

Corporatism: as democratic strategy, 35–6; and health and safety policy-making, 101–3; and New Deal, 90; and Progressivism, 32–3; in strategic planning, 133–4, 140. *See also* Greenhouse Compact; Public-private partnerships

Cost-benefit analysis, and administrative regulation, 67

Courts: and regulation, 70, 87, 94; role in public interest regulatory regime, 90, 92, 95–6, 99; complicity in national security state, 179, 180

Covert operations, 177–9, 183, 194; during Reagan administration, 185–6; proposal for elimination of, 194

Criticism, insulation of national security state from, 189

Debt: third-world, 150, 162, U.S. fiscal, 150, 151

Defense industry, recoversion of, 194

Deindustrialization, 114–5; political dimension of, 115–6

Democracy: authoritarian definition employed by national security state, 183; constitutional, 168, 195; contemporary crisis in the U.S., 16, 18–21; contemporary theorists of, 21; as cure for problems of government, 198; historical crisis in the U.S., 17; and liberalism, 33; state's role in promoting, 200; struggle to realize in U.S., 41–2, 168–9; traditions of in the U.S., 19,

Contributors

Jeff Faux is President of the Economic Policy Institute (EPI), a Washington, D.C. "think tank" that conducts research and promotes public discussion of critical issues facing the U.S. economy. Faux is the co-author (with Gar Alperovitz) of *Rebuilding America* (Pantheon, 1984), the author of *New Hope of the Inner City* (Twentieth Century Fund) and the co-author of *The Star-Spangled Hustle* (Doubleday). His articles have appeared in a wide variety of anthologies, magazines, and newspapers, and he has made numerous television appearances. He has been a consultant to governments at all levels, businesses, labor unions, and community and citizen organizations.

John Kushma has taught history at the University of Texas at Arlington and is a long-time local Democratic Party activist. He has written and edited works in the field of American history and politics.

Marc V. Levine is an Assistant Professor in the Departments of History and Urban Affairs at the University of Wisconsin-Milwaukee, where he has taught since 1984. His research and writing focuses on urban political economy, state and national economic policy, and language policy. His scholarly work has appeared in *The Journal of Politics, The Journal of Urban Affairs*, and numerous other academic journals. He is completing a book tentatively titled *The Transformation of Montreal, 1960–1985: Language Policy and Social Change in a Bilingual City* and is at work on a study of redevelopment policy in Baltimore. In 1983–84 he was an American Historical Association Congressional Fellow, serving as an economic policy advisor to Senator Edward M. Kennedy, and he has advised numerous candidates and elected officials at the local and national levels on issues of economic policy.

Carol MacLennan is Associate Professor of Anthropology in the Science, Technology, and Society Program at Michigan Technological University. Between 1979 and 1985 she worked in the federal government as a social scientist for the National Highway Traffic Safety Administration, Department of Transportation. During that time she was active in Local 3313, American Federation of Government Employees, and became its vice president. As an anthropologist she has published articles on the automotive industry, government regulation, and plant closings. As a government worker she has been an activist in union efforts to organize federal employees, seek civil service reform, and democratize the federal workplace.

Charles Noble is Associate Professor of Political Science at California State University at Long Beach. He writes on political economy, public policy, and American politics and is the author of *Liberalism at Work: The Rise and Fall of OSHA*, (Temple University Press, 1986).

Marcus G. Raskin is Senior Fellow and co-founder of the Institute for Policy Studies in Washington, D.C. He is co-chair of SANE-FREEZE, a former member of the White House National Security Council staff under President Kennedy, and author of a dozen books on government, international affairs and political philosophy. His most recent books are *The Common Good* (Routledge & Kegan Paul, 1986) and *New Ways of Knowing* (Littlefield Adams, 1987)